# DAUGHTER
## *of the*
# TERRITORY

*Jacqueline Hammar*

ARENA
ALLEN&UNWIN

*This book is for 'Old Darwin' and the remaining few who still live there. For me, they are not names in history books but real people I knew and cared about.*

Arena Books
Allen & Unwin
83 Alexander Street
Crows Nest NSW 2065
Australia
Phone: (61 2) 8425 0100
Email: info@allenandunwin.com
Web: www.allenandunwin.com

Cataloguing-in-Publication details are available
from the National Library of Australia
www.trove.nla.gov.au

ISBN 978 1 76029 251 5

Map by MAPgraphics
Set in Goudy Old Style by Bookhouse, Sydney
Printed in Australia by Griffin Press

10 9 8 7 6 5 4 3 2

# Contents

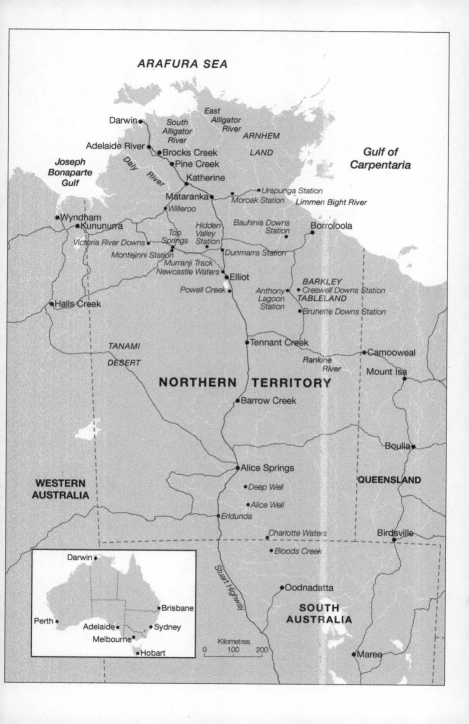

*There's the land. (Have you seen it?)*
*It's the cussedest land that I know . . .*
*Some say God was tired when He made it;*
*Some say it's a fine land to shun;*
*Maybe; but there's some as would trade it*
*For no land on earth—and I'm one.*

ROBERT W. SERVICE

# Prologue

Close to a hundred years ago, a young man not yet twenty years old rode with the Afghan camel teams over the red sand of the Centralian desert into the Northern Territory. He went on to ride the wild miles of the Territory as a trooper in the Mounted Police, when less than forty mounted men patrolled a country larger than Great Britain, France and Germany combined. He was to become my father.

When our family took root in the Territory, it was largely unpeopled, and inhospitable to Europeans. Men like my father came for the great adventure. The bush tracks they travelled were recorded as uncertain pin scratches on maps.

Four generations later, our family still flourishes under the guiding stars of the Southern Cross. We have ridden the hard ridges of the inland, travelled cattle through the old forgotten stock routes, and pioneered country where barefoot cattle kings, with no thrones but their saddles, patrolled their vast pandanus-bordered kingdoms. These adventures have been part of my life for nearly ninety years, passing through with the clink of spurs, the pad of bare black feet, and the night sounds of horse bells and corroboree.

In records of the Northern Territory's Genealogical Society, my parents are recorded as Pioneers of the Territory. As Pioneer Number 0376, my name has also been enclosed in these dusty files that are possibly never to be opened again, and never to tell of the births, deaths and tragedies of the lives within.

But I have tales to tell of pioneering in our time, of lonely white men and gentle black women, of murder and suicide, of animals and children, fire and flood. Men of the bush loved their hard, unbound life; wouldn't have considered another. The freedom and farness of the Outback suited them fine.

White women were very few and very far between on the hard ground of the old Territory. They dispensed hospitality to all who travelled bush roads. Newspapers repeatedly stated that: 'A far greater need than railways, naval bases, gold and garrisons is the Territory's need of white women.'

In 1928—before the days of radio, telephone and real medical aid—my mother came as a bride to live in a wide, wild-man's country. A trained nurse, she cared for the bush Aboriginals when they were sick: naked people wary of new ways, suffering the white man's diseases such as measles, yaws and leprosy. Late at night, many a lubra would come seeking my mother's help, guiding her through darkness with the light of a kerosene lantern to their camp.

The bush Aboriginals of our time were ever eager to hear a good yarn.

'Tell me a story, Jack-a-leen, true-fella story,' they'd say to me.

So gather around with the shades of these long-ago people of the old bush and I'll tell you our story—our true-fella story.

# PART I

'Overall brooded the silence and loneliness of the north,
a land of appalling distances and the fastest and only
way to bridge them, a man on a galloping horse.'

GLENVILLE PIKE

'These sand hills are suggestive of death
by fatigue, thirst, and famine.'

ERNEST FAVENC

'Amazing is the record of heroism, and endurance,
that is the history of the North Australian Mounted,
they lived the hair-raising thrillers of a boy's dream—
dashing in their uniforms and wide hats—hats that
more than once had been the target of showers of
spears, they laughed over stories that would electrify
an author of adventure tales, scarcely one has not
a life and death story to tell, but rarely tells it.'

ERNESTINE HILL

## CHAPTER 1

# North to the Territory

My story begins with my father, Arthur Edward (Jack) Sargeant. Queen Victoria was still sitting steadfastly upon her throne in the early months of the year he was born. He and the twentieth century began their journey through time together.

At fifteen he left his home in South Australia and joined the army. There was no conscription during the First World War, with young men joining for adventure, for patriotism, or both. Perhaps my father presumed life in the army wouldn't differ much from life as the youngest of seventeen children in a strict Presbyterian household.

After lying about his age, he was given an ill-fitting uniform and sent on a 20-kilometre fitness march that resulted in the army doctors diagnosing ingrown toenails. These were smartly removed (and never grew again) and he was soon on a ship sailing off to war.

And what a war it was! One of guts, no glory, no glamour, and such appalling horror that a child soldier could only return from mud-filled trenches and bayonet charges on the battlefields of France as a man.

In his journal, my father tells a little of his war:

*We went up through the Hindenburg Line recently taken by Australians, we were in trenches up to our waists in mud, I was on Lewis Guns, we were there for a week, it was my sixteenth birthday, and the men celebrated my birthday with sixteen lighted matches in a loaf of bread.*

*We were relieved by the first American troops to come into the front line, the 32nd Battalion. They seemed not to have good leadership for they tried to get through the barbed-wire entanglements where they were caught, and the Germans machine-gunned them, every one.*

*We were ordered out; the only way through the wire was to climb over the dead bodies of the Americans. There was no other way. There was a moon that night and it was a sight I'll never forget, men caught on the wire, their frozen grimacing faces, white in the moonlight.*

My father caught the Spanish flu that killed thousands of fighting men. While he was lying in an army hospital, yet another flu victim was placed in the bed beside him. In the morning, seeing the bed empty, my father said with the naivety of a bush lad, 'Has he gone home, Nurse?' The nurse replied, 'Yes son, he's gone home.'

He was invalided out to hospital in England, later onto a hospital ship back to Australia. They called in to Colombo, but he was too sick to go ashore. Then the ship set sail right into a cyclone, during which everything on top of the vessel was blown away—showers, toilets and sadly, their entire cargo of potatoes. The men remained battened down below or they would have gone too. Blown hundreds of miles off course, they finally sailed into Albany rather than Fremantle.

At war's end, my father was still a teenager. The years that followed his return held a diversity of adventurous pursuits for him.

In 1919, ten years before a railway line linked Oodnadatta in South Australia to Alice Springs, my father rode into the Northern Territory on the back of a camel. Eighteen years old, a soldier returned from war, he had been directed north by the British Australian Telegraph Company to work on the Overland Telegraph Line. This was an amazing feat of human achievement that linked Australia across more than 3000 kilometres, from Port Augusta in South Australia to the far tropics of Darwin. There it joined with the cable that ran along the ocean floor to Java, and so to communication with the rest of the world.

My father left Adelaide on the slow train that crawled through dust and heat every two weeks, taking an overnight break to the relief of passengers at Marree. Originally the area was named Hergott Springs—the story goes that a German explorer was the first man through and exclaimed in horror, 'Herr Gott!' at the desolate scene. It was in fact named for Hergott, an artist in John McDouall Stuart's exploration party who'd found water there.

Next day the train moved on to Oodnadatta, where the rail line stopped dead in the sand. A collection of dirty Afghan tents and a tin mosque defined it as little more than a camel camp. From there, my father travelled with the Afghan camel train over the red sand dunes of Central Australia, a journey of around three weeks. Like desert caravans of ages past, camel trains regularly travelled this route, one of the hottest and driest in the world. Turbaned Afghans packed their long strings of camels with every conceivable form of goods, furniture, building materials, grog—you name it, they found a way to load it.

My father wrote in his journal:

*My travel documents stated, 'Train to Oodnadatta, connecting with mail to Alice Springs.' With expectations of a mail truck to continue on, I found no such thing—there was no mail truck, not a sign of a mailman, so back to the railway station.*

*'Where's the Alice Springs mail truck, mate?' I asked.*

*'That's it up there; see those camels? That's how the mail gets through. A lot of sand between here and the Alice, a motor vehicle couldn't handle it.' He went on to explain, 'There are two camel teams, this one goes as far as Old Crown Station, that's about halfway, there they change to another string to continue on to the Alice. They return the same way.'*

*My baggage consisted of a suitcase, which went into one of the boxes located on each side of a pack animal, and my swag, which I carried on my camel. 'When you mount you'll find a waterbag on one side, and on the other a satchel with food,' I was told. On inspection, food was revealed as a packet of SAO biscuits and a can of sardines.*

*Loaded and ready to travel, we set off at what could be described as a fast amble—a shuffling sort of gait, the best way to travel, too fast, loads might shift, too slow, a feeling of motion sickness could overcome those so inclined. The camels were joined, nose to tail, in a long string, heavily loaded for settlements along the way. A big bull could carry half a ton and go without water for a week if conditioned to do so. We left camp before daybreak. Sometimes we travelled into the night; sometimes spent a day unloading.*

*When we finally reached Old Crown Station, the halfway point, the camels were unpacked, with blissful thoughts of some dinner and rolling out the swag for a few hours' sleep before continuing. It was not to be: the new team, ready to travel, was preparing to leave, so reluctantly I remounted, settled myself as comfortable as possible, and with a 'Hoosta' my new mount swayed to its feet and we were away again.*

My father's route followed the watering places that explorers had first marked about half a century earlier: Bloods Creek, Alice Well, Deep Well and, just across the present Northern Territory border on the 26th parallel, Charlotte Waters. A story of hardship and loneliness goes with each one. At that time even Alice Springs—or Stuart township, as it was then known—consisted of the telegraph station, a ramshackle pub and a couple of stores, along streets of red sand.

In 1870 the South Australian government had undertaken to build the Overland Telegraph Line in eighteen months. The British Australian Telegraph Company would finance it and lay the undersea cable to Java, with a penalty clause of £70 sterling a day if work proceeded after 1 January 1872. Charles Todd, the South Australian superintendent of telegraphs, was appointed to lead and organise the project.

At that time, the interior was virtually unknown country. In 1862 John McDouall Stuart's exploration party had crossed the continent from north to south on its sixth attempt. Information gleaned from their records wasn't encouraging: hundreds of miles without water in the dry season and flooding rains in the wet, and the country was peopled with Aboriginals who were not about to make welcome these strange pale debil-debils.

So when the OT Line was proposed and the contract signed, newspapers said it couldn't be done. They published derisive cartoons and made great fun of such an impossible project; of Charles Todd's need for thousands of insulators and permanently manned repeater stations that would be necessary to convey Morse code along the line.

Todd's men went out with swag, water bag, bullock drays, wagons, and horse and camel teams across empty land with no cattle stations, little wild game and uncertain delivery of supplies. For $2.50 per week in today's money they toiled northwards through spinifex plains into the tropics, where they were marooned for weeks by torrential rains. Bogged down, they subsisted on damp, weevil-infested flour, and boiled and ate their leather gear and greenhide. Volunteers made a boat of sorts from a tarpaulin-covered dray and careered crazily down the Roper River to hurry back the supply boats to the starving workers.

Still the poles went up, the wires sang in the wind, the line moved steadily forward. The project was completed in just two years.

As a Territorian, I admit to a thrill of pride, that prickles along the spine, when I read that with a twist of wire at Frew Ponds, England and Australia were joined in communication. In Adelaide, on 22 August 1872, with the town hall's bells ringing, Charles Todd's message was tapped through by Morse code:

We have this day, within two years, completed a line of communications two thousand miles long through the very centre of Australia, until a few years ago a terra incognita believed to be a desert.

Now there would be no more waiting months for the blue flag to flutter from Adelaide Town Hall, heralding the arrival of the P&O ships carrying stacks of English newspapers.

My father knew and spoke with men who had worked on the construction of this great line. Now his work was to help maintain it. As a linesman he travelled with packhorses from the Barrow Creek to Powell Creek telegraph stations, climbing the poles to test and repair. With handsets that attached to the main line, he could make contact with the nearest base. A break in the line meant a serious disruption in overseas contact, so constant surveillance was necessary.

The line was also vital for contact within Australia. When a man lay dying from spear wounds after an attack on Barrow Creek, his wife in far-off Adelaide farewelled him through the Morse code of the operators. Can it be imagined today, farewelling a husband with dots and dashes?

CHAPTER 2

# Mounted Constable Jack Sargeant

In Central Australia, Sergeant Robert (Bobby) Stott was The Law and The Order. As police commissioner for the region, he was known throughout the country as the uncrowned King of the Centre. He dispensed justice decreed by the times, by the isolation and with the small police force of the day.

My father always claimed, with some amusement, that he was shanghaied into the Territory Mounted. Sergeant Stott—ever on the lookout for recruits to swell the ranks of his small force—jovially persuaded my father to sign his little form: maybe in a few years, when he was older, Jack would be called upon to join the police force. Thinking nothing would come of it, my father signed.

A few weeks later, a telegram from Stott was tapped through to my father by Morse code:

You have this day been appointed Mounted Constable Northern Territory Police Force, a horse plant is being sent from Newcastle Waters to convey you to Rankine River. You will change horses at Anthony Lagoon and the plant will return to Newcastle Waters.

Just like that, with no specific qualifications for the job, no educational or health requirements—certainly no training period— my father was officially policeman, stock inspector, mining warden, protector of Aboriginals, registrar of cattle brands, receiver of dingo scalps from doggers, issuer of permits to employ, gravedigger for spear wound and fever victims, and supplier of rations. And he was still employed by the British Australian Telegraph Company.

Territorians have always referred to Alice Springs as 'The Alice', Katherine as 'The Kath-Er-Ryne', and the high stony ground of Newcastle Waters as 'The Ridge', so when my father set off with his horse plant to take up his first police post, it was to 'The Rankine'.

The Rankine River on the Barkly Tableland is dry for most of the year. The fierce cold wind of the dry months made a drover's life hell, plodding along in the dust of a thousand head of cattle. But with the flooding rains of the wet season, all of the Tableland's rivers and creeks come to life, and its nearly 300,000 square kilometres of grassland could gladden the heart of any cattleman. Amid the nutritious Mitchell and Flinders grasses of the Barkly, huge cattle stations were established early, and a packhorse mail run came through every six weeks.

12

The arm of the law was very long on the great plains of the Territory in 1921. A meagre police force patrolled more than a million square kilometres of country that spread from desert borders in Central Australia to the jungle tropics along the Arafura Sea. Within these boundaries were arid desert, lush grassland, rivers and mountain ranges—mirage and desolation, unmapped, unpeopled.

Police outposts had no outside communications except for those stationed along the Overland Telegraph Line. Officers spent months patrolling over hundreds of kilometres with packhorse plant and native tracker. Roads were rough or non-existent in the dry; impassable even by horseback in the wet.

When my father came to the Rankine in 1921, there was a bore for water, with a turkey-nest holding dam, and a store catering to drovers. The police station was a small iron building, hot as an oven within. Over its entrance hung an indomitably authoritative sign: *Police Post GRV* (George Rex V). Was King George, on the other side of the world, even aware that this small speck of habitation on the great plain existed?

Bush police posts left much to be desired and in some cases were merely iron sheds or worse. Nicholas Waters, the first Commonwealth Inspector of Police in the Northern Territory, protested in a 1922 report:

> Better quarters should be provided, so as to allow them to get married, as most stations are unfit for occupation. When last heard from the Constable at Lake Nash Station, he was occupying an old tent and bough shade for over two years.

The cattle station there had promised to improve his quarters, but nothing has been done. There is no means of securing prisoners except by chaining them to a post or tree. I submit lockups should be erected at Timber Creek, Rankin River and Roper River.

Rankine was a two-man station; my father joined Alf Stretton, who years later became superintendent of the Territory police force. Born in Borroloola, Stretton was one of the many children of W.G. Stretton, an early Territory policeman who'd endeavoured to tame the lawless gangs of travellers taking the Old Coast Road to seek fortune in the goldfields. In 1872 Wentworth D'Arcy Uhr had established this track when he made a trip from Charters Towers with 400 bullocks for Palmerston; pioneer cattlemen had followed with great herds.

At Rankine, Stretton and my father, along with two trackers, were the only police presence within thousands of square kilometres. Later John Creed Lovegrove took Stretton's place. The arm of the law was very long indeed.

As stock inspectors the Rankine police were responsible for dipping the big herds coming through the Barkly Stock Route during the droving season. They used an arsenic dip for tick and kept a close watch for the parasite's attendant red-water fever. They also administered to the health of Aboriginal people: yaws and leprosy were common diseases, and it was no easy task persuading bush Aboriginals to leave familiar country for medical treatment; unless detained, they silently disappeared into the night and were never seen again.

Anthony Lagoon Station, some 220 kilometres across the Barkly Tableland, was a breeding depot for police horses; from there the policemen restocked their plant with horses bearing the broad-arrow government brand.

Supplies for the Rankine police station came from the Camooweal store. Once, an item on their account caught my father's eye: ten sets of horseshoes that had neither been ordered nor received. He drew the storekeeper's attention to this. 'Oh! The horseshoes: the bookkeeper couldn't remember who bought them, so we charged for them on every account! You are the only person to remark on it. Everyone else paid up.'

One morning at the height of the droving season, a big wagon drawn by twenty horses—with loading for Alexandria Station— pulled up in Rankine. On board was a brand-new Ford, sent down from Darwin for police use by Captain Bishop, chief veterinary officer of the Territory and a Boer War veteran. Fifteen years later, the dear old captain, with his clipped white military moustache, would chaperone me to my first school ball.

The Ford proved a godsend for police on the downs, where the country was hard and flat; it cut travelling time on the long distances between cattle dips. Although bush patrols were still carried out with horse plant, the motor car brought my father and his colleagues into the modern world of the early 1920s.

For most Territorians, the motor car was pretty much a novelty until the early 1930s. But, in 1912, Administrator Gilruth and his chauffeur had made an epic car journey over horse pad and bush track to Borroloola, which says something for the early travellers and something for the early motor car as well.

# CHAPTER 3

# Old Darwin Town

In 1825 the boundaries of many Australian states and territories remained unfixed and land that includes the current Northern Territory was incorporated into New South Wales. Between 1825 and 1838 the British made three unsuccessful attempts to establish settlements on the coast of what is now the Northern Territory. In 1846, the British government considered creating a colony of 'Northern Australia' but later that year all plans for settlement of this proposed colony were abandoned.

The current boundaries of the Northern Territory were formed from the 'leftovers' of Western Australia, South Australia and Queensland establishing their borders between 1829 and 1862. In 1862, on the sixth attempt in four years, John McDouall Stuart travelled the length of the Northern Territory, thereby earning a £2000 reward from the South Australian government. The

Northern Territory was incorporated into South Australia on 6 July 1863, with the British reputedly glad to be rid of what they saw as unprofitable and inhospitable country.

Unique among Australian colonies, South Australia had been established by free settlers, not convicts. Perhaps with a transcontinental rail line, the Territory's pastoral, mineral and other resources could provide a good means of revenue for the colony. In February 1869, George Goyder, the surveyor general of South Australia, arrived to survey a town site on Port Darwin, which he named Palmerston for the then British prime minister. He enthused: 'South Australia has no reason to fear her connection with this place.'

The new town was settled in splendid isolation at land's end atop rocky cliffs, the harbour at its feet; a harbour with few equals, it's said. But the town has no close, surrounding hills to snuggle into; no hinterland of cool mountains for its residents to escape the vicious heat. It lies like a hide pegged out to dry. Town of perpetual summer, its seasons are 'the wet' and 'the dry'. After monsoon, the curtain goes up on cooler dry weather until October, when heat descends with its usual ferocity, and one hears from its brow-mopping citizens, 'By God! I wish it would rain.' And by December, it usually does.

In 1869 the good citizens in their settlement high above the port had rejected the name Darwin. They refused to live in a town named for a man who said they were not created in God's image, but were descended from monkeys. Unbeknown to them, the name Palmerston had a rather more unsavoury cloud about it.

Queen Victoria disliked her prime minister, apparently because at an advanced age he revealed a penchant for parlour maids of great English houses, which created a bit of a scandal back then. Rumour has it that he died on a billiard table at Brocket Hall, Hertfordshire, in enthusiastic sexual dalliance with yet another maid. He was given a state funeral. The residents of Palmerston, thousands of miles distant, could hardly have heard about the salacious and fascinating aspects of its namesake.

Poor little town. Not much of a complimentary nature seems to have been recorded about Palmerston in its early days, except of the considerable gold extracted from its environs. We're presented with a grim picture of daily life. The heat was unbearable for white men and women, encased in their European dress. Residents also had to contend with the isolation, the debilitating fevers and the deplorable filth of Chinatown.

Very few of the Territory's pre-war European citizens were Territory born. They came from all over—from China to the American goldfields—to join the gold rush that began in the early 1870s.

Palmerston's seemingly limitless capacity for booze drew comment from almost every visitor. The town became no place for the righteous. Its churches remained forlornly empty, while hotels overflowed. Drunkenness upset worthy clergymen endeavouring to tend their wayward flock. One Methodist minister of early days wrote: 'It is a town sunk in iniquity.' But then by all accounts he wasn't one for much fun.

A Reverend J.A. Boyle wrote in his diary of having preached twice in Palmerston to a congregation of four, in a church full of snakes and mosquitoes, with rain battering the roof. 'It rather spoiled my sermon,' he wrote glumly. He added, with apparent bitterness, that in a population of 600 whites, the bond stores held 3000 gallons of spirits and wine. 'I cannot help but feel discouraged at this dreadful apathy. Lord stir up thy people.'

The residents of Palmerston did manage a faint stir, but only enough to write cheeky letters that depressed the poor old thing further, and did nothing to staunch their unquenchable thirsts and indifference to his services.

⌒

There was considerable traffic in opium in Palmerston. Unlike cocaine and alcohol, opium is mild, pleasant and relaxing. It intensifies thoughts and eases pain. Where men lie with pipes, in dim shadowy surrounds, there is a curious smell—like toasted nuts, even faintly chocolaty. But this drug is seductive; it can slyly take hold, sink its claws deep, and you are lost.

Opium came to the Territory in the mid-1800s. Aboriginal people had largely been written off as a workforce, and the small European population still lived with the belief that the white man couldn't work in the tropics. Bringing in workers from India was considered, but the Chinese 'coolie' was finally settled upon as a source of manual labour.

In 1874 the ship *Vidar* arrived with the first batch of 176 coolies. They cost £9 7s to introduce and, with provisions, were to work for £3 per month, ten hours per day, not on Sundays. Many, some say all, were opium addicts; they also brought with them smallpox and leprosy.

Leprosy remained, and was disastrous for the Aboriginal people; having never been exposed to this disease, they had no barriers against it. Opium also became their scourge; the Chinese used ash from their opium pipes as payment for Aboriginal women, and their need of the drug was born.

By 1879 the Chinese far outnumbered Europeans in the Top End, and numbers were boosted further when railway construction began. The District Council of Palmerston allotted the Chinese a camp to the north-east of town, as the wind never blew from that direction. It was a shanty town of tin shacks with small odorous backyards, appallingly filthy, sanitation non-existent. Medical men condemned it as unfit for human habitation as leprosy took hold.

The smell wafting out of 'Little Canton' was awful and remained so for years; Cavanagh Street was referred to as Lavender Street. But Chinatown continued to grow right in the heart of town; gambling flourished in iron-walled alleys, where a wager was possible on anything at all.

In 1901 with the Immigration Restriction Act, many Chinese were deported and some suicided in preference to deportation, while others returned to China with new-found wealth, enabling them to live a good life with several wives.

As a young police officer in the early 1920s, my father suffered great embarrassment when he was ordered to observe a Chinese mother suckling her infant in her home, to ensure the child was a genuine resident, born in the country.

In the late nineteenth century, after a succession of unprofitable endeavours, the Territory was proving too expensive for South Australia and the state sought a way to divest itself of what many South Australians referred to as its 'white elephant'. After a visit to the Northern Territory in 1888, J.C.F Johnson, the South Australian minister for the Territory, said, 'It is a bad job that we have had anything to do with the Territory—a bad thing for the Territory, a bad thing for South Australia—we should get rid of it!'

Finally, on 1 January 1911—just eight years before my father's arrival—South Australia was rid of the Northern Territory when the Commonwealth government took over. Two months later, on 3 March 1911, the name Palmerston was changed and the town of Darwin was born. By then the name was already in common use, with no heed paid to monkey ancestors.

Darwin was a tropical colonial town in every sense: a combination of coconut-plantation ports of the East and the old American west. You might have seen, through the swinging doors of the old Terminus Hotel, a hunter in from the bush, bandolier across his chest; Chinese in coolie pants jogging by with yoke and baskets; Japanese pearlers milling about in their glove-like boots; chattering girls of mixed race, with tropical blossoms in their hair; children of exceptional beauty, black through to palest coffee. A proliferation of colours, smells, languages—you could have been anywhere in Asia. Truly, it was as cosmopolitan a town as you could find, and those who knew it well loved it in all its colourful bawdiness.

There is no chance now of re-creating Darwin's past. Gone are the European men in immaculate tropical dress, white linen shoes, pith helmets; gone are the days when evening dress was de rigueur after sundown for men and women. No barbecues back then: white-jacketed Aboriginal houseboys attended in the evenings, and the punkah fan cooled every public dining room and bar.

Ships from the south and from Asia brought regular loading. A certain monthly ship from Singapore, my father fondly recalled, made the very best gin slings. The unloading of liquor generally took precedence—should a strike prevent further work, some shipping lines had the good sense to pack the cases of alcohol well down in the hold.

Work ground to a halt in the wet. For the government employees who could afford it, this was a time to take berth on a ship and retreat south. One heard the old refrain 'out of Darwin by Christmas'. However, there were those to whom Darwin was home, and to them it was exhilarating to catch the town in the wild season of monsoon, when rain crashed on iron roofs so you could barely carry a conversation within, and water rushed in torrents down streets and gutters. Children released from weeks of scorching heat were out splashing through it, with not a thought to the warnings of fever and hookworm—all of the kids already had hookworm and a variety of other tropical parasites as well.

Storm time was exciting, and this was a town where anything could happen, from murder to all sorts of scandalous mayhem, and not an eyebrow raised—although every indiscretion, secret late-night tryst and unlawful dealing among European citizens made for good gossip.

In a new country, awash with opportunities, people came seeking their fortune in gold or pearls, or on vast cattle runs. From the early 1920s, Russian immigrants grew peanuts and bananas. And in every isolated corner of the bush, an Irishman could be found—bred for export, my father said.

Drawn by the novels of Robert Louis Stevenson and storytellers of the swashbuckling Pacific, men took berth on ships bound for the East—for Singapore, Shanghai and adventure—and never made it past Darwin. Here was all the exotic colour they wanted. They came ashore for a drink and forgot where they were going. Some came for more serious reasons: a scientist devoting a month or two to research Darwin's abundant insects and reptiles; a writer bent on prising his first great novel from the romance of an untamed Territory.

They came for only a season, missed the boat, stayed on for the next 60 years, their ambitions foundering early in the lethargy and torpor of early tropical living. Darwin's motto was 'mañana'; no wonder it was known as the 'Land of Wait-a-while'. If you were curious enough to ask, you might be told, 'Bin here for Christ knows how long, mate.' That was all you would hear of it.

Drinking was the great avocation, from elegant evening cocktails to the remittance man with his everlasting gin bottle. He was from an aristocratic family, outcast to the furthest possible shores for some indiscretion or another—aimlessly wandering the East, coming finally to Darwin, where most of his days were spent in the coolness of a tropical bar, waiting for the next cheque to arrive.

A gentleman named Bleezer planted Poinciana trees along the coastal road opposite the old Fannie Bay Gaol, a canopy of intense scarlet to compete with the spectacle of the tropic sunset off Mindil Beach—where, did you know there was once an Aboriginal burial ground?

Sumptuous purple bloom of Bougainvillea ran rampant over seedy sights, as if in coy apology for their shambolic state, while the heavy cloying scent of frangipani, fragrant jewel flower of the tropics, soaked into the humid night air, along with the buzzing of mosquitoes and stinging sand flies: a languorously exotic background for Darwin's thousand coloured faces.

# CHAPTER 4

# Life Down Batchelor Way

After three years on the Rankine, my father was transferred to Darwin. His leg injuries from the war had worsened; the continuous horse-riding played havoc with these old wounds. Because a surgeon was visiting Darwin from the south, it was decided that my father should have an operation.

In searing heat and raging winds, he'd dealt with horse thieves, cattle dodgers and murderers; patrolled hundreds of kilometres with packhorse and tracker; helped settle disputes of drovers, cattlemen, teamsters, Aboriginals. He departed with barely a backward glance, and made a beeline to the tropical delights and urbanity of Darwin.

After as successful a leg operation as was possible at that time, my father was sent down to Batchelor, a small settlement about a hundred kilometres south of Darwin, to recuperate while carrying out light duties—mainly supervising the care of elderly Aboriginal people who were settled there in a compound.

Life was uneventful down Batchelor way, until Police Commissioner George Vernon Dudley arranged to meet with him and came down on the train. In his journal, my father told of his meeting with Dudley and what followed:

*One of his first questions to me was: 'Jack, can you drive a car?'*

*'I drove the car sent down to the Rankine for stock work.'*

*'Good,' he replied. 'I've got a trip for you.'*

*'Where?' I asked warily.*

*'Out to the Tanami goldfields,' he said.*

*'Tanami—hell, that's way out in the desert. There's nothing there but wild Munjong blacks, bad ones too.'*

*Dudley replied, 'We've received a report that the blacks have been raiding the camps of miners and prospectors. They've been stealing their rations and burning their camps. There hasn't been a police patrol out there since 1911 when the first miners took up small gold shows, so we've got to go out and investigate this, see if there's any truth in it. You'll be back in a couple of weeks. All you'll need is your swag and a rifle, be a nice change for you.'*

*And away back to Darwin he went.*

*When the train came down again, my old native boys drove me over to the station in the dray. Sure enough, there was Dudley and a new Ford motor car too.*

*'Look here,' I said, 'why didn't you bring one of those young fellas from Darwin down for this trip? My legs still aren't a hundred per cent, y'know.'*

'Well, Jack,' he said, 'none of them can drive a car. Besides, it's no use taking inexperienced men out to deal with bush blacks, you must know that.'

Later, with the car unloaded, we went over to my quarters and settled down to study the report.

'Now,' Dudley said, 'we'll go down to Katherine, load up with rations, then we'll head out to Wave Hill Station and pick up Frank Sheridan. He's the trooper stationed there. He won't like it either, but we'll need his help to get through—I'm told the roads are just tracks.'

Somehow I couldn't picture the immaculate Dudley in his tropical whites wielding a shovel in heavy sand, so I was all for Sherry joining us.

My argument against going had fallen on deaf ears, so nothing for it but to pick up my rifle and swag, and see if I retained my driving skills.

We loaded stores in Katherine and, with our cans of benzene [petrol] strapped on the running boards, headed out into the 'wild' blue yonder. After chugging along a road made by the passage of wagon wheels and camping by the roadside at night, we finally lurched out of the dust, sweeping grandly into the western sunset and Wave Hill Station.

A reluctant Sheridan joined us. Dudley suggested he bring plenty of ammunition, as we could be headed for trouble—not a happy prospect.

We drove on through miles of Wave Hill country until we reached Gordon Downs Station, managed by a man named Egan. We took a few days break as the annual Halls Creek Picnic Races were due to begin. There was a regular packhorse mail out this way, but it would be another ten years before there would be only three permanent motor cars in the area from Wyndham on the west coast to Katherine in the Northern Territory. With our arrival came the latest news from outside, and our popularity as visitors was assured.

Then back to Gordon Downs. Egan killed a bullock for us, so we had a good supply of salted beef, and with several loaves of bread baked by the station cook in our tucker box, we packed up and set off into the desert.

Leaving the grassy plains behind us, we came into scrub of turpentine and saltbush—this was the back country, the last Australian frontier. With bushes under the wheels for traction, and pushing from the rear, we made our way through dry sandy crossings. By now both Sheridan and Dudley had mastered the modern art of driving a motor car, and we rolled along making good time.

About halfway to Tanami, we came upon an old white man named Beckney. He was quite comfortably settled into a permanent camp by a spring, a small hut with a herd of goats and a good vegetable garden, and a few old Aborigines camped close by for company. We camped the night there. Visitors were always welcome in the bush—even policemen.

Approaching Tanami as the sun was setting, we could see the burnt-out shells of camps silhouetted against the evening sky, which wasn't an encouraging sign. As we drove up, the small company of miners came out to meet us; a fellow named Beckitt took us into his hut.

'So,' said Dudley, 'where are these wild blacks you've reported?'

Beckitt pointed out toward the ranges. 'See that smoke? That's their hunting fires. They burn a patch of country, pick up small game in its wake—that's about all they live on. It's a hard country, not much water, not much tucker, they're always hungry.'

Beckitt explained how, during one raid, he and the other miners took refuge deep in a mine shaft, hiding there until the raiding party had gone, taking most of the rations with them. After much discussion, it was decided the miners had a just complaint and were in need of protection.

Dudley turned to me and said, 'Well, Jack, it looks as if I'll have to leave you here.'

'Hell, you can't leave me here—not in my condition. Anyway, all I have is my rifle and swag, no rations, nothing at all.'

'I'll arrange for the people here to provide for you until I can get some stores out. Sheridan knows what's required at a post like this—he can arrange an order for what is necessary at Halls Creek and find a way to get it out here. I understand from the miners there's a bridle path of 200 miles that goes directly to Wave Hill Station. It won't hurt Sheridan to do a couple of hundred miles on horseback; he's got a good strong plant of horses there.'

So they packed up and away they went, with Sherry showing off his newfound driving skills.

Dudley, plump and polished still, lifted his white pith helmet in farewell.

I stood and watched them depart until even their dust had gone.

I was twenty-four years old, had unsound legs, and I was sole protector of a group of miners who were regularly attacked by wild blacks—desert Munjongs, the worst kind. Did I hear a whisper, 'You'll be back in a couple of weeks, be a nice change for you,' or was that the wind blowing over the sharp desert sand? I picked up my swag and settled in with the miners.

There had been a police presence at Tanami when mining boomed there in 1911. When my father arrived, the gold rush had petered out—there were other goldfields that offered a less harsh environment. The few remaining miners, working their small diggings, were left to fend for themselves.

They led a terrible life of privation and hardship. So far from civilised life, they had to deal with diminishing water supplies—although eventually the government dug them a well—and poor food. At times their rations could be down to flour and a few rats, certainly no vegetables, and this caused that old scourge of the bush, Barcoo rot—a type of scurvy with appallingly painful skin ulcers and general poor health. On top of all this was the trouble of dealing with the marauders. My father wrote of the camp and its difficulties in his journal:

*About a month after my arrival, a chap by the name of Frank Castle rode into our camp with a heavily loaded plant of horses and mules.*

*'Where's this bloke Sargeant? I've got a hell of a load of stores for him.' I was right there and, with help from some of the miners, we unloaded and arranged my gear where I decided to settle camp. Castle brought all the basic rations: tea, salt, sugar, flour, saddles, ammunition and camp gear.*

*Sheridan had sent Paddy, one of his trackers. A sensible choice—a tracker would not venture far from his police post in the territory of hostile tribes.*

*Camp was quickly set up: a small horse yard, a bough shed with* a tarpaulin covering one end to protect from wind and rain, and a table of thin saplings supported with bush timbers. Cooking, as usual in bush camps, was done on an open fire outside; a kerosene tin made a bucket to boil beef, a billy-can for tea, and a camp-oven.

Camp complete, all that remained was the final touch: Paddy and me in our police uniforms, ready for duty. For this 'accommodation', the government chose to delete twenty-five pounds per year from my salary for rent, quite a considerable sum in those days.

Later, Sheridan and his trackers made their 200-mile trip out through the bridle pad from Wave Hill Station; he had all the necessary mining information sent down from the mining warden in Darwin. Dr Cook had sent quinine, bandages, Condy's crystals for snake bite, and other medicines—including that old standby, 'Guts Ache', popular with the blacks, with all of us. We had nothing else: with no refrigeration, meat—mostly dry-salted—suffered in the scorching temperatures of the hot season. The pitiful complaints of 'Me gottem cuts ache' from the blacks called for some treatment, however basic.

Sherry settled in and camped with us for a few days, before starting on the long trip back. In those days, when asked about track and travelling conditions, there was always the question of water for horses or stock, and an added, 'Bad nigger country mate,' or perhaps it was good. Here it was bad, and if a traveller was overdue, it was a reasonable conjecture that he had been killed by blacks.

Sheridan didn't risk the trip again; he and his trackers were too small a band to travel that long lonely track.

Among my loading was chain with locks. In these isolated outposts, a lone trooper and his tracker needed to be vigilant as

*they travelled for days through the bush, outnumbered by prisoners;*
*an attack was likely unless the prisoners were bound in some way.*
*Police tended to overlook lesser crimes; did not take prisoners in*
*these distant places unless in the case of murder.*

On Sherry, the June 1922 progress report by Inspector Waters states:

F. Sheridan—a very good man in procedure—unreliable in town as
he is fond of alcohol. He is stationed where no liquor is available.

Such consideration deserves comment: how civilised of the force
to take into account the social shortcomings of its members. I can't
imagine such solicitousness for one's weakness in today's force.

Even so, I never knew of anywhere in the bush that some
form of liquor wasn't available. If none was to hand, and the
need was desperate enough, the men were quite innovative in
their endeavours to produce something with an alcoholic punch.

There were concoctions from the kitchen and, of course,
methylated spirits, either alone or with various additives. Out
bush, where loading came only a couple of times each year, metho
came in 20-litre tins. It went down the throat like hot lava, and
bore the quaint cocktaily name of White Lady.

For those who drank it regularly, some processing of the raw
spirit took place; it was strained through bread and underwent
other measures to render it more palatable. But metho it remained,
and was not everyone's choice of spirit.

# CHAPTER 5

# Searching for Gold

'It is that eternal curse on gold, which
changes the soul of man in a second.'

B. TRAVEN, *THE TREASURE OF THE SIERRA MADRE*

Wandering the bush in the 1920s and 1930s were the
prospectors of the Territory. You might find them travelling
by camel or horse, but they were usually solitary wanderers on
foot, carrying their quinine and meagre provisions. With gold
dust before their eyes, they were dismissive of the sweltering heat
and harsh terrain.

The prospectors sought gold everywhere. Sometimes they found
it, most times not, and sometimes they unearthed other things
like copper and tin, and once in the rugged gorges near Alice
Springs there was a memorable discovery of rubies—thousands
of them, barrow loads of them, and a ruby rush began. Sent off

to London, the rubies from near Alice Springs were valued as highly as £42 per carat, but back in Australia they were found in such overwhelming quantities gem dealers stopped accepting them and old prospectors stacked sacks of them in sheds because they'd become passé. A prospector was even reputed to have cemented the floor of his outhouse with gravel made from rubies. Who else could boast such a floor?

Soon after setting up camp in Tanami, my father had a memorable encounter with one of these prospectors:

*Paddy and I rode out on our first patrol to familiarise ourselves with the surrounding country. Keeping an eye on distant fires, we rode far into the desert. Travelling east, we came onto a big body of water, heavily stained with leaves and debris, covered with a thick green scum. Our horses had a drink, but we decided not to risk it. This was known as Green Swamp.*

*Further on, we came to a clear pool and stripped off our clothes for a swim, only to find the water so salty we popped up like corks.*

*I gave the name to Rabbit Flat out there—whether they were rabbits or the desert rats, I later wondered, the name made its way into permanence on the map.*

*One morning Paddy called out, 'Camels coming!' and through the shimmering haze a dust cloud rose up. Ghostly mounted men took familiar shape and rode into our camp. It was a well-known prospector, Jimmy Wickham, with his string of camels, a half-caste named Alec and a young Aboriginal boy.*

*They unpacked and settled into camp. Jimmy was excited about a strike he claimed to have made. He tipped from a saddle bag* some fine gold samples, but refused to report a find to the mining authorities, fearing a rush.

Jimmy was an avid prospector, but unfortunately no bushman. He planned to leave Alec to care for the camels, take the Aboriginal boy and bring back men and supplies. I lent him horses and gear, and he set off, fuelled with excitement, for Halls Creek. Alec tended his camels and gave Paddy a hand with the horses. If unused to camels, horses won't drink at the same trough; generally they tend to be uneasy in their presence.

Paddy and Alec were inseparable, rode out together and spent hours playing card games in camp. Late one evening, Paddy reported that Alec hadn't returned to camp. I thought maybe he had cleared off, not wanting to return to the desert with Wickham, so didn't give it much thought.

A few days later we saw smoke out toward Rock-Hole, a water-hole about five miles out. It didn't auger well for anyone out there alone. We decided to take a look, armed ourselves and rode out, keeping a sharp eye and taking no chance of a spear in our backs. We saw recent burnt-out campfires, then Paddy called out, 'Boss, Alec, im ere,' and there among the cold ashes of a fire was all that remained of poor Alec. He had been speared and presumably eaten. The bones hadn't been there more than a few days, and there was clear evidence the remains were Alec. We buried all that we could gather together; with the far red dots of fires along the distant range, we hastened our pace towards home.

Paddy took Alec's death very hard; no doubt the manner in which he died made it so much harder to accept. As anyone would tell you, 'Give an old-time tracker a rifle, and he was an unrelenting hunter of villains.' I didn't fancy the chances of these Munjongs if Paddy came across them while armed.

When Wickham returned from Halls Creek, he had in his party Albert Schultz, uncle of Charlie Schultz, the well-known pastoralist of Humbert River Station. Jack Laurie, a local miner, joined Wickham's party, leaving his brother Tom to work their diggings. Early next day, the party rounded up their camels, packed up their camp and, full of that optimistic enthusiasm peculiar to gold prospectors, departed with the sunrise to claim their great discovery.

A few weeks went by—not a sign of them—and then late one evening Paddy called, 'Smoke come up close that place Green Swamp.' This was not the way Wickham had planned to travel; this was way to the east. Something was wrong there. Then, in they straggled. The first thing I noticed as the camels approached was that Albert Schultz wasn't among them.

'Where's Albert?' I asked Wickham.

'He died two days ago of fever. We buried him at Green Swamp.'

'Why where you there?'

'We got bushed,' he replied. 'Luckily the camels smelled water and led us into the swamp. Albert got sick that night and died—if Alec had been with us, we'd have been on track. He was the only one who really knew that country.'

In the party was another man with fever. We got him down; made him as comfortable as possible. It was Jack Laurie. I went down to the diggings and brought his brother up to camp. We decided that in the morning we would lay Jack in the buckboard and take him to Gordon Downs Station, then try to get him to Halls Creek, where there was a small clinic run by a nurse.

*We set off at a very steady pace. We camped at No. 2 well that night, only about twenty miles out, but we had travelled slowly: it was a rough track, and a horse-drawn buckboard would not be an easy ride for a sick man.*

*Next morning on daylight, Tom and I went to take a look at him, and 'Damn me' if he wasn't dead too. All we could do was bury him there and return to the depot.*

*Three good men had died as a result of Wickham's so-called fabulous find: had he done the right thing in the first place, this would not have happened and he may even have found his gold again. I am convinced there is gold out there, just waiting to be found. Perhaps Lasseter did come by a serious gold seam.*

*I've had Munjong blacks come into my camp—naked, primitive tribesmen from the desert, with not a word of English. They brought in good nuggets of gold; somewhere in that wilderness they learned the white man coveted it.*

*They held the gold there on the palm of the hand. A nod, a grin. 'Tabac, tabac,' they said, tobacco already something of value to them.*

*I asked these Munjongs, 'How far, which way?' waving my hand out yonder.*

*'How far, which way?' they repeated, imitating exactly without understanding.*

*I pointed to the gold nuggets. 'You got more, this kind?'*

*They repeated again, 'You got more, this kind?'*

*'I give you tobacco,' I said.*

*'Tabac, tabac.'*

*They took their tobacco and silently drifted on back into the stony ridges and the desert beyond.*

The Wickham party had buried Albert in a very shallow grave. Paddy and my father reburied him and placed a cairn of stones above the spot, as a marker and to keep dingoes away. Charlie Schultz was grateful for this clearing of his uncle's grave and through the years always remembered it.

Some years later, Charlie's father went out to bring back Albert's remains. It was a comfort to him to take them to Victoria River Downs and lie them beside those of another of his brothers, Billy. Charlie's father had strong suspicions that Albert had been murdered by his prospecting partners, perhaps poisoned, but my father was sure that fever had killed Albert and Jack.

In those days, 'fever' covered a wide range of unrecognised illness. A stiff dose of 'Old Gulf Cure' had its followers. This was concocted from:

> 2 weights of quinine (for fever)
> 60 drops of laudanum (opium)
> 60 drops of spirits of nitre in water (potassium nitrate)
> 1½ packets of Epsom salts

The mixture was usually carried in a rum or brandy bottle, and given a vigorous shake before patients were liberally dosed. If you recovered, all credit went to the Old Gulf Cure—failure was put down to bad luck.

# CHAPTER 6

# Murder in the Desert

One morning a very old Aboriginal man appeared in my father's camp. He must have travelled some distance as he was dirty and footsore.

'Boss,' he said, 'you know that old man Beckney, near that spring, gottum goat and garden?'

This was the old fellow the police party had spent the night with on their first trip out.

'I know him!' my father said.

'Well, him dead. One bad nigger come night time shoot him, take everything he want, then he bin run away.'

'Which way him bin run?'

The man pouted his lips to the west. 'That ai, sun go down.'

My father gave the old man food and a place to rest, then hurried to pack, took Paddy with them and set off to Beckney's camp. They rode all day, coming into camp in the stillness of early evening. A heavy silence lay over the camp. The old natives, Beckney's companions, were nowhere to be seen; they would not linger in a place where a death like this had occurred.

My father's party dismounted and, leading their horses, cautiously approached the doorway of the hut. Sure enough, there Beckney was, shot through the head. They buried him beside his garden and made camp for the night.

My father continues:

*Next morning we rode on towards Gordon Downs. From there I sent word to Wave Hill to advise Darwin of Beckney's murder by an unknown Aborigine, who had then taken off into heavy limestone country.*

*I received this reply:*

This native to be captured at all cost; am sending someone from Wave Hill to assist you. Please await his arrival.

*I waited a few days, then late one afternoon Tracker George— whom I knew—and another police boy, both armed to the teeth, came jogging into our camp, driving their packhorses. George was a perfect shot, and would happily shoot anyone at all in the line of duty.*

*I explained about the murder and that the murderer must be found.*

*'Alright Boss, we find him.'*

*'Now! If he comes along peacefully, we'll take him prisoner,'* I said, *'but if he tries to escape, shoot him. Remember, he has a rifle too, and he has killed a man.'*

We mounted and headed off into the rugged ridges, riding slowly and carefully. But before long the razor-sharp limestone proved too much for the horses' feet, and we had no choice but to turn back and plan an approach on foot.

At Gordon Downs, Egan suggested I let the trackers go out alone, but that wouldn't do—I had to be certain the murderer had been caught; I had to see him, not just have their word on it.

I went down to George's camp, sat with him and asked what he thought about going without me.

'Uwai (yes), we can walk faster, track him better than you.'

'If you find him, you must bring him back. I have to see his face, you understand?'

'I understand!'

We sent them off with a good supply of tucker and ammunition, and awaited result.

A week went by and they hadn't returned, so it seemed I would need to go out after all, but we decided to give them a little more time.

Then one afternoon there was a hell of a fuss from the station blacks' camp: dogs barking, piccaninnies excitedly calling out, the usual noise that heralded an arrival or unusual happening. The lubras were calling, 'Police Boy come up! Police Boy come up!'

We saw them in the distance, but without a prisoner. They sat down a short way off, as was their way, then George, alone, came toward the house. He carried a large hessian sugar bag over his shoulder.

As he drew near, I said, 'You nomore bin catchum that boy, eh?'

'Oh, we bin catchum alright, Boss.'

'But I told you to bring him in. Now I'll have to ride out there to see him. I told you I must see his face.'

'Him a big boy,' George told me, 'too heavy to carry, but you can look his face alright.'

With that he upended the bag and out rolled the murderer's large, odorous head, quickly covered by a swarm of flies.

George grinned at my reaction. He was extraordinarily pleased with himself and in the satisfaction of a job well done.

Over time I came to have a lot of respect for George. Although heartless with a rifle in his hand, he was always in good humour and his loyalty was unquestionable. He proved to be a good man to have behind you in a tight corner, and we later faced quite a few such times together.

George's grizzly prize was identified as the native who killed old Beckney.

I said to Egan, 'My report will sure cause a stir when I say his head's been cut off.'

'Don't mention it; just say he was shot in the execution of duty, no need for gruesome detail.'

Off went this report to Darwin, and that was the last I heard of it.

My father and George called in to Beckney's camp, collecting the goats and the old blackfellas who had returned there. Like a nomadic tribe of ancient times, with a slow-moving herd of goats, people on foot and a few horsemen leading the way, they came back to Tanami.

CHAPTER 7

# Hard Times

There was much for a white man to learn about life in the desert. In the freezing nights and the scorching hot season, we came to understand why the naked tribes were lean, and hard as the stone of their desert country.

Their lives were spent in the constant search for food and their skinny bodies could travel enormous distances. With spears and throwing sticks, they were accurate hunters of snake, wallaby and goanna, as well as the desert rats that had sustained the early miners on the Tanami diggings.

In the wet season there was a greater diversity of food than one might imagine. Berries and edible plants sprouted in the early rains. There were fat round honey ants, and the lubras dug huge quantities of small frogs out of the ground and threw them live onto hot coals. Those that sprang off were, with the flick of a hand, quickly returned by women sitting in a circle around the fire. The frogs were a special delicacy, eaten guts and all.

According to my father, the desert Aboriginal people were cannibals. When riding in the ranges, on several occasions he came upon blackened human remains in old fireplaces. They were mostly of children, but not always.

The tribes were always on the move; the old and sick were left behind, with a little food and water beside them, to die alone. What else could the tribes do? They had to wander, burn the country for small game, wander on—the tribe must survive. It is an easy thing for us to pass judgement.

In the western regions, the Aboriginal word for horse was *yowerda* (it also meant 'ears'). Horses were easy to kill, and a towering feast compared to the bush animals that for centuries had supplied the protein in the tribal diet.

My father wrote of this in this journal:

*One day an old Aborigine came rushing into the police depot in a hell of a fuss. 'Allabout blackfella killum horse, Boss!'*

*'How he killum?' I asked.*

*He described in grim detail, with talented theatrical mime, how the horse was caught by its neck strap, its throat cut, then left to gallop about in a frenzy of terror until it fell dead.*

*We had good horses; kept them hobbled at a spring out from our camp. We could not afford to lose any, as they were our only means of transport, packhorses carried our gear, and in a life or death situation we relied entirely on our horses for a quick getaway.*

We rode out to the spring to see if the situation was as bad as described—sure enough, the old fella was right. We found one of our packhorses dead, its throat cut and a haunch cut off. They had taken enough for their immediate needs and left the remains to rot in the sun—as always, never a thought beyond the next feed. Meat was not cooked or sundried to be carried on, to provide for leaner times. The blacks often killed for sport or ran cattle off pasture and burnt it out. Worse was when a large portion of flesh was cut from a living beast that was left to roam—a slow cruel death. This came to be referred to by cattlemen, with much bitterness, as 'Abyssinian steak'.

We knew the Munjongs would be back for another easy kill before too long, so we fired shots that reverberated around the stony gorge, hoping to warn them off. George and Paddy were ready to go right after them, but I felt our shots would keep them away—for a few weeks, anyway.

We had continuous trouble, our horse numbers dwindled alarmingly, and it became necessary to take further action. So, one morning when we found our quiet old packhorse killed, George, Paddy and I made early departure for the spring, armed with our Martini-Henry .310 rifles, which were police issue at that time. We settled down to wait. The sun moved slowly; shadows lengthened through our hideout.

We heard a horse snort and then bolt out in fright. The Munjongs—I counted sixteen, the late sun catching the sweat streaks on their naked dusty bodies—were driving the horses, who were plunging and circling in confusion toward the Gorge where they could easily be caught.

We waited until we were well within the rocky barrier, then rode in behind the Munjongs. They spotted us, turned, let fly with a shower of spears; we fired among them; they retreated up the stony sides of the enclosure and climbed to where they found a good position to again cast their spears. Those that got away clambered higher; they turned to watch us, the old men angrily chewing on their straggly beards. They realised they were out of range of our rifles; stood there on a high ridge presenting their buttocks to us and making obscene gestures.

We camped hidden among rocks that night, intending to bury the dead next day, and we were completely unaware that the dead had all been silently removed in the darkness.

George had received a shoulder wound in the skirmish and was seething for revenge. The Munjong drove him mad, keeping just out of rifle range, taunting him with gestures and ostentatious boldness. He was all for following them; Paddy too—no doubt Alec's death, the manner in which he died, tormented him, but I felt our horses would have a couple of months' reprieve, and we turned back to camp.

Later we were issued with .303 rifles—more powerful, with longer range—and George and Paddy had their revenge on their tormentors, with some superb buttock shots.

Sometime later, toward the end of the dry, late one afternoon, the old cry, 'All about packhorse coming, Boss.'

'Whatname?' I asked (the native way of asking who or what). 'Him whiteman?'

'No more, (no) him policeman!'

Aborigines admired the uniformed troopers, respected their authority in the bush. One could ask, 'Who that man?' and be answered, 'That nomore man, him policeman.' If a part-Aborigine were approaching, the answer would be a disparaging, 'That not man, that arp-carse (half-caste) or that yella fella.' A derisive term for the pale-skinned mixed blood. Half-caste children born in tribal camps were not received with much joy, and sometimes were disposed of early—I know this to be so, for I have found their remains on more than one occasion during early years, in various parts of the bush.

Well! The police troopers were Don Hood and Ben Toohey; they had appeared right out of the blue to relieve me with a casual, 'I believe you're going on leave.' I hadn't had leave in seven years of service, and this with their unexpected arrival was all good news.

Hood and Toohey were to begin establishing a permanent police depot on my camp. I prepared to leave; there wasn't much to pack. I told them of the tribes who roamed the distant ranges, that our horse numbers were down, and that some must be returned to Gordon Downs Station.

George insisted he leave with me; Paddy was to remain on duty at the depot. After farewelling my mining mates, we rode off towards Gordon Downs, then later on to Wave Hill Station. There George and I said goodbye; he was happily back in his own country again.

I couldn't have chosen a more reliable and loyal companion to ride beside me in those harsh times. We sat together and talked awhile, then shook hands.

With his hand on my shoulder, he gave me a steady look and said, 'My good old boss.'

We never met again, but I had news of him from time to time through police channels.

Soon after my father left, the local Aboriginal people attempted to burn out the police camp by lighting dry spinifex grass. Hood's best riding horse was speared; in his report, he said that he followed the tracks and shot the man responsible.

CHAPTER 8

# My Parents Wed

My father returned to Darwin, where he took berth on the *Marella*, a P&O passenger ship, to Adelaide. He had met my mother, Valeska Marie Hese, who was generally known as Marie, years before, and they renewed their old friendship during this visit, which led to their deciding to get married.

My mother's father, Heinrich Hese, was born in Silesia, Prussia in 1861. On 24 February 1882 he left Plymouth, England on the sailing ship *Clyde*, and arrived in Adelaide almost four months later on 6 June 1882. In 1889 he married my grandmother, Ernestine Henrietta Totschek, in Hackney, South Australia. My grandmother's parents were from Katowice in Poland. In the years after they married Ernestine had seven children. Of this large brood, my mother—who was born in 1902—was the youngest.

All three of my mother's brothers went off to fight with the Australian army in the First World War. According to my mother, in the very anti-German atmosphere of that time, it became a family joke that the large portrait on their drawing-room wall of Emperor Franz Joseph I, complete with gold epaulets, copious medals and drooping moustaches, was passed off to the curious as 'our old grandpa'. It remained there unchallenged all through the war years.

By all accounts Papa Heinie ruled his large family with an iron rod. He refused to allow my mother to study medicine with a view to becoming a doctor. When she reached 21 he did, however, consent to her training as a nurse, which he considered a more suitable pursuit for a woman. Perhaps he had a notion that nursing only entailed bandaging injured limbs, a la Florence Nightingale, and genteelly dosing with medicine—not poking about on naked male bodies, as he supposed a doctor must do.

After four years my mother graduated as a fully trained nurse from the Royal Adelaide Hospital, and went on to complete midwifery training at Yorketown Hospital in South Australia. This was to be of immense value to her in the remote country where she would later live.

In 1927 my parents were married in the Alberton Methodist Church in Adelaide. A newspaper notice listed my mother's parents as living at 'Murray View' Caloote, River Murray at the time. In the manner of the times, it went on to say, 'The bride was given away by her father, and wore a dress of white Milanese silk and georgette, with silver shoes and hose to match . . .' and so on, right down to a detailed description of her veil and the bouquet she carried. My mother's brother Theo was the best man. A lavish reception followed. The guests were almost all my mother's friends and relatives, as my father had lost touch with his large family since the war. He was not particularly close to them and told me once that he had an older brother he had never seen. In the newspaper notice my mother's travelling dress was described as 'of fawn georgette, with a bodice and overskirt of silk lace, and she had a silk straw hat to match'.

With his savings my father bought a new cloth-hooded Dodge touring car, the very latest model, and my parents spent their honeymoon exploring the country areas of South Australia while they waited for the wet season to end so they could travel to Darwin.

My father was devastatingly handsome in his youth, with the dark looks of his Scottish ancestry. He was generous, good fun, a born raconteur, but not a commendably attentive husband. He was away on bush patrol for long periods and—alas!—in the fashion of the times and the country, he drank too much.

Drinking was the great unifier in the Territory. If you didn't drink when you came there, you sure as hell did by the time you left—that is, of course, if you ever got around to leaving. But it didn't do much for a harmonious marriage, and my parents' marriage could never have been described as such.

⌒

With the wet season over, movement began on roads north, and it was time to take the trip back to the Territory. Mother had never been bush and thought it was a great adventure. They loaded rations, benzene and a good many spare parts for their car, then set off, taking much the same route my father had travelled with the Afghan camel train in 1919.

Along this route the Afghans still carried freight, but now Sam Irvine brought mail in his truck from Oodnadatta to Alice Springs (still officially named Stuart) every six weeks. Roads were somewhat improved, but heavy sand was always to be a problem for a motor vehicle. At Marree, the storekeeper suggested that my parents hire his coir (coconut fibre) matting to negotiate the deep sand. On arriving in Alice Springs, the mats were to be left at Fogarty's Store for a returning motorist.

When my parents were ready for the road, their tucker box and water replenished, an old desert-dusted Aboriginal man approached Mother. Thin and very dirty, he was rubbing his stomach and chewing on a dirty sock. 'Me 'ungry, Missus, no tucker.' Mother, shocked at such need, freely dispensed food, then returned to the store to restock, much to the storekeeper's amusement.

It transpired that the old man was an accomplished actor and, with neat addition of the dirty sock to chew, did very well from soft-hearted new chums.

For my mother, first bushman, first lesson.

My parents left Marree with coir mats strapped aboard and had a fair run to Oodnadatta. Barely out of town, their problems began. They set the mats under the wheels, crawled forward, transferred the rear mats to the front and continued on through long stretches of deep sand. This route had twice been tough for my father. I always thought it a great pity he never travelled on the modern train that glides effortlessly over the camel pads of the old Afghan trail.

⁓

The Afghan cameleers were settled in Australia from 1860 to attend a mode of transport more suited to the harsh desert interior where horse and bullock teams were proving unsuccessful. It is written that without the camel, European settlement within the centre of our dry continent would not have been possible on the same scale for a further 50 years.

The Afghans were victims of prejudice and religious intolerance. Alienated by both Aboriginal and European, they remained secreted behind their religion in their Ghan town communities, but they were also hospitable and giving.

There is a much-told tale of the first camel track seen by Aboriginals of the central desert, who were familiar with the tracks of everything that moved in their world. They were thoroughly bewildered by this strange print in the dust. After much consideration, the elders decided it resembled a baby's bottom; when an infant of the tribe was brought to the spot and set upon it, the fit was perfect. All was explained: a debil-debil piccaninny had taken a moment to rest awhile on this dusty path on his journey through another time.

The Afghans brought loadings through the Barkly Tableland. They were a common sight out west in the Kimberley too, where there is still a well-tended Afghan cemetery. They came through Alice Springs up to Newcastle Waters, but took their teams no further north, for there grew the Cooktown ironwood tree, whose round green leaves were poisonous to their camels.

My parents had an endless fund of anecdotes about these remarkable men, and about their camels too—some of whom, with head held high, looked out upon the world with a cool disdain, but were gracious enough to accept titbits from children. But the camels could also be dangerous: my father once saw a cameleer killed, his head crushed by a bite from a rogue animal.

Travelling through the Barkly, an Afghan had an altercation with the manager of Alexandria Station, Cay (C.A.Y.) Johnson. After a loud and angry argument, the Afghan departed to his camp, returning soon after with two long stiletto-type knives. He presented them with great formality and dignity, for the manager's choice of weapon. 'Mr Johnson,' he said, 'we fight, one man die.' My father witnessed this drama, and remarked that it said something for the persuasive powers of Johnson that he was still there years later—and so was the old Afghan, travelling his regular route.

It can truly be said that Afghans carried everything in their loading—building material, stores, furniture, household items—but no pork or bacon. In the bush, bacon was an easily stored food, in high demand, so before presenting it to Afghans to load, it had to be disguised in heavily wrapped parcels.

Other parcels would have benefited from more careful wrapping. My mother once ordered from Adelaide a rather fancy hat to wear to the annual Rankine picnic races. For weeks she waited anxiously for the cameleers to arrive, and in her impatience was standing at the yards when the packs were opened.

The box containing her long-awaited hat was crushed, the contents a total disaster—with no shopping and rare occasion to socialise, this was a tragedy of vast proportions, as any woman will understand. Mother sat right down in the dust, among the kneeling camels, and wept great tears of disappointment.

Later she admitted that the picture she presented of a respectable lady of that period, of whom a certain dignity was expected, sitting in the dust, clutching a crumpled hat to her breast, surrounded by camels regarding her with their long-lashed soulful eyes—which she swears were full of sympathy—and encircled by uncomfortable, turbaned Afghans, was, no doubt about it, an event to be retold with wonder around many a desert campfire.

Of course, everyone knows that if you see an Afghan standing close by his camel's head, chances are they are discussing the 99 names of God—only a camel knows the hundredth name, which accounts for his arrogance and superior attitude.

# CHAPTER 9

# My Welcome to the World

In 1928, when my parents arrived in Darwin as newlyweds, a welcome to my mother on behalf of the city's residents appeared in the only newspaper, mentioning that they'd had to deal with a very boggy road through the town of Mataranka. My parents settled into their first joint home in the new stone police barracks, overlooking Darwin Harbour. This was quite a change from when my father had first joined the force—back then, troopers had slept on camp beds behind the police station and eaten at a local Chinese café.

After six months of sea breezes and harbour views, my father was posted to Brocks Creek, a dry little settlement lying desiccated and exhausted under the tropical sun, and here my mother's true bush life began. Brocks Creek provided a pretty raw introduction to Territory life for a young woman fresh from the city, and she was thrown into the deep end, so to speak.

With the gold rush over, Brocks Creek's only excuses for existence were the surrounding cattle stations and railway station. It was a hard police posting, with long horse plant patrols that could take weeks. All had to be dealt with by a lone trooper: Chinese opium dens, buffalo hunters, Aboriginals and prospectors.

Across the road from the police station stood the Federation Hotel. Although in slow decline, it was a reminder of the town's palmier days of goldmining. The publican was an old English woman named Fannie known throughout the Territory as 'Cockney Fan'. She had come with the gold rush of the 1880s and built the Federation Hotel with her parliamentarian husband, Thomas Crush, who died long before my parents arrived in Brocks Creek.

The arrival of a police trooper and his wife right across the road from her hotel wasn't an occasion of great joy to Fannie and the patrons of the Federation Hotel; however, they would provide diversion enough to keep any policeman constantly on duty.

Fannie ruled Brocks Creek—the whole 160 kilos of her—and few dared defy her. She out-drank the most seasoned drinkers, and her repertoire of obscenities was the envy and admiration of the most hardened miner or teamster.

She kept pigs, ducks, chickens and dogs—all roamed unchecked indoors and out. She also ran the post office from her hotel, and if her ever-vigilant eye fell upon a letter addressed to someone who owed her money, she opened it in the hope it contained cash or perhaps a cheque; she would then remove the amount owing her, return the change and reclose the letter without a word said.

It wasn't long before she fell afoul of the law, as far as my father was concerned. The town's bore water was rationed, everyone expected to keep within their limits. Not Fannie—she let water flood freely so her pigs and ducks could wallow about, and of course this caused a general shortage. My father, after many confrontations with her, cut off her water for a short while, hoping to make her aware of the serious situation they all faced.

When drunk, which was often, Fannie had a tendency to remove her clothes. On this occasion the public was presented with the vision of Fannie clad only in a tiny singlet, with her abundant rolls of flesh jiggling about her, staggering drunkenly across the road with a small bucket over one finger, desperately gasping, 'Water! Water!' This created a scene of much pathos and interest to onlookers, but there is no knowing if it changed her attitude to the town's water problems—possibly it made not the slightest difference at all.

On one of the rare times my mother happened to enter the hotel, she was confronted with the sight of Fannie stretched upon the floor, drunk and as naked as the day she was born. Four of her regular patrons were seated on the floor around her, the enormous pink mound of her stomach providing them a table on which they nonchalantly played a game of cards. I believe Mother fled the scene never to return, quite shaken by such a sight so early in her Territory experience.

The well-known author Bill Harney, my father's good friend, told another Fannie story. She was serving lunch of roast beef to a fastidious Englishman travelling through by train. The flies were in clouds, so Fannie produced an insect spray of her own concoction and gave his dinner a thorough spraying, with a jolly, 'It's alright, it won't hurt you much but it'll kill the little bastards.' And so it did, for they lay thickly upon his dinner, their little legs in the air, as dead as dodos.

Fannie remained in Brocks Creek until the outbreak of the Second World War, whereupon the town became a military depot. When civilians were evacuated from the north, she had to be forcibly removed by the army. With a gun in her hand and the vast expanse of her back to the bar, she defied them to remove her, though remove her they surely did. She had met her match at last! Only the army had the manpower to do it.

Sadly, Fannie never returned; dying in Sydney where she'd gone to live with her sister. I say 'sadly' because, old harridan that she was, Fannie was one of our own, a real character of the old Outback, her like never to be seen again.

⁓

The sizeable Chinese community of Brocks Creek gathered remnants of miners from the gold-rush days. Their camp was referred to locally as the Rice Garden; it was settled on land dangerously pitted with old mine shafts, through which only the Chinese were sure to negotiate safe passage.

On a certain dark night, my father was called out to investigate trouble at the Rice Garden. Afterwards he was following a narrow path back to town, gripping two Chinese miscreants by the collar, when suddenly they both disappeared from his grasp and couldn't be found in the gloom. Later they were hoisted up unhurt from an old shaft that lay directly beneath his path into which they had fallen.

Of much concern to police at that time was the effect opium had on Aboriginal people. One night my father had reason to police a noisy group of Chinese being threatened by Aboriginal people who were half-crazed on opium ash—a situation where a lone policeman could easily have taken a spear in the liver. A spear was thrown out of the darkness: it tore through the cloth of my father's uniform, grazing his shoulder. With that, he took out his pistol and fired in the general direction the spear had come from, hoping to deter any further missiles.

He continued on to the crowded shanties of the Rice Garden, where he unearthed a cache of opium. Returning with his Chinese prisoner, he found he had wounded the spear thrower, so he took them both back to the police station.

The Aboriginal man was obviously wounded quite badly, so my father decided to head straight for Darwin, where soon afterwards the man died in hospital. The Chinese man was released, and my father was suspended from duty on a murder charge while an inquiry was held.

In due course, the magistrate brought in a verdict that the man had met his death by a revolver bullet fired by a police trooper in the execution of his duty. Having given his verdict, the magistrate then said—and my father always remembered this—'Should any man ever accuse this man of having murdered this native, I ask he be brought before me, and I will deal with him accordingly.'

In the midst of dealing with her husband's suspension and murder charge, my mother travelled to Darwin for my birth. She must have wondered just what she had taken on with her marriage into the Territory police force.

Having trained as a nurse in a large modern city hospital, my mother was to give birth in the Darwin Hospital, a little old iron building perched high on cliffs above the Timor Sea. The hospital was staffed by Dr Cecil Evelyn Cook and four nurses. The five of them had been responsible for a couple of thousand Asiatics and Europeans, and hundreds of Aboriginals camped about the town and beaches. They'd treated everything from malaria and leprosy to spear wounds and crocodile maulings. Cook operated without the assistance of an anaesthetist; instead, chloroform was administered by one of the nurses.

I was born early in 1929 on a proverbial dark and stormy night, at the height of monsoon. Dr Bruce Kirkland, who had lately joined the hospital staff, was called upon this night, and a long and arduous undertaking it was for him and my mother. The end result—puny, weak and undersized—must have seemed poor reward for their efforts.

Regardless of gender, my mother had wished to name her child Murray after the Murray River: a river dear to her heart that flowed through the country where she'd spent her youth. However, when the good doctor brought me forth he announced, 'We'll call her Jacqueline,' and would brook no argument, not even from my mother—so, that was that.

Oil flares lit the sky above Darwin that night in 1929, and those with a romantic turn of mind might think this an ardent welcome to this white child born into a Territory with only a few thousand Europeans scattered over its wide landscape. However, the oil flares were in fact beacons to guide aviators during the great air races of the day.

Of course, in 1929 the birth of a child was always a good excuse—if an excuse was needed—for prolonged celebration. My doting father thought I was the best thing to come out of that year of disaster and financial mayhem. The completion of the Alice Springs to South Australia railway line had to come a close second.

I was duly welcomed into the Christian faith in Darwin's small stone Anglican church. The famous old hunter Harry Hardy, a man as dry and tough as the wild buffalo he chased on horseback, was chosen as my godfather. Harry and his brother Fred were the most successful and well-regarded buffalo hunters of their day. With Aboriginal companions, they rode the wetlands of Arnhem Land and could ship out a thousand hides in a season.

~

With the murder case resolved, my father was reinstated into the Territory police force, and my parents returned to Brocks Creek with me.

Soon after our arrival, the local Aboriginal women presented my mother with a coolamon, carved from the outer trunk of a tree, to carry her new infant as their babies were carried. But my mother would never have learned the knack of carrying a coolamon on the hip, and it was left to the nurse girls.

Infants were barely visible in the coolamons, covered with bits of cloth and clothes to keep off flies and the sun. One wonders that they could breathe, but they seemed always to sleep peacefully in their snug cocoons. If they stirred or fretted, the mother scratched with her fingernails on the underside, which soothed the baby within.

# CHAPTER 10

# The Many Ways to Die in the Bush

My mother's nursing training proved useful at Brocks Creek and a steady stream of patients, black and white, presented with a wide range of ills.

Throughout her years in the bush she had never been employed by, nor connected in any way with, a health or government service, but Dr Cook sent her medicines to treat yaws, Barcoo rot, ear and eye problems. With no doctor in the area, her medicines—though basic—were in demand; much of her treatment entailed constant care for each phase of illness as it presented.

On one occasion she had the unenviable task of dealing with a man who had cut his throat in a suicide attempt. He was left on her verandah in a very bad state—the only course for her to take was to get him through to Darwin Hospital.

A rugged trip lay ahead: the road was rough, thick with dust and unsealed all the way. With my father driving, their infant daughter with them, my parents set off in their open touring car and travelled through the night. My mother made the journey holding together the man's ghastly wound and doing whatever else one does to staunch excessive bleeding. Incredibly, they succeeded in delivering him alive to Dr Cook the next day.

With the patient progressing quite well, he was brought into court to face charges for his suicide attempt, which the law in those days considered akin to murder. It was too soon for him to deal with the stress of a court attendance, and he collapsed and haemorrhaged his unwanted life away.

On another occasion, Mother had to deal with a man perishing from thirst. Searchers found him wandering naked, for clothes are early discarded in this situation. The sight of mounted rescuers sent the thirst-maddened man running: he was caught, wrapped in wet blankets and delivered to my mother. A long drink was out of the question, so she gave him a wet flannel to suck and kept him moist. He lost a great deal of skin from dehydration, but he lived—or so my mother told me.

She had an uphill battle convincing Aboriginal mothers to prevent disease through cleanliness, especially the need to keep flies from clustering in eyes, ears and noses. But it was cure for their ills they sought and they had great faith in the 'Missus medicines'. Often they presented for treatment when illness was well advanced; with no doctors and no antibiotics, the outcome could not be good.

Bush medical cases in the 1920s and 1930s could seem quite unbelievable to a doctor or nurse newly arrived from a far city. For the first time in their careers they might be called upon to deal with a man dying from the power of suggestion or one whose kidney fat had been ripped out to be used as a magic potion.

A person could be 'sung' by a power from within the tribe. A bone is pointed at the unfortunate one—to be truly effective, it must be human and the magic words must be chanted over it before use. The pointer's back is always turned to the victim, the bone pointed from over the shoulder or between the knees. The victim is unaware of the pointing but he will hear of it, this is certain—then the terrible curse begins. He sits alone, this ill-fated man, and slowly, slowly, he withers. As his life fades, he imagines his blood is seeping away or his liver is drying out to become nothing within him, and he obligingly dies—a triumph of suggestion. There is apparently no way to survive the death bone.

My father took one such fading man to Dr Cook in Darwin. At a loss to know how to treat him, the doctor anaesthetised him with chloroform. After awakening from his induced sleep, the man was told the curse had taken its course and worked through to its end. He had died. Now he was reborn to occupy the same body—a reborn life can take any form—and could never be cursed again.

He returned to his tribe full of confidence. What arrogance he displayed! He was untouchable, need fear no authority and showed little respect for Elders. Never before had their power been thwarted; to them it was unbelievable. They retired in anger and bad grace, and with much loss of face.

A patient my mother always remembered was an elderly Aboriginal woman found dying and neglected in the native camp. She lay on the ground, children and dogs tumbling over her in play, and not a person cared. My mother had her brought up and settled in a bed on her verandah.

The woman had obviously been exposed to Christianity at some point, perhaps on a mission station. Sensing her end was nigh, she begged Mother, 'Sing me Jesus song, Missus.'

Mother's repertoire of hymns was limited, so she gave a shaky rendition of 'Onward Christian Soldiers'; the comforting word here was Jesus, so 'Onward Jesus Soldiers' was rendered somewhat off-key. Another hymn she recalled from her days of wartime church services, when her brothers were away fighting at the front, was 'For Those in Peril on the Sea', which brought comfort to a woman who couldn't have had the slightest notion of what a sea was.

When death was imminent, she had forsaken her old beliefs and sought solace in an alien faith.

⌒

When I was three months old, my father joined the police patrol to track down Moodoorish, an Aboriginal man who had murdered a young white man named Renouf.

Recently arrived in the Territory and set on seeking adventure in the wild, Renouf had teamed up with a bushman named Nichols. They bought a small launch and set sail out of Darwin, south-west down the coast. At Point Blaze they sprang a leak and beached for repairs, and it was there that their short-lived adventuring came to an abrupt end.

Renouf was alone on the boat, Nichols away on shore, when Moodoorish and his right-hand man Nijooli crept silently up on the man bending over his cooking pot and shot him in the back with his own gun.

So the police hunt began. Two mounted constables, Hoffman and Hemmings, from Daly River and their trackers set off on horseback with orders to pursue and capture the murderer. They tracked through bush for days, but the crafty Moodoorish was always just ahead. They were told by Brinkin tribespeople that he had reached the coast and was boasting to all of his shooting the white man. He was regaling the gathering tribes with his threats to kill all the pursing police and take the kidney fat of every tracker in the patrol.

On 19 June 1929 the patrol reached the coast, hobbled out the horses and made camp. Around midnight, settled under mosquito nets in their swags, they heard a call on the still night air—a long, low animal call, not quite that of a dingo—and presently an answering call from the other side of camp. Fully alert, they edged out of their swags and took cover. 'Who's there?'

They were answered with a shower of spears. They fired into darkness; the spearmen retreated through trees. All was quiet again.

Tracker Charlie was wounded in the leg. In darkness they removed long splinters of poisoned mangrove-wood spearhead, but Charlie was already poisoned, becoming fevered and confused.

In the morning twenty spears quilled up out of swags, fireplace and surrounding trees. In spite of their cunning, it hadn't occurred to the attackers to kill or run off the hobbled horses. A good thing this was too, for it would have been more than 150 kilometres on foot with a wounded man, through country rapidly filling with overexcited tribespeople come to join the corroboree telling of Moodoorish killing the white man.

The policemen decided to abandon the patrol temporarily. Hemmings would take Charlie into Brocks Creek, while Hoffman went on to Tipperary Station to shoe the horses and refurbish the plant. So Charlie was brought in to my mother—more than 150 kilometres on horseback had been a hard trip for the wounded man. Later my mother sent him to hospital in Darwin, where he recovered from his wounds and returned to work as a tracker in the force.

With two more constables, my father and Constable Don, and additional trackers, the strengthened patrol rode straight back to the coast, where growing numbers of tribespeople were performing the triumphant corroboree that told of Moodoorish's victory, along with the withdrawal of police.

The new patrol made camp on clear ground surrounded by mangrove and bush, and waited expectantly through the night. The sounds of corroboree continued with increasingly feverish excitement until morning, when over a hundred gaudily painted participants gathered among the mangroves—howling, threatening with clacking spears, chewing wildly on their beards. More than two hundred feet were stomping on the ground.

The patrol prepared to stand. The spearmen moved forward, rhythmically chanting; retired en masse; moved forward again, spears poised; and then fanned out, intending to encircle the camp.

'Aim at the ground,' Hemmings said. 'When I say *fire*, fire in front of them and keep firing.'

Four white men facing a hundred naked, armed black men. It would have been so easy to take a spear in the gut and the trackers no doubt dwelled on unsettling thoughts of their kidney fat being unceremoniously ripped out.

Spears showered in at them. 'Ready, fire, keep firing!' They took aim, fired into the ground; bullets ricocheted; spears curved in a high arc at them; the blacks turned, fled into the mangroves. That was close! 'If they'd had the courage to stand their ground,' said Don, 'what a mess they'd have made of us.'

Moodoorish was arrested for the murder of Renouf; his close brotherhood for the wounding of Charlie. It was a long, slow return trip with eight prisoners. For about 120 kilometres the patrol was closely shadowed by Moodoorish's tribesmen. The constables and trackers remained tensely alert throughout the night, and surely it can be seen why they had to manacle their prisoners.

The Aboriginal men were tried in Darwin. They were dismissed and returned to their country on the grounds they were all implicated and couldn't be witness against one another.

On his return, Moodoorish's fame spread from the Daly to the Victoria River. He was hailed a great warrior, but he had only shot a new chum lad in the back and, with a hundred armed men around him, retreated before four mounted troopers.

In a book called *Man Tracks*, Ion Idriess wrote a detailed account of this patrol in 1929, telling of how Hemmings, Sargeant, Don and Hoffman coolly stood their ground in remote country. It is quite a tale.

In Brocks Creek a nine-month-old baby lay feverish in its cot, very sick with a severe case of bronchial pneumonia, and there was little hope she would survive the night. Despite my mother's nursing prowess and success, she had been unable to return the baby to health.

My father, who knew everyone's comings and goings, heard that the fortnightly train from Darwin had arrived. Its passengers, among whom was an English doctor, were settled for the night at Fannie's Federation Hotel. My father raced over to seek the doctor's help. Unfortunately, the good doctor was heavily loaded with rum and refused to leave his card game, whereupon my dear father, never one to dally about, produced his trusty service pistol. With this hard cold instrument jammed uncomfortably behind the reluctant doctor's ear, my father marched him to the young patient's bedside.

To his credit, when he realised the severity of the baby's illness, the doctor sat with her all through the night—but then in view of my father's earlier method of persuasion, perhaps he thought it politic to remain.

Obviously the patient recovered, for here I am telling of it today.

# CHAPTER 11

# Newcastle Waters

In 1930, when I was a year old, my parents left Brocks Creek and moved to Newcastle Waters, known to Territorians everywhere as the Ridge, which turned out to be my father's last police posting. In the early days of the Territory, it was possible for a town to set its foundation on a bottle of rum, a couple of drinkers, a swag rolled out beside a waterhole; later, a bough shade could lend a homely touch, as well as protection from the elements. They could sell a bag of flour or a horse to someone passing. Other travellers might unpack the old horse for the night, find the company congenial and stay on through the wet. The place could take a name like 'The Four Mile', 'Paddy's Lagoon', 'Ryan's Bend'—and so it was that a small settlement would begin, perhaps to grow larger, probably not too large, but a tiny fly-spot on the map it would remain, and an infant town might be born.

Back then roads weren't gravelled and there was certainly no Stuart Highway with bog-proofing bitumen. Instead, two-wheel tracks led through spinifex from Alice Springs to Darwin, and you took your chances and battled on as best you could. In the wet you bogged; when river crossings went under floodwater, you camped 'till they went down'.

About a half-mile from the Newcastle Waters Station homestead, a small store catering to drovers, and licensed to sell liquor, was flourishing. It was run by Jack McCarthy, widely known as Irish Mac, a teamster who carried loading through Elsey Station and whom Jeannie Gunn had written of in her book *We of the Never Never*, published in 1908.

Mac was unequalled as a bullock driver; he possessed the extraordinary facility of nursing his team of 22 bullocks through floodwater and over long waterless stages. The freight cost from the railhead at Pine Creek to Daly Waters (before the line was extended to Birdum in 1929) was £35 per ton, and further on to the Powell Creek telegraph station it was £45 pounds. It was hard work and, when the going was rough, goods could be twelve months on the road before delivery.

While Irish Mac was away with his wagons for many months at a time, his wife ran their store very capably. Her method of dealing with obstreperous drunks was a hard jab in the mid-section with a stout stick, kept behind the door especially for this purpose; as her target doubled over, she followed through with a mighty crack to the head. This, accompanied by a loud tirade of Irish-accented invective, kept her customers in reasonable control.

After a couple of years on the Ridge, my parents could see a profitable future there and with £1000 (a considerable sum then) borrowed from a Territory eccentric by the name of Harry Bates they bought the McCarthys out—lock, stock and every last rum barrel.

While my father awaited his replacement in the force, he remained the resident police officer, and when necessary would arrest a noisy drunk and haul him off to sober up in the police cell—the stout stick long gone from behind the door. There was some local puzzlement here: the publican serving grog and the policeman in his uniform looked so alike, it was even suggested by confused drinkers that they might be brothers.

My mother transferred her household—which consisted of me, the cook, my nursemaid, a pet brolga and dog, and the fine linen and silver of her trousseau—from the reasonable comfort of the police station to the less-than-luxurious house of the store, with not a pause in business. This house was definitely a temporary dwelling; its walls of tree bark were an open invitation to white ants to come, feast and frolic.

But Mother never in her life let her standards of genteel existence slip. I still have a small brass bell she used at the dinner table; it was an ornate replica of Nelson's flagship *Victory* in full sail. It was not pretentious in those times to have staff serve at table, even in the most modest of bush homes, and colonial traditions persisted as they did in India and other far reaches of empire.

There was no shortage of household help; Aboriginal women were curious about working in a house. But it was a doubtful blessing, for with them came numerous relatives—mothers, sisters, an assortment of piccaninnies—and in the early days they could be unreliable. If the mood took them to go bush, off they went without thought; it was quite beyond them to understand the endless futility of work that occupied white people. My generation had the early Missus to thank for the competent house staff we inherited.

In the colonial household, children were fed their meals separately until of an age when good table behaviour was observed. Usually we had our own child-sized table and chairs, with meals supervised by a nurse girl. I went on to continue this tradition with my own children.

The lubras vied for table duty, which entailed no more than removing dishes and serving the following course. On big stations the uniformed staff stood throughout the meal, in the fashion of an English country house, so wild kids of the old Outback grew up with exposure to certain refinements.

The Missus was head of the household—her word was law—and it was expected she do no wrong. House staff everywhere looked to the Missus for their care, to sort out their problems, settle arguments, attend their ills. They brought new babies up to the Missus to hear their white-man names. The Boss might get drunk at the picnic races, and cavort in a less-than-dignified manner if he was so inclined; the Missus—never!

In the constant rain of the wet season, life within the walls of our bark dwelling was damp and uncomfortable; still, when the occasion arose Mother entertained with great verve. Once with cans and basins placed to catch rainwater dripping through a

leaking roof, she gave a creditable dinner party for Lady Somers—
the wife of the Victorian governor—and the pilot of her plane.
In fact, they had such an enjoyable time that they stayed on a
further few days.

Lady Somers and my mother went riding in the huge station
horse paddock. They were disinclined to have an Aboriginal groom
ride along, so my father locked the paddock gate with instructions
not to go out—what a national disaster if the wife of the Victorian
governor had been lost in the bush while in his care.

Beginning around April, when rains had cleared, drovers passed
through the Ridge, heading west to take delivery of cattle. They
restocked their tucker bags at our store, which had flourished
since my parents had bought it.

Apart from the usual liquor and canned goods, the store stocked
clothes, saddlery and a strong cotton fabric called 'turkey red'
which was popular. Boiled sweets, the only kind one could expect
to find in bush stores, came in 10-pound tins and were doled out
into paper bags. In the heat they tended to stick together in hard
lumps and needed a good deal of thumping to separate, and the
Aboriginals loved them.

No R.M. Williams boots in those days—the Johnson boot
was first choice of the ringer, and the Koorelah was popular too,
with elastic sides that were prone to sag with age, hence their
nickname 'laughin' side boots'.

Capstan tobacco came in round pocket-sized tins, as well as a
dark square plug called AZ—'nigger twist'—which was moist and

strong-flavoured, and stamped 'For Aboriginal Use Only'. The Aboriginals chewed it, formed it into marble-sized balls, rolled it in ashes and settled it in the mouth along the back of the lower jaw, which bulged the cheek and caused much objectionable spitting of tobacco juice; when not in the mouth, it was often carried behind the ear. Sometimes one or two of these 'wannoo' were carried about in a small tin of powdered ashes—metal wax match tins were popular for this.

The Aboriginal people newly arrived from the inland Territory bush would advance carefully and full of wonder into the store; naked, or girt with a thin belt woven from human hair, from which often hung a naga (loin cloth), lean-bodied, with stick-thin strong legs, peg in nose, carrying their spears, two or three in the left hand, woomera (throwing stick) in the right. They had not a word of English. If I placed my small hand on their arm or hand, as our house lubras said I should, they erupted with loud, delighted laughter, their nose pegs stiffening upwards with their wide smiles until their eyes disappeared into folds of flesh. They pinched my ribs to indicate I was in good condition, and mimed that I might make a succulent meal, with great humour and nods all around.

They gazed in awe at this Aladdin's cave of goods—axes, red cloth, knives sharp and shining—and they offered carved weapons, shields, spears, ornaments of dogs' teeth and coloured seeds, and cleverly woven hair and grass armbands, in exchange for sugar, flour and tobacco. If careful watch wasn't kept, small items disappeared into mouths, hair, and a favourite hiding place, the armpit.

Within their tight small tribes, no half-caste nor mixed-blood person had a remote chance of acceptance, and the welcome mat wasn't put out for visitors from other tribes either. Apart from an occasional exchange of goods and the 'dancer man' who travelled about demonstrating his new dances, the tribes kept a wary and possessive eye on their territory.

But in what seemed like no time of contact with Europeans, an Aboriginal man would be out of his naga and into shirt, trousers and hat; and a lubra would cover her nakedness, donning the floor-length, high-necked fashion of early days. Only the piccaninny remained clad in dust-covered skin.

When European fashion became less rigid, the lubras' skirts shortened accordingly, but they remained very modest and preferred their dresses to have sleeves. 'Want im gotta arm,' they would tell you. 'Me chame [ashamed] no arm.'

⁓

After his first wet season on the Ridge, my father started building the present pub. He used the angle-iron of a windmill he'd purchased from the Department of Works to form the frame, bought corrugated iron for roof and walls, and laid a cement floor. Apart from its doors, no timber was used in the pub's construction, to avoid white ant infestation.

My mother's brother Bill Hese and the author Bill Harney were my father's helpers. Harney and his part-Aboriginal wife, Linda, rigged their camp on the Ridge, and he spent the wet season working for my father.

With bar, dining room, kitchen and three-bedroom living quarters, the Junction Hotel was ready for occupation and business. It was so-named for being the junction of the main north–south road and the east–west stock routes, and was comparable to a saloon in America's Wild West. No swinging doors here, but gunfights and wild brawls aplenty.

To the drovers travelling their big herds to southern markets, the pub meant that the open downs country of the Barkly Tableland lay ahead and the Murranji Track was behind—a once-forbidding stock route that snaked westward through Bullwaddy and Lancewood scrub for a couple of hundred kilometres to Top Springs on the Armstrong River.

Perched on its stony ridge, the pub was fronted by a wide gravel road. Open country bare as a billiard table—the cattle mobs and pub goats saw to that—ran down to the white, clay-coloured water of Newcastle Creek.

These days, a plaque outside the Junction Hotel informs tourists it was 'built by Arthur Edward (Jack) Sargeant with help from those owing him money'. Not so, a total fabrication! No doubt a story concocted by a writer hoping to create a little local colour—you know the sort of thing: I heard it, I liked it, I wrote it.

## CHAPTER 12

# He Redeemed his Vices with his Virtue

This is a tale of the eccentric Territory man who loaned my parents the money to buy the McCarthys' store.

A white man with a long white beard, he'd first ridden into the Territory in the late 1880s, bearing the name Harry Bates. Later he'd changed his surname to Bathern, although he was known mostly as Bullwaddy, in honour of the hardy, ugly shrub that grows densely in that region. Name changes weren't so unusual then—a new name was something to hide behind if one had a dubious past; it could smooth the way to a new life. Some had two or even three aliases, but the Territory never held a man's lawless past against him.

Although I was very young when I knew Bullwaddy, I remember him quite well—perhaps because he gave me a beautiful taffy-coloured pony, which after long deliberation we imaginatively named Taffy.

A successful cattleman when he loaned my parents money, Bullwaddy was the owner of several stations and lived on Beetaloo Station, quite close to Newcastle Waters. Like many old bushmen, he had no white women in his life. He reigned over his kingdom of dark concubines and the prodigious issue of his loins, their skins of all shades. Were they really all his? He liked to think so and loudly boasted, 'See those cattle? Bred 'em all. The horses? Bred them too. And see those fine men riding 'em? Bred the bloody lot.' Perhaps a little wishful thinking there, but with some truth to it.

They all had little schooling. Bullwaddy could neither read nor write and saw no reason his children should. Later he employed a bookkeeper in the belief the man was impotent due to First World War injuries. How wrong he was! The bookkeeper was soon given his marching orders, to be replaced by someone deemed more suitable.

Bullwaddy was looked upon with much respect and affection by his large family, although he wasn't overly generous. On the occasion they requested jam, bottled sauce or anything else on the dinner table he thought excessive, he would tell them sadly, 'Of course you can have it, but you must understand the great risk to your good health. Perhaps even blindness is possible from such indulgences. But if you desire it, you can have it. Have I ever denied you anything?'

Silence! Not another word. Fear of such calamity ruled out any arguments or further requests, and that was the end of it.

At the same time, Bullwaddy provided well for his children and everyone on the station. They butchered their own cattle, goats and chickens; were excellent cooks and bread-makers; and had a large vegetable garden. They worked their cattle—their brand ZTZ—and maintained their properties well. Although Bullwaddy's word was law, I never heard of him being harsh. I guess he was too small and too old by then anyway.

On a trip to Beetaloo to attend someone sick, my mother spent the night in their only fully enclosed bedroom. A wild storm blew up with thunder and flashing lightning. Bullwaddy, brave as any bushman with horse or rushing cattle, was deathly afraid of lightning. The little man rushed in panic into Mother's room and straight under the bed, where he huddled, shivering with fright.

All the while, Mother told us, she reclined regally on her pillows above, like a feudal grande dame with her servant at foot. She hadn't the heart to send him forth before the storm quietened.

Mother often told this story of continuing to read her book by the light of a kerosene lantern, while a frightened little man with a long white beard cowered beneath her bed.

Bullwaddy died in the Junction Hotel during the Second World War, and the story goes he left instructions for his boys to bury him in a particular spot that was especially hard digging. His word was law unto the end, and none dared disobey. Who knew what he could do even beyond the grave?

He'd also ensured that his considerable wealth was distributed in such a way that all of his descendants were provided for. Many years later they were still profiting from his estate, still cashing their cheques at the store.

His eldest son, Wattie, regularly made the trip into Newcastle Waters in an old red truck he referred to as the 'Dieselene'. He and his chief offsider, Whitefoot—probably named for the marks of leprosy from which he later died—grandly took their places in the cab. Along with as many people as could cram on board, they all set off for their trip to town. Wattie could neither read nor write, but he could make his mark on his cheques and this was good enough for Mother. After a day visiting relatives and spending money in the store, the old Dieseline chugged on home to Beetaloo.

Wattie had a bottomless fund of tales to tell about old Bullwaddy, who'd always been ready to compare the hardships of his own life, as a young fella roaming the Outback, to the good fortune and what he considered the easy life that his hard work had provided for his children.

I have among my books a collection of drawings Wattie presented to my mother, including scenes from his life in the bush, cattle, men on horseback and a small aeroplane of the 1930s—Dr Clyde Fenton's plane on a mercy flight, perhaps. All the action of life on the old Territory cattle station by a man of the bush who could neither read nor write, remarkably well drawn; perhaps I will entrust them to a Territory gallery.

A young soldier, my father
Jack Sargeant, just before
leaving for France in 1916.

My father took this photo of the camel train he travelled with as he rode into the
Northern Territory in 1919.

My father's police camp at Tanami in 1925. He is in his police uniform.

My father in the centre, preparing for a long patrol.

The Territory Police Force in the 1920s with my father at the extreme right front row.

My father taking the police car across the McArthur River.

My father's truck returning through the bog from the buffalo camp. Everyone had to join in to pull it out of the swamp.

My father took this photo of Aboriginals from Alexandria Station.

My mother, Valeska Marie
Sargeant (nee Hese).
The Missus.

The grog truck in the early 1930s.

From left, my mother, myself, Lady Somers and local nurse girl with Lady Somers' plane in 1931.

The first 'Pioneer Tours' in Australia taken outside the store at Pine Creek in the 1930s.

My mother, myself and an Aboriginal girl being pushed across the floodwaters.

The nurse girls had a great time dressing me as a young child. What a sight to behold!

Our store in Pine Creek in the 1930s.

Aboriginal tribesman like these often wandered into our store at Pine Creek.

# CHAPTER 13

# Daughter of
# the Mounted

I was to remain my parents' only child. Spoiled? Sure! You know what they say—everything under the Christmas tree is for you alone.

My father called me Jackie or Jock; my mother Jacqueline or, when irritated or angry, a shrill 'Jacqueleen!' in the French fashion. To the Aboriginal men, lubras, nannies and ringers, I was always Jack-a-leen, never Jackie, for reasons I know not.

Little white girls were rare in the remote Territory of my childhood, so I received lots of special attention. I still possess teddy bears, silver mugs and books to attest to my bevy of surrogate uncles in the Mounted: Tom Turner, Tas Fitzer and Wally Langdon, to name a few. All are familiar names sprinkled throughout the pages of old police records and histories of the Territory's past. I was 'a true child of the old Mounted', my father used to say.

He was determined I should be a girl. It's said that when a man has a son, he becomes a father; with a daughter, he is a daddy. I had a daddy for 56 years who thought me quite marvellous and always referred to me as his beautiful daughter. How could you not love such a man?

He believed a father should spoil his daughters or they would grow up disliking men. It's a good thing he did just that, for a large part of my life has been spent in the sole company of men, mostly hard men of the Australian bush; they were my protectors, teachers and trusted friends.

⁓

Not long after we'd moved to Newcastle Waters, Polly—a Mudburra woman from nearby Montejinni country—had come into our lives. She wasn't a young woman, had no children of her own, and was my nurse girl for the next few years. She happily carried me about in my coolamon and, I am told, fussed possessively over her piccaninny.

As a young child I was always in search of wannoo tins for Polly. These were accepted, whether suitable or not, with a gracious, 'Good gel, Good gel,' and tucked away in her dilly bag.

In those early years I was taken on hunting expeditions with women of the local tribe. I was taught to dig yams with my own yam-stick, what bush tucker one ate (or didn't eat), and what berries were 'cheeky bugger' (poisonous). We had many a bush feed of greasy goanna on ashy coals.

One day my mother came upon Polly giving me a lesson in hygiene. After taking up a handful of sticks, she carefully laid one down. When quite sure she had my full attention, she said, 'Ghish un, im dirty bugger,' then another stick in a separate pile, 'Ghish un, im clean bugger,' and so on until she was satisfied that the difference was noted.

One fun memory of my early childhood is of lying on the ground in a great tumble of lubras and piccaninnies, gazing skyward and conjuring images in the shifting clouds. 'Look, there horse, see his tail? Im gone now, that un now him helephant, see his long nose?' Not that any of us had ever seen an elephant, but we had my picture books to aid our imagination.

I remember the vision of the koala bear, because it so amused my father that he often brought it up. Clearly formed in cloud, this image caused me to excitedly announce to all, 'Look, qualabare! Qualabare!'

'What that un qualabare, Jack-a-leen?'

'Well, he's a bear,' I put forward uncertainly. 'He got fur like kungaru.'

'You bin lookin for this un qualabare one nutja time, Jack-a-leen?'

With all attention hanging on my superior knowledge of such matters, I wasn't about to admit I knew not a thing of koala bears.

'I bin see pictures,' I countered tentatively and changed the subject, with a mental note to consult my father regarding qualabears.

A popular pastime was smoothing the dusty ground and imitating animal tracks: 'See ghish un, im lighard foot,' and the spidery mark of a lizard was there in the dust. You could make a baby's bottom or footprint, or press down on the outer side of a clenched fist, dabbing in the 'toes' with thumb and fingers.

Cat's cradles were another skill; string interlaced through fingers created a wide range of designs. With a quick flick of a finger, a twist of string, another picture appeared. An anthropologist once told me that he had recorded over 200 designs of string pictures.

The women were ever curious and showered me with questions. When Uncle Bill Hese of Harpers Springs Station came to visit, they asked, 'Jack-a-leen, what name you call that brother belong mother belong you?'

'That uncle for me.'

'Ay-na-yah, *uwai*, that un huncle for im,' they agreed, with understanding nods all around.

'Ay-na-yah'—I'm at a loss to spell this sound. It was an exclamation of surprise, irritation, praise, alarm: a warmly familiar acknowledgement of anything at all. I still think 'ay-na-yah' when I'm truly surprised by something.

The women didn't always speak aloud. Periodic silences were imposed on individuals for tribal reasons, and finger talk—a special sign language, more complex and conveying a wider range of information than one might think—was learned early and used often. A heated disagreement could take place without a single sound uttered, and be quite entertaining for me to observe.

There was much to know. I learned early that secrets must not be told if a willy wagtail should alight on a branch nearby, because it was a well-known fact they carried tales and caused trouble; of course, this was obvious from the way they tilted their heads to listen to what you were saying. Another rule was that the name of one departed must never be spoken, or he might hear from that dark place beyond, and perhaps think you were calling him to come.

We bush kids retrieved objects from the ground with our toes as the Aboriginals did, pouted our lips toward an object, or pointed with the chin when asked directions. We stood with a bare foot resting against the opposite knee—I still do this barefoot. All of which irritated our mothers, of course.

The nurse girls gave loads of attention to their charges; they seemed to have infinite patience with European children. If I incurred my mother's wrath or the world was unkind, I stomped off to their camp by the house to tell of the unfairness of it all, and be petted and fussed over: 'Ay-na-yah, poor pulla Jack-a-leen!' Maybe I'd be fed a bit of 'sugarbag' (wild bush honey) or other titbits from a grubby dilly bag, until ruffled feathers settled.

My father took delight in telling the following little tale, much to my mother's discomfiture. One day, with her patience sorely tried by her unruly child, my mother slapped me. Polly took offence at such treatment of her beloved charge, and sprang into battle with serious intent.

Mother was going down fast; her only defence was to take up a saucepan and bounce it off Polly's woolly head. My father came by and intervened: 'Oh bugger off, Pol, and take your piccaninny with you.' We were banished from the house until tempers cooled. Although the fault lay with Polly, she returned with me on her hip and haughtily treated Mother with magnificent forgiveness.

After a few years in Newcastle Waters, my parents leased the Junction Hotel to Max Schober, a tubby little German ex-seaman, and bought a store with a liquor licence in the gold-mining town of Pine Creek. North of the Ridge on the main north–south road, and about 230 kilometres from Darwin, Pine Creek had the advantage of being on the railway line.

The farewells of our Aboriginal friends were dramatic in the manner of old tribal people. The lubras wailed and cut shallow wounds into their arms and foreheads until the blood flowed down. It was reasoned that blood must be shed to show real sorrow and grief must be heard to signify sincerity.

Polly didn't accompany us. I still remember looking over my father's shoulder at her dear old face as I was taken from her. She was sitting cross-legged on the ground where we'd played every day, swaying back and forth, blood streaking her face from the cuttem-cuttem marks, loudly lamenting the piccaninny she believed she would never see again.

CHAPTER 14

# North to
# Gold Field Country

What a gentle bucolic scene the name 'Pine Creek' conjures. Forget it! Several large gold mines were working around the clock and there was nothing placidly pastoral about a mining town of those days. The wild ringers were replaced by mad miners, and in a town where the booze flowed freely, there were quite a few to rage and rampage about.

As well as gold mines and my parents' store, Pine Creek had another store, a Chinese bakery, a bush pub, a railway station, a small school and a bush hospital run by one nursing sister.

To the end of her life, my mother wasn't domestically inclined. I never saw her cook anything, not even a piece of toast. Probably during her nursing training she'd learned something of invalid cookery, but she always declared she couldn't cook, and that was that.

Instead, Mother was totally involved in her business ventures, so my general day-to-day care fell again to nurse girls, some of them Malay amah. I have good memories of all the women who cared for me—each left something special to remember with affection.

A great favourite was Rosie Cheong, a mix of Chinese and Malay and, as my father put it, an Aboriginal was looking over the fence as well. Pretty and good natured, she laced my food with the hottest chillies, so that very early I acquired a taste for highly spiced Asian cuisine—and with this added to Polly's bush tucker, I developed a cast-iron digestion.

Bet-Bet, another Aboriginal nurse, accompanied us on our only family holiday to Adelaide. On our return she, who had never had a shoe on her foot, refused to be seen not only without shoes, but also the white cotton stockings that were in fashion and disappeared regularly from my mother's wardrobe.

Still another was Daphne Alright, a European girl who was later married at our house, my mother's wedding ring borrowed for the ceremony. Daphne's husband became a well-known hotelier in the Territory.

Maggie, a half-caste girl, was with us a very long while. She had a glass eye that shattered in its socket, and my mother spent a good deal of time probing for shards.

After her marriage, Maggie and her husband trained their pet pig to perform a wide range of clever tricks, all of which impressed me no end. He could retrieve things and carry them about on command, and was about as talented in a piggy way as it was possible to be. I found it all great fun when he was put through his performance for me, and I always brought along a good supply of treats for him.

I was utterly crushed by the vagaries of adult behaviour when I found out he'd been eaten for Christmas dinner—it fostered in me an early distrust of adults where pets were concerned.

～

I started my education at the tiny Pine Creek school. My little terrier, Wuffles, would accompany me as far as the railway line I had to cross on my way, and in the afternoon was always waiting there to escort me home.

Miss Pearl Heine was the sole teacher: a gentle, gracious lady who lived in quarters behind the classroom. We launched straight into the alphabet and sums, and though my arithmetic made little progress, I could read quite well at a very early age. Our schoolwork was done on slates that, grubby lot we were, we spat on to erase, instead of using the neat little damp sponges provided. We also spent a lot of time eating from under the desk: ginger plums and dried watermelon seeds, all bought from the Chinese bakery.

My schoolmates included a tough element from among the mine workers' families in town. On a few mornings as I made my way to school, I fell afoul of the Sullivan brothers, who lay in wait for me. They divested me of my lunch and whatever else took their fancy.

My father smelled a Sullivan rat when I refused to go unescorted to school—they were a pretty well-known bunch—so one morning he lay in wait near the railway line and, with the assistance of Wuffles, frightened the bejaysus out of them. I had safe passage ever after. Paddy, the eldest, went to reformatory for nicking something that wasn't his'n.

Mr Sullivan, a small jovial Irishman, went to the mines to defend his daughter's honour against a man who 'done her wrong'. Big mistake—he shot the wrong man and was taken off to the Darwin gaol. We Pine Creek kids went down to the railway station to wave our little hands sadly as he was carried off. When war broke out he was set free, as were all the prisoners in the gaol.

I had an eclectic treasure house of friends in Pine Creek—children of many races and backgrounds, adults too. For a time, Bob Pearce was my very best friend whenever he visited. He was a liquor salesman who travelled down from Darwin on the train with his samples, order book and all the latest Darwin gossip for my mother. Poor Bob's enthusiastic imbibing of his samples, and much more besides, was the ruin of him. One wet season in Darwin, with no escape from the unending rain on the iron roof, he beat his liver to it and shot himself.

Joe was another firm friend. He was an Englishman of good education, who in his youth had travelled the world in some luxury. Now he lived in a little hut in the bush, and often came to see my father. My mother thought him disreputable; I thought him a knight in the shiniest of armour. He gave me a beautifully bound book of English children's poetry, and was always quite happy to have me engage him in serious child's conversation. His departures from his hut, and the town, were often and lengthy.

Years later, my father told me he'd died in a Chinese opium den in the hills behind Pine Creek.

While all the most fun and interesting people I spent time with seemed to be 'disreputable' in one way or another, I'm sure I must have also had some friends of whom my mother did approve!

～

Into the Territory of the early 1930s came tourists fired up by the exploits of adventurers in Ion Idriess's novels, in country referred to as outback of beyond.

Pioneer Tours brought their first motor vehicles in, and my father photographed such a novel thing. Those tourists saw their trip through, in spite of heat, dust, rough roads and unaccustomed proximity to raw nature. Some of these early tourers found little other than a country too unfamiliar, with a surplus of uncooked birds and animals, and should not have left home at all.

Those of harder stuff set off to discover the undiscovered, and have left records of their adventures in old photo albums—standing bravely tall, doffing their pith helmets beside a giant ant hill or an ochre-painted Aboriginal person.

～

There were some notable frequent visitors to Pine Creek. A Catholic priest made visits to his Pine Creek flock, arriving by train, as most everyone did, and returning to Darwin a day or two later. There were a number of Catholic households in town, but he preferred to stay in my mother's, although we were not of his fold. The food was better, he said, and he could indulge in a game of bridge; my mother was an avid bridge player all her life.

Dr Cecil Evelyn Cook was another keen for an evening of bridge. He was the chief medical officer of the Territory and chief protector of Aborigines. As mentioned earlier, he was also the sole doctor at Darwin Hospital for a number of years. Although he repeatedly requested a colleague to assist him, Darwin's reputation was such that no one would take the job.

Cook learned there was a doctor on board a ship in harbour— there he found Clyde Fenton on the *Koolinda*, due to sail south next day. Fenton later wrote that he was practically shanghaied, for when he sobered up, his baggage was ashore and the ship had sailed.

Dr Fenton became the Territory's famous flying doctor, who flew in to attend patients when necessary—and, if in a playful mood, bombed our house with small bags of flour. He was an audacious, flashy daredevil who could land his plane in the most unlikely stretches of bush.

A Chinese community was well-established in and around Pine Creek. Out-of-town gardeners tended their fruit and vegetable patch, working hard with simple tools and removing the bugs by hand. Some of their fertiliser was their own nightsoil, and their fruit trees flourished. During the dry, a quiet old buffalo drew their produce cart around town, filled with mangoes, guavas and bananas.

Then there was the Chinese bakery across the road. I was always reluctant to venture over there, because Mr Ah Yu, in coolie trousers and slip-slop sandals, would be reclining in his hessian bag-covered deck chair, right at the entrance. He was very old and thin, and as wrinkled as a dried salty-plum. A long grey beard of only a few hairs hung straight down from the point of his chin, topped off by a gapped, yellow-toothed grin.

Mr Ah Yu had come out from China years before to work as a coolie on the railway line, then in the mines. He had practically no English, but a diabolical chuckle could erupt unexpectedly when one was quite unprepared for it. As far as I was concerned, his chief function in life was to terrorise me. He had a homemade turkey feather fan, and I think only one exceptionally long fingernail—perhaps there were more, but I never dared a longer look to establish this fact.

Each of my visits was the same. I drew near, heart thudding, and just as I reached the door, as if on cue, he burst forth with his demented-sounding cackle and shot out his arm to point his fan at me. I almost wet myself in terror, and scuttled through the door into the dark little shop, to the kindly and much younger Mrs Ah Yu. Clutching my bread, I departed at full speed, too quickly for him to do anything but collapse with laughter.

Looking back, I'm sure my infrequent visits provided Mr Ah Yu with welcome diversion from the tedium of his day in the hessian chair.

Now his descendants are Territory business and professional men. The iron bakery building still stands, deserted now, and a plaque outside the door tells of its origins, and of the Chinese family who lived there. When passing through this old mining town, I sometimes stand awhile at that door and feel nostalgic; I remember Mr Ah Yu and my nervous approach, 70 years ago.

As well as those gentle ladies who helped tame the bush and kept colonial civilisation alive in the Outback, Pine Creek was not without those memorable few who were looked upon with disapproval and considered 'fast'. Gossip would have it that they were given to taming the lonely miners around this riotous town, where they had wide choice of companions.

They weren't professional ladies, but their social lives were certainly more exuberant than was considered appropriate. For my part, I'm inclined to agree with Robert Graves, who said, 'For a woman to have a liaison is almost always pardonable, and occasionally, when the lover chosen is sufficiently distinguished, even admirable: but in love as in sport, the amateur status must be strictly maintained.'

These ladies had good looks and charm, and liked a good time. They gave little thought to their reputations, long sullied beyond repair, and ignored the pursed lips. Swanning around, enjoying their notoriety, they continued to beguile and bewitch with their abundant curves, and gave not a damn for anyone. They caused much disharmony and jealously, and loads of scandalous gossip that they seemed to enjoy; they were the cause of fist fights and vicious brawls, and once a man was shot and wounded. There were husbands in the dim background who presented no hindrance to their social lives.

Among them was the Spinifex Queen—who, gossip had it, was quite amenable to a frolic in the spinifex grass, in spite of its sharp and prickly nature.

But for me, the Cullen Queen was the most memorable, so named for the Cullen River district where she lived. She had great dark eyes lined with kohl and light golden skin, and on special occasions she wore a sari, perhaps to make the point that she was of Indian extraction and not Aboriginal. She was like a hot-house orchid growing in a bush konkerberry patch, and I thought her very beautiful. She always smiled and wiggled her fingers in my direction as if we were old friends, and I was delighted to be noticed by such a fascinating creature, although I was hushed if I asked about her.

I know not what became of those women during the war. I didn't ask my mother, but my father, who knew everything, thought that they might have continued in good times with the incoming army, or were evacuated out of the Territory with civilians at the beginning of the war.

⁓

Pine Creek was a base for buffalo hunters, who would periodically set off from there for their camps in Arnhem Land. Others passing through this old town, who took time to spend a pleasant evening in congenial company, included men who'd come into the country during its golden heyday, and elderly men who'd travelled the Old Coast Road.

In the evenings we gathered outside for coolness and company. People came by to sit awhile and talk late into the night; that's what we did then, all over the bush, without radios and with only one another for company. Everyone had something to tell: their latest bush travels, odd happenings, adventures. Well, life in the

Outback was always an adventure, although we were probably unaware of this at the time. Every day some drama unfolded that those settled in southern suburbia could never imagine.

How lucky I am to have known such a variety of people as I did when so young. I learned early to accept the non-conformist. I rather regret I was born too early for that unconstrained period of the sixties when bohemians metamorphosed into uninhibited hippies.

# CHAPTER 15

# Buffalo Shooting

In 1934 my father left Pine Creek to go out into the Territory's Arnhem Land and hunt buffalo, taking up a grazing licence of around 3000 square kilometres between the South and East Alligator Rivers—country now known as Kakadu.

No roads led to the Alligator Rivers. Oenpelli Mission had been settled out there, very little else. The lugger *Maroubra* came up the river several times a year to deliver supplies and take out the buffalo hides.

Shooting feral buffalo from horseback in swampy country was as dangerous an undertaking as one could imagine, and hunters were few—the Gaden brothers, Harry and Fred Hardy, my father and Tom Cole, who went out with the Hardy brothers to learn the ways of the buffalo and later wrote about his time there.

Harry Hardy, my godfather, had long urged my father to head

out to buffalo country, as it was generally known. Hides were bringing 5 pence per pound, and buffalo were in the thousands. Accompanied by Mick Madigan, an Aboriginal-Irishman, and with some trained shooting horses from Harry, my father packed his old cabinless truck; with the jarring action of the crank-handle, it coughed into life and he set out through bush to buffalo country. The horse plant of 30 horses and about twenty Aboriginals followed a few days later.

Camp was settled; their gear was prepared for the hunt. On good shooting horses, a bandolier of cartridges across the chest, the shooters were ready. They started their run at daylight to locate a mob of maybe a hundred feeding on the flats and cut out the young bulls, had them strung out. As the mob went sweeping by, the shooters—with .303 rifles sawn-off short and strapped to their arms for skilful one-handed control—always shot backwards over the horses' tails to prevent them taking fright, although a good shooting horse would become accustomed to this.

The two horseback shooters galloped close alongside the thundering herd; the lead rider leaned from the saddle, shot the first buffalo; the second rider picked off the next, the first rider took the third, and so on. The buffalo were always shot in the loins, to hit the spine and paralyse them. With a number down, perhaps twenty, the foot-shooter Aboriginals came in to finish off the wounded beasts.

The buffalo is a cunning beast, and its wide sweeping horns can disembowel a horse, injure or kill a man. In my father's camp, never was a man lost—although sometimes a good horse went down or was taken by crocodiles.

The foot-shooters and skinners removed the hides and loaded them on packhorses to take them to camp. They were thoroughly washed in a waterhole and hung up to dry, then rotated from bottom to top each day for ten days. When really dry, they were folded and taken to be loaded on the lugger for Darwin.

At the end of the dry season, just before the rains set in, they returned to Pine Creek to sit out the wet.

My father continued shooting buffalo until the outbreak of the Second World War. He did so well that the *Maroubra* started coming in every three weeks to take out hides and the price went up to 8 pence a pound. I remember being told that buffalo hide was used in Russia for railway carriage seats, and no doubt for a great deal else as well. On a cattle station, the hide made great boot soles that seemed never to wear out.

Those who hunted buffalo in the Territory were fine horsemen, excellent shots, and incredibly fearless and tough.

# CHAPTER 16

# Darwin
# Convent School

While my father was away shooting buffalo, my mother—who was of the Lutheran faith—decided to send me to board at the Territory's only boarding school, the Darwin Convent School, which was run by Roman Catholic nuns from the order of Our Lady of the Sacred Heart.

Off we went to Darwin on the train and settled into the Victoria Hotel as we always did. It wasn't to be the holiday I expected. After delivering me to the nuns, my mother left to return to the hotel, and it dawned on me that I was to stay there, that this was a permanent arrangement.

To my way of thinking, it wasn't! I turned tail and left at high speed, a desperate dash for freedom, and almost made it back to the hotel, which was a very long way down the road—but even with a good head start, capture was inevitable with a large posse of Convent kids in hot pursuit. I was returned, still valiantly struggling. Had I known what lay ahead, I may have fought even harder for my freedom. That establishment was right out of the pages of a Dickens novel, and I was five years old.

I've heard many accounts of friends' 'first day at boarding school', but never have I heard of a runaway; it has boosted my self-esteem somewhat that I didn't go quietly but had the gumption to make a run for it.

The extreme contrast of the strict and frugal Catholic boarding school to my life so far as an over-indulged only child might have caused some confusion in a more sensitive girl. Fortunately I was no delicate flower, and took what came.

I now feel sure the austere Convent life did me a lot of good, kept my feet firmly on the ground and enabled me to appreciate the insouciance of home life in the short holiday periods at Pine Creek—during which, unlike most of my classmates, I was still under the care of nursemaids.

In the primary school of Darwin Convent, two grown women, sisters from an outback cattle station, took their place each morning to learn with the first graders. They were big women, well used to hard outdoor work with their menfolk, but they took part in all our childish games; no one gave it a thought.

There was a variety of colours and a mixture of nationalities—Greek, Spanish, Portuguese, Japanese, Chinese, Malay and more—within the stern cloisters of Darwin Convent. Two

Portuguese boys with long sausage curls to their bottoms, tied back with pastel ribbons, could play a rough game of football, their curls flying in a tackle—and this in an era when no man, absolutely no man, would consider wearing his hair longer than a basin cut.

There were also many girls of mixed race sent as boarders to the Convent. The author Ernestine Hill, writing of Darwin in the 1930s, said: 'There are two schools, a Public School, and a Convent School overflowing with half-caste children.' Their white fathers—loving, responsible men—expected the nuns to send them out into the world educated in all the arts, and good Christians as well.

When we weren't praying or at our lessons, if the church needed cleaning—floors swept, statues dusted, pews polished—we were all expected to buck in and help. However, if there was a Catholic feast day or a church celebration, we non-Catholics weren't invited to attend the festivities. We sat at the far end of the refectory with our bread and jam (no butter ever passed through those refectory doors) and looked on wistfully, hoping a cake or cookie might come our way.

There seemed always to be a great number of these feast days from whose celebrations we were excluded, and I once made a half-hearted approach toward Roman Catholicism, but the nuns were no fools and saw through my self-serving intentions. I was banished back to that less fruitful end of the refectory.

There were several sessions of prayer throughout our day: morning mass, the Rosary and Benediction, and when the Angelus bell tolled daily, it was ruled that all movement must stop midstride. Wherever we were, we stood rooted to the spot like statues and lapsed into deep contemplation of the bell's holy message—or fiddled with our bare toes in the dust and thought about things less relevant.

It was years before anyone deciphered for me, the words—the fruit-of-thy-womb-Jesus—rattled off during prayers in one swift breath, almost as one word, and which we repeated like so many little parrots.

Each time we made the sign of the cross on our person, we were assured that ten of our sins were removed from our sentence of hopping barefoot from one scorching rock to another in the fires of purgatory—that halfway house to heaven—where our sins were gradually cleansed before entry. A process of varying time, I imagine, depending on the baggage of sin accumulated along life's path. All this straight from the lips of Sister Mary Damascene, so it had to be true.

As it was possible to store these sin-cancellers, we kids spent much time 'doing' our signs of the cross in readiness. All this at an age when we weren't yet aware that some sin might be well worth braving the hot-seat for.

The nuns threatened us with the fires of purgatory if we neglected our prayers. Before lights out in the dormitory, we knelt in our pyjamas before an elevated statue of the Virgin Mary holding her child, all pastel blues and gold, her gaze benevolent and gentle. Her plaster foot was placed firmly on the neck of a serpent, its shiny black scales paradoxically aligned to the glory above.

From where I knelt, the serpent's eye caught mine with an evil penetration, and I often requested an extra shake over my bed from the holy water dispenser to quieten my nervousness.

Children of the old Outback like me, who had spent so much time with the lubras and piccaninnies, knew the legends and felt the magic, our naughtiness held in check by nursemaids with dire threats of debil-debils.

After our prayers were said and holy water liberally sprinkled on our beds, the dormitory lights went out. Some of the older girls would then climb the high Convent walls and spend the night in dubious pursuits around town, returning in the early hours, removing smudged lipstick and delivering such terrifying threats to us little kids if we dared tell that not a word passed our lips.

The nuns were well aware of what they were dealing with. They were exceptionally strict and did their best to educate us all and make good Catholic, God-fearing girls of us.

Every Saturday morning a large tumbler of Epsom salts was downed under supervision—and if it made you sick, you were presented with another.

On the odd occasion I wet my bed, I was sent in disgrace to the laundry; with sheets billowing up and around my ears, I dabbled my hands about in the suds in an attempt to wash them. How I missed Bet-Bet, who retrieved my clothes and everything else I cast about.

One of the most curious practices I encountered at the Convent was an accessory to our modesty, the so-called 'bath dress'. A sarong-type garment made from heavy calico, it was tied around the waist in an effort to protect little girls from gazing upon one another's naked loins. After use it was discarded in a wet heap by the last wearer, then wrapped cold and clinging around the nether regions of the next in queue, before she slid off her knickers in an action that would arouse the envy of any striptease queen, then took her turn in the tub. Same bath water for all, of course, but we were too young to find this distasteful.

My children refused to believe this quaint gem from the Convent bath ritual until I met Joan Peterson, a charming lady who lived in Katherine, and my credibility was restored, for she too had taken her place in the bath queue of old.

I also have fond memories of the excursions we took, which were unlike those of other schools. We had our own large and sturdy lugger, the *St Francis*, manned by a Catholic brother, Andrew Smith, who'd been in the navy during the First World War. Brother Smith would sail out of the harbour and take to the open sea, sometimes dropping anchor at Shell Island, a small cay composed of tiny sun-bleached shells. We'd shovel them into bags and take them back to make dazzling paths around the church.

~

As a non-Roman Catholic I felt quite left out when my school-mates emerged from church arrogantly sin free after making their confessions. So when a visiting priest arrived for a time, my friend Geraldine and I thought it an opportune moment to purify our souls too. With a little tutoring as to procedure, I went forth alone—for Geraldine had chickened out, as they say.

For me it went thus: 'Forgive me, Father, for I have sinned,' then when it became apparent one's sins must by enumerated, I became tongue-tied with nervousness and could only recall that we—heavy emphasis on the *we*: it was necessary he realise that Geraldine was steeped in this sin too—had purloined Sister Mary Xavier's large and baggy checked bloomers from the clothesline, and hidden them in the kitchen wood-box.

'Unholy child! I absolve you of your sin. Ten Hail Marys and one Our Father, and off you go now.'

What a relief, but a certain disappointment too, for I had envisioned the Holy One behind the screen, waving a hand over my sinful brow, and in a great flash of heavenly light retreating from His presence, pure and beatific as the angels in the painting above the church altar.

In a superior attitude of holiness, I saw to it that Geraldine joined me in the Our Father and made sure she said five of the Hail Marys.

~

We Convent boarders were always on the prowl to supplement our diet, usually with the odd mango from trees within the grounds, or perhaps a coconut or two from the derelict plantation just a short walk down Smith Street from the Convent. Can you imagine an unkempt coconut plantation in Darwin's Main Street? We could also earn a few sweets from the nuns, if we caught and plucked the fleet-footed, free-roaming chickens for their dinner table (but never a taste).

Sadly they never did come within a fragrant whiff of our refectory. Maybe the heavy, medieval, all-encasing habits they wore in 50-degree heat affected their attitude toward their charges, or perhaps it was just the times.

Pocket money, provided by our parents, was doled out by the nuns at one penny each week, and we were encouraged to head straight on down to the rectory—or Bishop's Palace, as it was called—where Father Henschke would do his best to sell us a 'holy picture'. But if we were quick and applied a little cunning, we could evade capture and make a dash for the store—quite out of bounds, of course—and spend our penny on delectable lollies.

For years, Father Henschke was our resident priest, and I have the clearest image of him still; to my child's eye he was tall and rather stooped about the shoulders. He was a solid man with bushy, untidy hair, big grey teeth and rimless spectacles. As he strode about, his soutane flapped and flowed around him like black wings. We kids crowded onto his huge boots—as many as possible in our bare feet, clustered one upon the other—and he would amuse us by attempting to walk slowly along with us clinging like bats to his robes. He was gentle, kind and vague, and sang very melodiously in a fine soaring baritone during his mass, which is more than can be said for other priests whose mass I attended.

Another marvellous old fellow was a Dutchman, Edwin Verberg, known to everyone as Daddy Verberg, who had a market garden at Adelaide River. Laden with all manner of luscious food, he came often to the Convent to visit his two daughters, Ada and Madeline. We eagerly awaited his visits, not entirely for altruistic reasons. Poor man, we fell in behind him in Pied Piper fashion and gave him no peace, fixing our beady eyes on his bags of goodies. But he seemed happy to entertain us and was always generous. A bridge over the Adelaide River bears his name today and reminds me of his visits and the largesse he dispensed to us voracious Convent kids.

One of my fellow boarders, Madge Gaden, spent much of her childhood in the camps of swampy buffalo country, where her father hunted with the Hardy brothers, my father and Tom Cole. After Madge contracted leprosy, she entertained us by piercing her toes with needles and declaring no pain; we found this trick quite riveting and unsuccessfully tried it ourselves. A talented pianist, Madge was sent from the Convent to the leprosarium on Peel Island, off the Queensland coast. A Darwin business house presented her with a piano to help fill her lonely life on the island.

Eileen G., also a talented pianist, was an attractive and popular young woman whose white father had taken her from her Aboriginal mother's camp and placed her in the Convent School to grow up with the nuns. After she completed her education, she taught for a while at the Convent. Eileen was a special friend to me; she taught my class and rather spoiled me. I have included a photo of us together. When I knew her, she was always stylishly dressed in the fashion of the 1930s. Later she married a successful businessman and went to live in Adelaide. A happy ending for one who could quite easily have spent her life in the Aboriginal camp, living on the periphery of traditional tribal life, perhaps to become one of the wives of an old man. It would have been tragic to leave her there.

In the end, I regret to report that I wasn't one of the Convent's successes on the religious front. After years of praying to St

Anthony to retrieve lost possessions, to St Jude as a fix-it man who dealt with a higher authority to right lost causes, and to St Christopher to ensure I had a safe trip home at holiday time, any Christian inclination I may have had disappeared entirely, and I remain forever bereft of the comfort of religious conviction.

CHAPTER 17

# Leaping Lena

'I do not believe that I shall live to see a railway
made from Adelaide to Port Darwin, or even
that younger men than I will do so.'

ANTHONY TROLLOPE, 1875

In 1877 a resolution moved by A. Landseer in favour of a rail line from Palmerston to the Pine Creek goldfields was accepted. Built mostly with Chinese labour, the line was completed on 13 June 1889.

Eight times a year for five years I travelled this line to and from boarding school in the 1930s. Am I the last person living who travelled so frequently on this old line? The train I took was officially named *Sentinel*, but to her passengers she was Leaping Lena because of the violent lurching one endured. More than once she leaped clear off the tracks and ploughed into the bush. But each week she busily huffed and puffed, jolted and rattled along at 30 kilometres per hour amid great clouds of soot, taking a full day to cover the distance from Pine Creek to Darwin.

There were two passenger carriages, each with long continuous seats facing each other across a passageway. Then there was the guards' van, manned by Len Scott. Known to everyone, he passed along news and delivered packages of the newspapers and books that were shared around bush settlements. Our Aboriginal workers on walkabout sent letter sticks with him to deliver to my mother for rations, which he brought to them on the return trip. The markings on a letter stick conveyed little: the accompanying spoken message said it all.

The third carriage was the 'blacks' carriage', and here a wide-eyed Aboriginal man sat with a tight grip on his bucking seat, uneasily taking in the scene through the window, passing faster than he could ever have imagined. Behind this carriage was a prison van, then a leper van when one was needed.

Leaping Lena was the only train on the bush line, and need not make way for anyone. She could make an unscheduled stop anywhere, if hailed by a horseman or someone sick who required transport to a hospital. There was never a rush.

Lena always stopped at Adelaide River for lunch when travelling north—the iron refreshment room was right alongside the line. Of supreme interest to me was a tiny patch of green lawn at its entrance with 'Adelaide River' cut into the growing grass; Pine Creek was undersupplied with green lawns, especially ones with writing.

Inside the refreshment room, tables were set for lunch: sparkling silver and glass, and snowy starched tablecloths with ornately folded damask serviettes. A punkah fan cooled the entire room, operated by a 'punkah wallah'—a bored Aboriginal boy who sat on the floor by the kitchen, pulling the rope with his toe. Sometimes the arrival of travellers distracted him and the big old fan slowed almost to a stop, whereupon a light poke from the toe of a passing waitress caused a burst of action and the fan flew enough to make the soup flutter.

While lunch was in progress, Leaping Lena took on water from the canvas 'elephant trunk' that hung from the high water tank. If passing by the stationary engine, a loud, unexpected and forceful burst of steam could shoot out at your feet from somewhere within her iron-clad belly, as if she were a living angry thing.

When ready to depart, a slow grinding *grumph*, a final exhale of steam, a laboured gathering of speed—off to Darwin and back to school. Without any cooling system in the train, it was a temptation to lean from a window for a whiff of fresh air, but soot from the engine soon put that out of mind; rarely was the trip completed without something in your eye.

A family of railway sleeper cutters worked along the line just out of Darwin. Several were women; big hardy women, well able to wield an axe as well as any man. Working in the heat, they did as the men did—removed their shirts, baring their large pendulous bosoms, without any thought other than to keep cool, which was unusual public exposure for white women in those days. They were of great interest to travellers on the train, which slowed down and gave a toot of its shrill little whistle in passing. In their baggy khaki bloomers, the sleeper cutters stopped work, leaned on their axes and good-naturedly waved to passengers craning from windows, often with cameras busily clicking. Perhaps there are photographs in far-distant albums of these sleeper cutters along the old Territory rail line.

Convent-indoctrinated child that I was, this cheery scene brought to mind Sister Annunciata—she who ruled in the Convent bathroom and policed the bath-dress ritual. This state of unashamed undress would not sit well with the good Sister, I was sure of that. I once almost told her about it—and that I didn't 'cover my eyes' either—but courage, always in short supply in the presence of Sister Annunciata, deserted me entirely, and she never did hear of it.

~

My mother once rode from Pine Creek to Darwin in 'the Quad': a small, flat, roofless wooden platform on wheels, propelled along the line by the slow back-and-forth pumping of a long handle. It was used as a means for railway workmen to travel the line; I can't recall the emergency that called for Mother to undertake such a journey, for it was extremely uncomfortable and the last thing for a 'lady'.

For Mother's journey, a straight-backed chair was placed on the Quad, and manpower for its slow, jerky progress was provided by two sturdy railway workers. She sat there all day in the savage heat until, at sunset, they rolled rather grandly into Darwin Railway Station, Mother still sitting sedately on her chair, holding her parasol aloft.

Today is 5 March and I am 86 years old. Just as bush Christmases remain in the hidden nooks of the mind where the best memories are kept, so do special birthdays. My eighth birthday shines in my memory as if it were yesterday.

My father made a special trip to Darwin on the train, and charmed Mother Superior into allowing me out for the entire day. He took me down to the Chinaman's shop and bought me a shiny new Malvern Star bicycle, then off to the Botanic Gardens to learn to ride it. Along these shaded paths, he met a mate from his police days and they decided to take me to the old Vic Hotel for dinner, but first I must have a party dress, for 'Didn't all little girls like party dresses?' Of course they did! Off we went to buy one.

I was in school uniform, so a new dress seemed a good idea to me too. But the pink voile creation, with stiff, wide-tiered frills from waist to hem, was perhaps an unhappy choice. Of course, my father and his friend were thoroughly pleased with themselves, especially when the saleslady kindly adhered a large pink satin bow to my straggly hair, rather like the star atop the Christmas tree.

We headed on down to dinner—me pushing my bicycle, which I was very proud of and not about to let out of my sight for even a moment.

Dinner was a happy time of reminiscences between these two troopers of the old Mounted; memories warmed by a gentlemanly intake of liquor. After dinner, a walk, they decided, to clear the head, and off along the less-travelled paths of old Darwin town we went.

When we passed by a small wooden gate, part-hidden by tropical shrubbery, this seemed to trigger old memories in my escorts. They paused awhile, exchanged a few brief words, and we turned back and entered into a small garden lit with Chinese lanterns that cast a soft shadowy glow among the trees from which they hung. We were met at the door by an elderly Chinese lady dressed in sleek black silk trousers and high-necked jacket, her hair severely pulled back in a bun. With her long cigarette holder and silk fan, which she languidly waved, she remains clear as a photograph fixed in my memory.

She appeared to know her visitors, but cast a stern eye on the eight-year-old apparition in wilting pink frills that ended abruptly above scuffed, knobby knees and heavy school shoes, a pink bow like a tired butterfly drooping over one ear—and could she believe it, pushing a bicycle!

She took my father aside for a whispered conference, with much headshaking and agitated waving about of the cigarette holder—then abruptly she nodded and held open the door: bicycle outside, please.

The room was small, adorned with the Chinese decor with which any Darwinite of the day was familiar: inlaid chests, hanging scrolls, much red and gold. There I was left with four young Chinese girls with flowers in their hair, dressed in long qipaos—a dress with mandarin collar and butterfly buttons. Very pretty, I thought.

At first they seemed unsure, but soon warmed to the novelty of a small visitor, giggled and clustered around, all of which I thoroughly enjoyed. I took them outside to see my new bicycle, rang its bell, and made quite sure they were aware of the skirt guard—coloured netting across the back wheel.

I told them it was my birthday; I was eight years old. This brought forth much clucking and fuss. I was given a colourful paper fan and familiar Chinese sweets. Sitting amid my attentive audience, unwrapping my salty-plums, I told of the purchase of the party dress, which appeared to engender sympathy rather than the expected admiration. They retied the pink bow and threaded the red ribbon of good luck through my hair.

They seemed to know my father quite well, which was nice, I thought.

They came to the door when we left; fluttered their hands and farewelled us in soft girlish voices while I wheeled my bicycle off through the garden. I had enjoyed myself immensely, as would any child when the centre of attention.

I asked my father if I could return sometime, but never did. A child of those times learned many things; dark stories came with strange men out of the bush. One learned early to be circumspect, or as my father succinctly put it, 'Learn to keep your mouth shut.' I emerged out of my early years much enlightened, quite unscathed and feel I had a rather wonderful childhood.

CHAPTER 18

# A New Darwin Emerges

Old Darwin Town died with its destruction during the Second World War. The city that emerged from the turmoil was a far cry from that of the past, and those who came there to live after 1945 would never know it in the full chaotic tropical flamboyance of the small frontier town it had been.

For years people complained about the Territory and its capital. Darwin the damned, some called it. A sheet of newspaper was all that separated it from *hell*, they caustically declared; it would be profitable to export its mountains of discarded liquor bottles. As late as 1942, Professor C.J. Hart of Toronto, in an open article, told the world that our Territory was not worth owning, describing it as: 'A land of vast empty spaces marked on the map with rivers that contain no water and towns that contain no people . . . one of the most hopeless in the world to live in, and one of the most difficult to get away from.'

But we liked the old place; had been born impervious to its discomforts. You nodded agreement to their complaints, looked sternly upon your outrageously rambunctious little town, and pretended to be ashamed of it.

Out of Chinatown came Darwin's gossip, information on business developments, mining news, cattle movements, pearl and peanut prices—scandal, too. One heard, 'It must be true, got it straight from Cavanagh Street.'

A town without a Chinese community must surely be dull. Chinese New Year was an exciting festival that we all looked forward to: the fantastic dragon with a hundred legs—the longest in Australia, we were told; cymbals clashing; crackers to ward off evil thrown under your feet; food in such abundance to warm every child's heart.

Somewhat more intimidating to me were the small dark shops of old Chinatown, where idols sat with smiles on their painted faces, the pale smoke of incense lazily drifted, and enigmatic, unsmiling old men in high-necked frogged jackets, cloth shoes and small black caps smoked their water pipes, while trousered women gave a gold-toothed smile behind the abacus on the counter and sold you liquorice plums, salted ginger or a pennyworth of roasted melon seeds, all taken from big glass jars on dusty shelves and doled out into tiny white packets. And perhaps if a man were known, a little opium could change hands too.

The mother goddess Kwan Yin, giver of fine sons, was obviously appreciative of the offerings on her shrine, for the Chinese had large families—a Chinese man could have several wives—and children overflowed the cramped, small houses of old Chinatown.

In their shops Chinese tailors padded about in bare feet and could make a perfect linen suit for a few shillings. My mother had a favourite tailor who could turn out a garment in a day or two. When working on the front of a jacket, his finger would hop-skippity down the button line: 'What you want, Missus? You want button, button, button, or you want button, button nothing, button, button nothing?' And in no time it was finished, buttoned to request and perfect.

So Chinatown remained until its destruction during the war. From those early Chinese who'd come as coolies to scratch a living from gold, tin and hard manual labour on railway construction, ever industrious, minding their own business, planting their vegetable gardens, bamboo and mango trees by springs and waterways, came respected citizens, business and professional men. Harry Chan, a handsome Darwin-born accountant, was the first elected president of the Northern Territory Legislative Council in 1965. Alec Fong Lim, he of the effervescent personality and generous spirit, was my good friend for many years before his early death; Alec was one of Darwin's greatest lord mayors.

Now all that remains of the original fine gardens are enormous mango trees and clumps of soaring bamboo overtaken by bush. The outskirts of old mining towns are still pitted with the shafts of Chinese diggings.

What an establishment was Zero in the Tropics, on the corner of Cavanagh Street. What child of the 1930s could forget it? Real ice-cream for the first time, served in a glass dish with a thin dry wafer and a tiny glass of ice water, considered an essential accompaniment. Luxury beyond belief for unworldly bush children in whose homes a refrigerator hadn't yet made an appearance.

For Territory kids, almost always barefoot, it was well worth putting your shoes on to be taken to the Zero, where you sat with not a word of complaint that your shoes or anything else were uncomfortable. With the punkah's gentle breeze lifting the sweat-damp hair on your neck, you slowly ate that gleaming white ice-cream. You wondered: Could life hold anything better?

After all these years, I can still describe the patterns on the stemmed glass dish. Visits to the Zero were treats extraordinarily special to a bush kid in the early 1930s, a time of sparse luxuries in Darwin.

Then there was the 'Squash Shop' run by Javanese. Long thick slabs of ice were shaved into curls with a plane, and added to big containers of freshly squeezed lemons and limes. I wish they were still there, and give them a wistful thought on hot days while trudging the streets of Darwin.

The enormous banyan tree on the corner of Smith Street, with its long, rubbery, snake-like roots descending from above to burrow in the surrounding earth, covered a corner block close to the Star Pictures cinema. The local kids saved their sixpences and we'd view the open-air movies from its comfortable branches.

Later, down it came, and a concrete bank building went up in its place—a building that still bears the pockmarks of Japanese machine-gun bullets.

~

In 1890 the Victoria Hotel had been built in Smith Street by Chinese labourers from the pale-hued stone of the sea cliffs; wooden pegs were hammered into the cliff face and swelled when submerged by high tide, forcing the soft rock to split into blocks.

From 1926 and into the 1930s, Mrs Christina Gordon and her two sons, Cookie and Wattie, owned and operated the Vic. As a young woman, Christina had travelled by buggy and buckboard through harsh country of the north-west, hundreds of miles over spinifex and desert with her husband and two small sons, to join in the gold rush of the waterless, miserable country of the Tanami desert.

Her husband, Walter, and his brother Hugh Gordon were brothers-in-law to Nat Buchanan, the explorer and cattleman who first took up and named Wave Hill Station. Walter and Hugh were inseparable and always travelled together, along with Christina who, besides May Brown and a few others, was the only white woman to have lived rough in the man's world of the desert gold-diggings.

At ten years old I was in awe of Mrs Gordon. She favoured long, high-necked Edwardian-style dresses with a cameo at the throat, and spent her days in her office at the foot of the polished wooden staircase. She was an imposing sight, sitting stiffly behind her window grille.

Guests received superior service at the old Vic. Ornately decorated china chamber pots could be found in a cupboard by each bed, and shoes were placed outside one's door at night, shined to perfection and awaiting their owners. Tea was delivered to one's bedside each morning—no preparing your own tea in those hotels. Mrs Gordon's dining room was starched and gleaming under the punkah fan, with its scalloped edging that gave it a lift from the ordinary. The waitresses wore black with little white aprons and small frontal caps like starched tiaras.

The Vic still stands, but how many know of its past glory?

Monsoons did more than make you wet. As Ernestine Hill wrote in 1930, 'To come into Darwin in the Wet Season is to tip-toe across the bounds of possibility into an opium dream.'

The oppressive heat and cloying humidity brought with them that scourge of the tropics, prickly-heat skin rash, all of which ensured sleepless nights on sweat-soaked sheets, enshrouded with netting to barricade oneself from mosquitoes, sand flies and myriad other creatures—small or large, with wings or crawling legs. Malaria and dengue fever were common ailments, and every home medicine cupboard contained quinine tablets.

For some, problems of depression and loneliness surfaced in those trying conditions. That abandoned character in the tropical setting of a Somerset Maugham novel—gin-soaked, unshaven, in dirty tropical whites, crashing his fist in despair on the table and mumbling, 'The rain, the rain, my God, the rain!'—has been well known to Darwin, although that romantic version is gone now.

These days he hangs out in the parks, in thongs and grubby shorts. The desperation for departure isn't so urgent when one can hop on a bus or take a flight out, whatever the weather: impossible back then in the wet, when berth on the monthly boat was the only passage out—if finances permitted, of course.

Monsoon was the time of year for suicide, oft-conducted with such flamboyance that these deaths are still yarned about. A graceful swallow dive from the high water tank behind the Victoria Hotel was a popular method, often during the busiest hour. It gave drinkers at the bar pause for a moment or two, but with no undue interest.

In the early 1920s a Japanese consul decided, for reasons unknown, to depart a cruel world. No half-measures here—he cut his throat from one ear to the other, and his head fell back over his wooden pillow. He lay behind wide glass windows, a ghastly sight for all who passed by. Unfortunately for my father, he was voted among troopers as having the strongest stomach for such things, so it fell to him to approach the poor consul's body with bag, needle and twine, with a view to temporary reconstruction before it was removed.

Perhaps one of the most memorable departures was devised by a gentleman who had a flair for the unusual. He wandered through the crowded bar-room with a cigar in his mouth, and in a jovial manner shook a hand here, had a friendly word to another, good will all around. Then, to disinterested drinkers, he said a theatrical 'Goodbye to you all!' and lit his cigar.

My father, who was there, said it fizzed a little. Then, with a loud retort, the man's head and cigar exploded together, above and beyond.

Exit Territory style.

A popular tree grown around Darwin was the cinchona; quinine was made from its bark. We also ate its berries, although who knows why, as they were bitter and acidic—perhaps we had a vitamin need in that direction. Tamarinds also put the teeth on edge, as any Territory kid will tell, but we devoured them with relish.

Darwin has a unique botanical gardens with giant trees seen nowhere else in Australia—specimens brought from Asia the century before, with unusual names. We would picnic under a huge 'Devil's Tooth' tree, disregarding the large white painted sign at the entrance saying, 'TRESPASSERS WILL BE SHOT'. Sadly Cyclone Tracy destroyed many of these wonderful trees in 1974.

In those pre-war days the gardens were maintained by prisoners from Fannie Bay Gaol. Armed guards strolled among them, rifles in hand. The gaol had been built in 1884 at a cost of £5600, and remained in use with its great sea views for years. This was quite sad really, for the inmates, incarcerated behind high iron walls, never got a chance to enjoy the view.

The gaolers of Fannie Bay had a very laissez-faire attitude to prisoners. They turned a blind eye on certain individuals who chose to spend their evenings outside in more conventional company than that of their cellmates. There were conditions, however: they must return in time for morning roll call.

Jack Buscall was one of the favoured ones. One morning, returning over the gaol's high iron wall, he fell and injured his back, never to walk again. With his sister to attend him, Mr Buscall opened a store close to the Convent School, where he sold sweets and curios from his bed behind the shop counter. It was said he used a wheelchair, and perhaps on occasion he did, but we kids never saw him other than dressed in a white singlet, sitting up in his bed, complete with white sheets and pillows, as he attended to his customers.

He kept a menagerie of animals—kangaroos, emus, other bush creatures—in a high-fenced yard, and right at the entrance to his little shop were overhanging cages of reptiles. To enter, one had to pass beneath a cage of light wire netting, sagging alarmingly with the weight of a gigantic Boa constrictor, whose great head, with bright beady eyes, was never shyly buried within its masses of piled coils, but always aggressively stiff and alert, ever watchful.

Mr Buscall sold many delectable sweets, but he was sole purveyor of a small hard lolly on a short stick, called a lamp-post, which cost a ha'penny each. If a lamp-post hadn't been such a gnawing necessity, I would never have ventured beneath that enormous snake with its steady, glittering eyes.

CHAPTER 19

# War is Declared

In 1939, on the eve of the one-hundredth anniversary of the *Beagle* sailing into Darwin Harbour, war was declared in Europe. Not long after this, my mother and I, like so many others, prepared to go to Queensland.

The only comfort I took from leaving my beloved old dog, who was the same age as me, was that Mrs George Stevens had agreed to adopt him. As she owned the local butchery, I felt his good life would continue, with the additional bounty of an endless supply of beef and bones.

However, there was nothing to ease the sadness of parting from people I had known all my life. Friends gathered on the small iron railway station.

'*Ma muk, ma muk!* Goodbye, goodbye!' cried Kati and Nym, an Aboriginal man and wife standing apart from the others, barefoot, forlorn; no loud weeping, no bloodletting as of old bush farewells, just a gentle hand on head, a sorrowful, 'I cry long my bingy for you.' I never heard of Kati and Nym again. When my father returned to disperse his shooting plant soon after settling Mother and me in Brisbane, they had left. They may have gone bush, back to tribal life.

This journey from Pine Creek was to be my last on old Leaping Lena. We lunched at Adelaide River Station as usual—where the punkah wallah still pulled the cord with his toe—then on to Darwin.

We took berth on the P&O ship *Merkur*. With the band playing on the wharf and streamers cascading about us, women waved our handkerchiefs, men their hats. The deep sonorous blast of the ship's horn signalled we were under way.

Our streamers grew taut. I gripped the coloured paper ribbon with a childish desperation, my last tangible link with home, until it snapped apart from those on shore. In silence I watched the cliffs above the harbour grow distantly dim, then disappear as the ship sailed into open sea and away from every familiar thing.

For me, a foreign land lay beyond that harbour. What did I know about a land that wasn't populated with half-naked Aboriginal people, and men who travelled on horseback? When I arrived in Brisbane, men everywhere were in military uniform. For a child of the bush, the transition was overwhelming.

How like a bush Aboriginal I was! My mother couldn't keep my shoes on—I discarded them in the most unlikely places, and often never found them again. She finally settled on oversized button-over canvas sandshoes, or plimsolls, and I flapped unhappily about in those.

I knew the Aboriginal name for most things and I was a dab hand at finger talk. I still retrieved objects from the ground with my toes and pointed rudely with the chin, but in all my ten years I had never seen a rose, a peach or myriad other things most European children took for granted. I gazed enthralled at pictures of Italian grape arbours in *National Geographic* and marvelled at the abundance of fruit hanging there—bush tucker never produced that luxuriantly.

I went about in a constant state of wonder. At night I stared up at the city's neon lights: Johnny Walker brandishing his whisky bottle and actually walking—how do they do that? Then a glittering polar bear, jerkily licking a never-diminishing ice-cream. The multi-coloured lights held me spellbound in this unbelievable world.

During the day there were flower and fruit stalls, pet shops—what was a hamster? No need for me to take in a fun fair: a ride on the escalator in Penny's Department Store or on a noisy tramcar was novelty enough.

Somehow, certainly in an unguarded moment, I was allowed to accompany my mother to a garden party at Government House. In the midst of an elegant, subdued gathering, I declared to all that there was a blackfellow's grave up in a tree. I would neither desist nor retreat from the spot until a kindly official explained it was the trunk of a large fern among the branches, by which time a curious crowd had gathered about this strange child holding forth in her sandshoes on Aboriginal funerary habit, and my mother thought it time to leave.

~

Then off to boarding school, high on a hill overlooking the city—just like that! But it wasn't really 'just like that' at all: it was a daunting undertaking for this child of the wild. Unlike mixing with the exotic and varied collection of inmates at the Darwin Convent, at my fashionable Brisbane girls school one had to weave a tricky path through the social hazards of its urbane students.

No tumblers of Epsom salts here. Instead, monogrammed china and good silver, all in a panelled Tudor dining room, uniformed maids, and our own Rolls-Royce, in which I was occasionally taken to the dentist. The central school building was a gracious old mansion, with marble fireplaces and tapestry bell pulls in rooms converted into dormitories for the younger students.

I took to all of this like a duck to a paddy-field. My mother's friends tut-tutted and said, 'Poor child, such a culture shock.' But it was a journey of constant discovery. The shock was in reverse; the other girls were fascinated and unbelieving. Their fathers were business and professional men. I told them that my father was a buffalo hunter and former mounted trooper who'd ridden hundreds of miles with his Aboriginal trackers. 'Such lies,' they said. 'Whoever heard of such a thing?'

At night I lay in bed and marvelled at the carpet of coloured city lights glittering far down beneath our hill. But then cold nights arrived and the wind screamed around our perch, rattling and clawing at the slatted blinds that inadequately covered the huge windows.

My first Brisbane winter was disastrous for my health. Tropical animal that I was, I had never experienced anything like it. I suffered the agony of chilblains, while nobody else had them. Playing netball on early winter mornings was torment, chronic chest problems plagued me, and I was forced to wear fleece-lined vests and voluminous bloomers, much to my embarrassment and the hilarity of the other girls.

Generally we teenagers in boarding school weren't a bad lot. Not nearly as sophisticated as we imagined, we lived under very strict rules: one just didn't do *this*, and you certainly didn't do *that*. We had excellent teachers and no doubt should have been more appreciative of their efforts on our behalf.

Our school motto was 'Guard Thine Honour', which I feel was generally done for us by the vigilance of the nuns. Our house motto was 'Born to Fly Upwards', which my mother found particularly hilarious in my case.

This fine girls school had a decidedly British tone; several of our teachers were English women. In moments of exasperation, our Maths teacher would reproach a student as an 'idle ass', but this came out as 'arse'. As my Maths marks were always abysmally low, I came in for an 'idle arse' more than most.

On Tuesdays we took our 'French lunch' with Madame Claire, a chic and gentle Frenchwoman who actually said, '*Oh là là!*' She provided us with wine glasses—for coloured cordials, of course.

What we didn't ask for in French, we didn't get, so lunch could be quite sparse for the idle student.

When France fell to the enemy in 1940, Madame had us stand solemnly to sing 'La Marseillaise'. We had the anthem word perfect; even today I can sing along with patriotic Frenchmen.

Our games mistress was large, loud and intensely determined to instil English traditions of good sportsmanship in her pupils. She sprang about in a short pleated gym uniform, with matching puffy bloomers that displayed a generous expanse of robust haunch when she took us through our callisthenics. Her special interest was her hockey team, and she quite embarrassed her girls, when one missed a shot, by loudly baying, 'Oh, you silly sausage!' Visiting teams sniggered behind their hands at our expense.

Latin was still a compulsory subject for us, and one wonders at the time we wasted mumbling our Latin verbs into memory before we faced 'The Bug', our tiny venomous teacher. I was actually fairly good at Latin, possibly because there wasn't the remotest need for it in 'real' life.

I recall with affection our gentle English tutor, who chided us when our voices became strident and unladylike by quoting Shakespeare: 'Her voice was ever soft, / Gentle, and low, an excellent thing in woman,' and hoping the message got through.

These women were untiring in their efforts to make 'ladies' of us, hopefully with some success. There was no television that might encourage unacceptable behaviour; an hour listening to war news on the radio was considered sufficient exposure to what might be happening outside our walls. Any thought of mutiny? Totally out of the question! There was also not the hazard of drugs; we thought ourselves quite daring to toss off a glass of champagne, or cough and choke our way through a cheap cigarette.

Together we managed a fairly harmonious existence. Occasionally a girl would appear among us whom we generally disliked; I remember a new student from a local, socially prominent family, who found us all too plebeian and treated us with a weary superiority. Her surname was Ramsbotham, and we were unworldly enough to think ourselves quite risqué to refer to her—among ourselves, of course—as Sheepsarse.

Times, they were a-changing fast! Petrol rationing meant our school car went up on blocks; dental visits and trips to the city now entailed a tram ride. Butter, tea, sugar, meat and clothing all required coupons, and we were issued with ration books and wore identification tags as bracelets or neck chains.

Word would filter through that underwear, coats or perhaps a consignment of shoes had just arrived at a certain store. Queues formed early, so with ration books clutched firmly in hand, we girls desperately hoped stocks would last until our turn came around. Clothing coupons disappeared so rapidly, and we'd watch sadly as the sales lady snipped them out with her scissors.

But gloves, even if holes in fingers must be patched, were deemed an absolute necessity for the well-groomed young lady—there was no way they were going. Woe betide any student seen in public without her gloves.

Silk or nylon stockings were to die for, but just not available, so they were painted on, the seams carefully drawn with eyebrow pencil; this required a steady hand and was a believable substitute for the real thing.

As the war progressed and clothing stocks dwindled even further, the nuns reluctantly permitted us to discard our thick brown cotton stockings for socks. This relaxing of the school dress code—and the very thought of their older charges displaying a bare leg in public—was almost too much for the poor nuns to bear, but nothing could be done about it. It's possible they considered it their major contribution to the war effort.

CHAPTER 20

# The Bombing
# of Darwin

A t exactly seven minutes to ten on the hot calm morning of
19 February 1942, a time etched deep in the memory of old
Darwin town, Japanese bombers and fighter planes flew in over
the Darwin Harbour in a neat V formation. They screamed down
so low that sailors could clearly see the heads and shoulders of
Japanese pilots machine-gunning their ships.

Earlier that day, American Kittyhawk fighter planes had set
off from Darwin to Koepang. Due to adverse weather conditions,
they turned back, flew right into an uneven dogfight and covered
themselves with glory. Their planes were all destroyed; several
pilots died in the battle.

More than fifty ships of all types were in the harbour that
morning—warships, flying boats, a floating dock, a hospital ship.

The Japanese made direct hits on the wharf and two ships moored there: the SS *Barossa* and the MV *Neptuna*, the latter of which was packed with explosives and depth charges. A naval officer on the nearby HMAS *Platypus* recalled a low rumbling from *Neptuna*, then a warning cry 'She's going up!' He dropped flat on the deck while *Neptuna* blew sky-high with an explosion that shook the entire town.

The wharf collapsed under the bombing and 22 of the 70 waterside workers died. A goods train and a loco engine were blown clean over the side. The hospital ship *Manunda*, with large red crosses clear on its brilliant white sides, took a direct hit but remained afloat. Among its casualties was 26-year-old Margaret de Mestre, the first nurse of the Australian forces to be killed.

The post office also took a direct hit, killing all within. Iris Bald, the postmaster's young daughter who'd just returned from boarding school, died endeavouring to reach her home. The blast tore every item of clothing from her body, yet there wasn't a mark on her—she died from concussion.

After the first raid that day, the Japanese swept in to attack again. The American destroyer USS *Peary* took a direct hit. With decks awash, she fought on. Another bomb exploded her magazine and finally she pointed her nose to the sky and sank. Her forward gunners were clearly silhouetted against the brilliant blue of the tropic sky still valiantly firing their guns upward as she disappeared beneath the sea. Eighty American sailors went down with her.

That day war came to Australia, and people I knew were in the midst of it. The Convent lugger *St Francis*, with Brother Smith commanding, arrived in the harbour just after the bombing, with nuns he'd evacuated from Port Keats Mission. Fearlessly they manoeuvred around the chaos, rescuing survivors.

Dr Clyde Fenton flew the wounded from the outer islands, while Dr Bruce Kirkland, who'd delivered me into the world and bestowed my name upon me, worked with patients in a makeshift hospital. Operating by torch and kerosene lamp, he boiled instruments on a Primus stove, all in the roughest conditions. He was later decorated for this work.

A message was relayed to naval personnel stationed in Darwin, its meaning crystal clear:

> The town and harbour of Darwin has now been designated a fortress area. As you are naval personnel defending your native land, you are now expendable. You will defend this fortress area until the last man. This is an order. An invasion of Australia is deemed inevitable.

How dispiriting to be told this so coldly!

In 1942 alone there were over forty Japanese air raids on Darwin, causing fearful damage. Enemy planes ventured as far inland as Katherine, where they strafed rocky outcrops they imagined were gun emplacements.

~

My parents had both joined the armed services; my mother entering the Nursing Corps, my father the Small Ships Division of the United States Navy. One wonders why, aged in his forties, he would return to active service after the rigours of the First World

War. But there he was, resplendent and *très debonair* in a smartly tailored khaki naval uniform and gold braided cap, ready to fight.

Delivering supplies to Pacific Island battle areas was a dangerous job, sometimes under heavy fire. In bad weather, my father wrote, the waves were mountainous; the small ship wallowed through troughs that blotted out the sky. But dangerous situations were always part of his life—and he always prevailed.

I rarely saw him during those war years, apart from the odd visit to him in American servicemen's hospitals. His legs were still a problem, but didn't deter him from sailing out with his ship—he made sure of that.

He once sent me an enormous unhusked coconut from New Guinea, my name and address in white paint on the outer husk. This was an impressive thing to arrive in the school postbag; few city girls had seen a real coconut.

~

Most students at my school had relatives in the armed forces, and a father, brother, friend, even a female relative, was sometimes reported wounded, missing or killed. This brought the war very close to us all. Telegrams were delivered by hand, prettily decorated for birthdays and anniversaries, but if you had a man at the front, the telegram boy on his bicycle could cause heart-stopping anxiety.

Letters came marked 'somewhere in Europe' or other vague destinations, so you never really knew where they were fighting, and every letter bore the stamp 'Opened by Censor'; sometimes large sections had been scissored out.

The popular wartime song 'They're Either Too Young or Too Old' became a standard joke among women at home. The only man readily available as an escort was either under eighteen or over 60. A young man not in uniform was a rare sight.

But although these were stressful times, parties and diverse entertainments proliferated. Civilians were expected to do their bit by helping to keep up the spirits of those in the armed forces—to work in canteens, perhaps organise a dance, or entertain in their homes where possible. There was a feverish determination to have a positive attitude and ignore the uncertainties of the times. Parties welcomed the return of troops, for however brief a stay, before they went on to another theatre of battle and a farewell party would be thrown.

Well-known entertainers hosted street parties where musicians performed for huge crowds. This raised money for numerous charities, among them a most popular cause called 'Smokes for Sick Soldiers'. Much money was raised to keep the hospitalised servicemen well supplied with cigarettes. We felt it our duty to contribute to such a worthy cause, so almost every serviceman had a cigarette pack protruding from his shirt pocket—it was a rare picture of Diggers at the front without a cigarette adhered to lip.

Much to our pique, we older school boarders had little access to all this social gaiety. We were also dying to leave school and enlist, our preference generally to join the Women's Royal Australian Navy Service: the dazzling white uniform, with braided gold epaulets and a natty little cap, was bound to appeal to young girls. We knew boys in uniform who had only just left school; one shot down in his aircraft over Milne Bay had been my escort at a school dance, so we were very aware of the war raging around us.

Streets were crowded with uniformed men and women: the hard, brown faces of Australian Diggers in their slouch hats, and soon Americans everywhere in smartly tailored uniforms, the sailors with gob caps squared on their foreheads. They cheekily wolf-whistled at every female over twelve. We thought them all wonderful; when they told us of their close relationships to famous movie stars, we believed them utterly, and hung on their every word.

With their arrival came novelties that are commonplace today, such as Coca-Cola in its shapely bottle—never heard of a canned drink in those days. We tea drinkers took to coffee with gusto, and until then we'd thought a Hamburger was a citizen of a German city. We were also introduced to such unfamiliar delights as pizza and doughnuts. But Colonel Sanders and his fried chickens hadn't yet made an appearance—for us, chicken was a special dish presented for the family Sunday lunch.

Through my father's American friends we acquired blue jeans from the navy stores, and through his nurses at the American hospitals, cosmetics and glossy magazines. These all gladdened the heart of a teenage girl when almost every necessity was rationed and luxuries were unattainable. Americans were also generous in the extreme with the abundance of their PX canteens.

We danced to the big bands of the day, cheek to cheek under dimmed lights to Glenn Miller, or jiving to Harry James and the Dorseys. We collected their records and lugged our wind-up gramophones wherever we went.

CHAPTER 21

# Our Hearts Were Young and Gay

Apart from spending occasional Christmas breaks with my mother in various places, I spent most school holidays at the houses of my school chums. Betty, Pat, Barbara, Elaine and me Jackie—what fun and good times we managed to extract from those trying years. Our hearts were young and carefree.

Betty's father was a hotelier in Brisbane and I recall roller-skating through endless hotel corridors, endeavouring to avoid expensive decor and disapproving, well-heeled guests. Unfortunately, those holidays were short-lived, for her father joined the air force and became one of the uniformed masses.

When last seen years later, Betty was driving a Mercedes-Benz sports car along the coastal highway, with the same disregard for anything in her path as she had on her skates in those corridors long ago.

Pat's family were city jewellers, but happily for us they owned a beach house on what's now called the Gold Coast. This timber cottage, with a small outdoor lavatory, stood on a rise directly opposite the famous Surfers Paradise Hotel, which had the popular attraction of a zoo within its grounds. The hotel was the only one in the heart of the city. Along Cavill Avenue to the beach were all private holiday homes, not a high-rise in sight, and we rode our bicycles around quiet streets. Now clustered skyscrapers rear up against the sea, and there are no timber shacks and certainly no outdoor privies.

Elaine's father was a theatre-owner who had met and married her mother when she danced in a chorus line. She was a tiny, dark-haired, effervescent lady who missed her life in show business. When her husband was away, she would take a little drink or two, strip down to minimal underwear that resembled her stage costumes and entertain us with her favourite dance routines. We were an enthralled audience, clapping our approval, yelling the odd catcall, and momentarily giving a thought to a stage career ourselves. It was all great fun, although when her husband was home she was the epitome of decorum.

Barbara, a great personality, life of every party, took up a medical career.

And Jackie? She went north into the wilderness, stepped off the edge of the world and wasn't seen by these old friends again.

The five of us spent weekends at the beach, lying about in the sun, baking to the colour of mahogany. Ruin our complexions?

Yeah! We'd exhibit our newly minted skills of flirtation by daringly displaying our two-piece costumes to wolf-whistles from callow youths. Those costumes rarely displayed more than a few inches of midriff, as the bikini was not yet born.

Weekending on the coast, we might spend a Sunday at Byron Bay to see the great whales brought in to be flensed, a fishy name for them being stripped of skin and blubber. They were looked upon as no different to any fish being prepared for market—try telling that to today's public!

George Patterson, a sun-scorched old beach bird, was a fixture at Surfers in the mid-1940s. He was known as the 'Mutton Bird Oil Man'. Every day he took up his post on the sand, close by his ancient, cut-down Rolls-Royce with its rough coat of silver paint. A mutton bird, dead for many years, dangled forlornly from the car's aerial, and drew attention to his special-formula suntan oil.

If business was slow, we teenagers might receive a generous and free spraying, and be assured it would do wonders toward acquiring a great tan. Well marinated with this vile-smelling concoction, we lay in the sun and fried.

My sixteenth birthday fell in the last year of the war, when my mother was stationed on an island off the Queensland coast. She arranged a dinner party for the occasion and, with donated coupons, I was able to purchase enough fabric from mainland stores to have a sixteen-year-old's dream party dress made.

It was an elegant party and everyone wore their dress whites. I sat in honorary splendour at the top of the table. When the officers in their handsome uniforms stood with glasses raised, it was like an echo of a Kipling poem.

This was a party to relate in minutest detail to envious chums on return to school—a story that weathered an entire term of 'after lights out' retelling.

~

Then Germany surrendered. The war in Europe was over. Living in the twilight days of a great war, we teenagers could no longer imagine peace-time living. What *is* life like, when there is no war? What does the radio broadcast? Can you just walk into a shop and buy anything at all? Will there be no one in uniform? It was going to be a strange and exciting life in a world at peace.

With the surrender of the Japanese in September 1945, the war was truly over. Victory in the Pacific Night was one of those public celebrations you could never forget. Ask anyone of the time and they will tell you exactly where they were. Brisbane went wild, on the streets and everywhere else—champagne corks popped and hotels overflowed, many distributing free drinks to the exuberant crowds. School boarders were allowed to join family and friends in the long lines spanning the city streets, linking arms, dancing, singing, throwing streamers, blowing whistles, totally ignoring any authority until dawn.

We were well aware of our good fortune in not having to fight a prolonged war on our own soil. When General de Gaulle marched back into Paris, Tuesday's French lunch was quite a party. With Madame in tears, we toasted victory with our elegant glasses of cordial, and were quite overcome.

Life changed quickly. Car charcoal-burners went as petrol became available, identification tags were removed, and gas masks were returned, unused except in drill. Blackout curtains were taken from windows; never again would an irate air-raid warden come pounding on your door late at night, warning that the chink of light at your window would cause the entire city to be bombed.

With rationing over, Christian Dior dropped the hemline to the ankle in an exuberance of fabric and created the 'New Look'. Then the glamorous Coco Chanel, who had been branded a collaborator with the Germans, returned all forgiven and with renewed force. She cattily declared Dior's New Look hideous: 'Look at how ridiculous women are, wearing clothes designed by a man who doesn't know women, never had one, and dreams of being one.'

We enjoyed this frivolous rivalry in the magazines; it was such a change from the anxious talk we had endured for years.

# PART II

'[A man's] heart must thrill for the saddle
and not for the hearthstone.'

THEODORE ROOSEVELT, 1916

'Out on the wastes of the Never Never—
That's where the dead men lie!
There where the heat-waves dance forever—
That's where the dead men lie!
That's where the Earth's loved sons are keeping
Endless tryst: not the west wind sweeping
Feverish pinions can wake their sleeping—
Out where the dead men lie!'

BARCROFT BOAKE

'In my wild erratic fancy visions come to me of Clancy
Gone a-droving 'down the Cooper'
where the Western drovers go;
As the stock are slowly stringing, Clancy
rides behind them singing,
For the drover's life has pleasures that
the townsfolk never know.'

BANJO PATERSON

CHAPTER 22

# Emerging from
# the Cloister

I was seventeen when I emerged from the cloistered custody of
the Anglican Sisters of the Sacred Advent. I was summoned
to take tea with Mother Superior in her private den, and gently
warned of the pitfalls that awaited the unwary in life—pitfalls of
which many of us were more aware than Mother Superior herself,
in the limited experience of her world. She hoped I would be
mindful of my training in ladylike behaviour—not something
uppermost in my mind.

Then, duly warned, I was sent forth to deal with the perils
ahead. If she only knew, I would no doubt have been the subject
of many of her late-night prayers. I had been in boarding school
since I was five, so freedom was heady stuff, and like many of the
freshly released I was determined to make the most of this new life.

With the war over there was an air of euphoria. We felt we could now make plans and get on with things, where previously we were in a sort of limbo, not knowing what to expect each day.

Service members were discarding their uniforms for civvies and endeavouring to fit back into uneventful civilian routines. My mother, released from the Army Nursing Corps, took up a nursing post in Darwin—a town still in upheaval, with the military encamped around its outlying areas. She was on the staff of the Civil Hospital, as it was known, and for a period flew out to medical emergencies with Jack Slade, who for so long was pilot for the Flying Doctor Service and well known to bush folk.

I reluctantly went into nursing training to please Mother, but after twelve months had to admit my only talent lay in decorating and design. A friend from Mother's fashion trade days suggested I become his house model while learning something of dress design, a career I regarded with much more enthusiasm.

Life settled into peaceful routine, all over the country.

My parents had formed a fragile marital truce and gone back into the hotel business—first in the business district of a tropical town in north Queensland, later on an island off the Queensland coast.

So soon after the war, there were no great holiday resorts. Islands that are now luxurious and quite famous holiday destinations were then completely barren, with barely a beachcomber's shack. Before the tourist trade gathered momentum, life on these tropical islands was ideal.

When my father gave me a casual 'come on up', I dropped everything and did just that. He was always ready to encourage you to have a good time, whereas my mother thought one should aim toward a more productive life—not always the most popular choice.

What a wonderful period in my life to look back on. My friends and I dallied through our days in bathing costume and sarong, with oleander flowers in our hair. We wore our long ropes of fine pearls entwined with shell necklaces on the beach, a la the French socialite Sara Murphy. Swimming at night in the warm tropical sea left dense starry trails of phosphorescence in our wake. A beachcomber's paradise!

An aimless lifestyle for a young person, perhaps, but after growing into adulthood throughout a long war, the sudden normality of peacetime had produced a certain world-weariness in me.

These good times were not to last, however. My parents took up a hotel further north on the Queensland coast and I settled in Townsville at a YWCA hostel—not unlike boarding school, but with more fun, more freedom, no nuns to disapprove when slinking home after curfew. I began work in cosmetics and beauty therapy, although it wasn't something I felt I would pursue for long.

When I flew up to visit my parents, my father usually found some minor adventure for us to go on together. 'Are you ready for some crabbing?' he would say, and clad in our scruffiest trousers we would advance on the rubbish bin areas of fancy seafood restaurants to collect fish heads, guts and discarded raw bones for bait. My mother forbade us entry through the hotel's front entrance in our smelly clothes, clutching our hessian bag of fish offal—although later, when our catch was delectably cooked and served, it was fallen upon with relish by all.

During one such trip, my fox terrier along for the ride, we rowed across the harbour to the mangrove-lined shore and cast our pots. When we turned for home it was almost dark, the water choppy, and we got into a predicament on the open sea beside ships moored at the wharves. Luckily our situation became obvious to sailors on a freighter close to where we were bobbing about. They waved for us to approach and then let down a rope ladder that hung loosely from the deck.

I was thirsty, hungry and dead tired, and the top of the ladder looked like Mount Everest. I discarded my shoes and, in spite of the bucking rowboat, managed to clasp the ladder. My father was right behind me, clutching the precious crabs, with the terrier in his shirt. I made it to the top with the help of the sailors, who came down a bit to keep the ladder from swaying with the ship's movement. I can't remember what became of our rowboat and pots. We trudged home to the pub's back entrance.

How many gals can say they climbed a long rope ladder in darkness into the arms of a bevy of sailors?

∼

Now and then I returned to the old haunts of the south coast to spend time with Elaine and her family. While there I met and befriended Miss Van Weine, a Paris-trained couturier who designed and made the most divine clothes. She was happy for me to wear them on special occasions, which ensured I always had something elegant to wear that I would otherwise not have been able to afford.

Van Weine made me the most gorgeous dress I ever owned, a strapless gown of a white sharkskin fabric, with metres and metres in its heavy skirt. A maze of boning and hidden tapes supported its shape, ensuring it hung just so. Sometime later, as its life was waning, I gave it to a hotel barmaid in Alice Springs who'd admired it. As women are wont to do, I remember it still.

# CHAPTER 23

# Back to Newcastle Waters

'Where there aren't no Ten Commandments
an' a man can raise a thirst.'

RUDYARD KIPLING, 'MANDALAY'

In 1950 my parents' German tenant Max Schober decided to move on from the Junction Hotel at the Ridge, which he'd been leasing since the early 1930s. He opened a store in the new town of Elliott. With no provision made for a caretaker to stand in at the pub, the only thing my mother could do was return alone to Newcastle Waters. She would see what could be done with the old place my father had built, which she hadn't set eyes on for sixteen years.

Mother found that the intervening years had wrought big changes in the old pub, which was rundown and dirty beyond belief. She quickly realised that she would need to take a very firm hand in dealing with her customers; the slightest sign of weakness and control would be lost, and there'd be anarchy.

Early on the first evening, with the old management still in place, she sat in the office behind the bar, listening to the buzz of laughter and high spirits echoing around the iron walls. Suddenly a deathly silence descended and she wandered into the bar to see what was doing—or undoing, in this case.

Bill Fulton, the enormously fat barman, was there alone, hanging from a rafter with a rope around his neck. He was red faced, his eyes bulging alarmingly, toes scrabbling for contact with the top of the bar.

Bill had been accused of a crime: something terrible, to be sure—maybe overcharging for a drink or watering the rum a tad too much. Ringer court had sat! The prisoner was pronounced guilty and sentenced. A rope was thrown over a beam and the prisoner hoisted onto the bar—no mean feat in Bill's case—there to be hanged by the neck, presumably until dead.

At this undeniably critical point in the proceedings, something of general interest had taken place outside on the road. Perhaps a fight had broken out or a new arrival needed investigating, and judge, jury and executioner had cleared the bar in seconds, the fun of Bill's hanging entirely forgotten.

At Mother's anxious insistence, they returned sulkily to cut Bill down. Resentfulness prevailed that anyone should take the incident seriously and spoil the fun. 'He's a good mate, Missus,' they insisted. Why would they harm old Bill, who'd suffered little more than a rope burn around his fat pink neck, and continued on serving at the bar as if nothing unusual had happened? And in view of the pub, the place and the times, nothing unusual *had* happened.

'What do you do when they get out of control?' my mother enquired.

'Oh, put the drunks in the monkey room until they settle down.'

The small monkey room, she discovered, was locked from the outside and fronted with a heavy, galvanised mesh grille. It closely resembled a prison cell.

That night Mother retired to a none-too-clean bedroom with some misgivings. If this was the first night, what was to come?

Tom Quilty, an old friend, said to her, 'I hope you know what you're taking on, here alone. If you can handle this lot, you're a better man than I am.'

My God! I can tell you that this was a place to intimidate the toughest bush publican. Another memorable night Mother heard about a drunken couple *in flagrante delicto* on a public pathway in broad daylight, she called her yardman. 'Remove them,' said she, and stood by as he cast a bucket of cold water on the love-makers. Was my mother, a genteelly raised lady, intimidated? Did she go pack her bags and depart a place of such immoral decadence? *Not she!* She handled it alone, and in her usual efficient and orderly way proceeded with her intention to clean the place up and sell out as soon as possible. She'd spent years as a hospital matron, terrorising probationary nurses and untidy interns in her wards, and wasn't about to be intimidated by unruly drinkers.

Mother set about proving she was equal to the challenge. She soon learned that staff were hard to find, with advertisements in southern newspapers either going unanswered or bringing unsuitable applicants. Sometimes after just one look at the miserable, lonely landscape of scrubby Bullwaddy, they were on the next trip out.

Newcastle Waters seemed like a town where there would never be anything to do you shouldn't be doing. But looks belie, for this town had a wild past, and a wilder future awaited the wary new publican.

There were good men to deal with, and bad; happy drinkers, and dangerous ones to be handled with tact. This was an establishment where the public played really rough. For years they'd behaved how they wished.

The pub's patrons were an unruly bunch to be sure, but big reforms were in the wind with my mother's management:

No spitting on the floor.

No excessive swearing in the bar.

No cheques cashed with the merest suggestion of rubber in their make-up.

No credit to anyone with the faintest unsavoury whiff to his character.

She also banned from the premises a small group of local women who'd spent most of their day settled on the verandah, causing trouble with drinkers.

*Shock! Horror!* was the response of the Junction's regulars, who had real trouble dealing with the passing of their 'good ole days'. And a woman to deal with too! How bad could it get? Were the days of undisciplined drunken revelry gone forever, when you could ride your horse into the bar to fetch a bottle of rum, cheered on by your mates? Were there to be no more mad gallops down the road outside, firing your rifle into the bar to give everyone a scare? Just for the hell of it, y'know. That slash in front of the bar was a reminder of the time you brought out your big bush knife to deal with someone similarly armed. 'What harm in that, eh? We both lived to tell of it.' Was all the fun to end?

When Mother was under siege from determined revellers, reinforcements were slow to arrive. The policeman and Long Tommy, his Aboriginal tracker, were rarely anxious to get involved in problems 30 kilometres away.

Tommy, who had once tracked for my father, was unusually tall and had a thick mop of snowy white hair, which he coloured a lustrous dark reddish-orange with powdered ochre. He was a sight to behold in his police uniform, with his old-style, high-crowned trooper's hat balanced precariously on top.

~

The next pub out through the Murranji Track was at old Halls Creek, hundreds of kilometres distant, so Mother had a dedicated clientele. Under her firm rule, they were no worse than drinkers anywhere else in the bush—just seeking company, a break from life in isolation. Sure, they were wild men at times, but if a drunk became truly unruly, his mates usually took him in hand.

The Ridge was a regular Territory cow-town, where drovers brought their big cattle herds right through. Copious amounts of rum were sold, and beer came in large bottles, each covered with a straw sleeve, four-dozen to the wooden case—always referred to as a case of beer, never a crate or box. When Cuban-heeled riding boots clumped on the pub's stone floor, and the rum and beer bottles began a-clinking, a wild night could be expected and stern measures were needed to keep control.

The law demanded 10 p.m. closing, and my mother saw to it that the doors closed right on time, in spite of desperate pleas: 'Aw, c'mon, Missus, gissus another ten minutes, will ya?' Banished from the bar, they would continue their big night, if in a serious party mood, right across the wide road out front.

In cold weather they made a big campfire, gathered around in a wide circle and settled right down to make a night of it. Supplies to see them through until morning were piled into the big hotel wheelbarrow and trundled across to the site of festivities. It was of little importance if the beer wasn't cold: 'Cold or straight from the case—doesn't matter, Missus, so long as there's plenty of it!' Mother ensured her stocks never ran out—sometimes low, but never out.

In the morning amid the powdery ashes and surrounded by high piles of empties, the revellers were to be found in various stages of inebriation or recovery. Often they would continue on through the next day, or they could even make a week of it, by which time the beer bottles were mountainous and the drinkers who were still vertical were subdued and very shaky of paw.

Throughout their revelry they sang, boasted, swapped yarns—and fought. A curious phenomenon among Territory ringers was that when they fought, it was with a suddenness and savagery, and for reasons they couldn't really explain; but, with the fight over and tensions released, camaraderie restored, they subsided back to peace and good will, mateship with no grudges held. The only evidence of it were the wounds of battle, rarely more than a split lip or black eye.

During such a battle, a top Territory cattleman, Elmore Lewis, took a more damaging punch than usual—it split his lip open right to his nose. A hawker known as Happy Wilson was camped with his van outside the pub, a good spot to latch on to retiring drinkers who may still have the odd bit of cash. With bag needle and strong black thread, Happy stitched Elmore's lip together. Antiseptic? None—only the alcohol that passed over it on the way down his throat during the remainder of the evening. But Happy made a neat job of it, with only a faint scar.

When drinkers got too rowdy my mother would call on the services of those still sober to act as gaolers. Occasionally two or three men would be incarcerated in the monkey room together. There'd be a loud protest and a few swinging kicks at the door, or perhaps a fight that bounced them off the walls and bulged the door, after which they'd settle and fall asleep until released in the morning.

~

In the late 1940s and early 1950s, cattle droving through the outback stock routes was at its peak. Herds weren't yet transported by motor vehicle, but trucks carried loading through the bulldusted roads of the Murranji to outlying western stations. The transport drivers were as given to off-the-track revelry as the stockmen.

The Martin brothers, Stan and Jim, were the Territory-born, station-raised sons of Alf Martin, long-time manager of Victoria River Downs Station. They carried loading through Newcastle Waters and the Murranji, and both they and their drivers knew how to party ringer style. To liven a dull evening, they invented crazy competitions of the reckless and dangerous variety.

On a prolonged binge, fuelled with enough alcohol to launch a rocket to Mars, they marked out a race course with the prime-movers of their semi-trailers. It led over a rough bush track and culminated in traversing a rickety bridge, of two narrow timber wheel tracks, that spanned a deep creek—with no side rails and a cavernous nothing beneath.

I can't recall which of the furiously racing monsters made it over the fragile bridge first, but surprisingly both brothers lived until a reasonably advanced age.

Of course, not everyone on the track played so hazardously. There were drovers through each year who rarely took a drink when they had the responsibility of cattle in hand, but it was a rare transport driver who couldn't be inveigled into a night around the campfire if good company was gathered and a bottle of rum was passed around.

Anyway, what is there to report on the commendably proper and hard-working? Is it not the wild and the rebellious who stand in one's memory?

The staff situation hadn't improved all that much. My mother applied for a permit to employ an Aboriginal yardman, which was grudgingly granted, though the law didn't allow him to put even a foot on the licensed premises. Prentice was a big, good-natured man who kept the grounds tidy and did all kinds of odd jobs.

When Prentice cleared the huge piles of empties after drinkers departed, he covertly drank the dregs. He also wheeled the big grog-loaded barrow across the road to where revellers were in full celebration. Given that full-blood Aboriginals weren't permitted liquor of any kind, there would have been reservations about the legality of this close proximity to alcohol if anyone had thought about it, or if there'd been a closer police presence.

Prentice had leprosy and dreaded being sent away from his people for treatment; he kept well out of sight if a government motor vehicle came into town. Eventually, though, he had to go and be treated at Darwin's leprosarium.

Another staff member was Cookie, a part-Aboriginal woman who lived locally and reigned over the kitchen. She was a good bush cook, but unreliable, for she had a fondness for a drink or two.

Part-Aboriginals had to be officially exempted from the prohibition order before being allowed into a bar. Publicans were issued with a list of those exempted, which had to be regularly brought up-to-date. Known colloquially as the 'Dog Act' list, it was tacked up behind the office door for quick reference.

Exemption could be rescinded if a person was found drunk and unacceptably disorderly. For those unable to enter a bar, there were always mates to supply a drink off the premises—but even if supplying liquor in complete innocence of the restriction, one faced the mandatory six months' gaol term.

When a part-Aboriginal man entered the bar, you asked his name if he was unknown to you, then checked the list to save the embarrassment of a direct: 'Are you exempt?'

After the grime of years had been scrubbed and polished into an unusual cleanliness, and my mother's law laid down, the lads generally resigned themselves to the new order.

Mother put aside her plan of early departure—she was not one to turn her back on a lucrative business—and remained behind her bar and in her store for the next seven years. But she still needed more staff.

One day I received a rather desperate telegram, begging my help. Though I wasn't sure what Mother expected of me, I decided to go anyway.

CHAPTER 24

# Anyone Can Do Anything

On the day I returned to Newcastle Waters, my old nursemaid Polly came down from the camp with a group of elderly lubras from my mother's household years before. It had been twenty years since I'd last seen Polly and she boasted to all who cared to listen, 'Him my piccaninn that un, I bin grow im up little bit—longest time now.'

Amid those remarks and the noisy greeting, 'Ay-na-yah,' I was hugged, hands were pressed gently on my head as of old, and I was much congratulated for the skill I'd shown in managing to grow up without Polly's supervision.

Polly invited all the lubras to pinch my breasts. They admired the changes that had taken place in me since childhood and gave one another serious nods. There was some laughter when they jointly offered to rectify any sagging the future might bring by inflicting the thick-ridged cicatrix or tribal scars, which they assured me would restore everything to its upright position. Polly and her tribeswomen had a solution for these problems that preceded silicon.

Polly considered herself family and settled down outside my mother's store, observing all who came and went, and what they did between times—all good gossip for the camp, with embellishments, of course; she relished her position as chief reporter of Ridge happenings. Sitting cross-legged at her observation post, wannoo bulging her cheek, occasionally spitting a stream of tobacco juice, Polly received, and expected to receive, a generous supply of handouts.

~

Soon after my arrival at the pub, I discovered with some uneasiness that I was to be the cook! There had been no mention of this until now. The cook? I was 22 years old and had not so much as made a cup of tea; boiling an egg would have been advanced cuisine of Cordon Bleu standard. Who was going to teach me how to cook?

Certainly not my mother, who presented me with an old, grease-stained *Country Women's Association Cookbook* she'd come across in a drawer. 'Just follow the recipes, nothing to it,' she said breezily as she departed the kitchen, giving the strong impression she didn't intend to return—it wasn't her scene—though she expected everything to be well cooked and presented on time.

What a baptism of fire this was! The hotel kitchen was big and had no sink—the washing up was done by two lubras in a dish on the table with water heated on the stove. There were a couple of ancient kerosene refrigerators and—'Heaven forbid!'—an enormous two-door, wood-fired cooking range: the very sight of it, with its interior aflame, terrified me. The cookbook was full of terms like broiled, braised and moderate heat, but there was no thermostat on the pub's oven—how could that enormous iron monster be moderate in anything? Luckily Cookie could stay on and teach me some basics.

At that early stage of our occupation, there was no vegetable garden, hence produce other than potatoes and onions was all canned. There were also no kitchen scales, so Cookie used a Capstan tobacco tin to measure things out—two tins of rendered beef fat to so many of flour; the same with sugar; for cakes and brownies, a handful of dried fruit was thrown in, always referred to as plums whatever size, shape or origin.

Corned beef was boiled in a 20-litre bucket, and I faced the frightening prospect of 10-kilogram roasts to be rolled up and stabbed with wooden skewers that could have stood in for fence posts, then manhandled into fat and placed inside that scorching monster. Steak was cooked without a pan: coarse salt scattered like chicken feed over the wide stovetop, then the meat cast willy-nilly on top. The kitchen was hot, *very* hot—no fan ever fluttered there.

An old Aboriginal man, Peterson, who'd once been on the road with teamsters, came early every morning to light the stove. After stacking wood and leaving water for the kitchen, he departed with his billy-can of tea. All the time I was there, I don't recall one morning without Peterson.

I muddled along with Cookie, who endeavoured to give me some training. Then came my big test. On their way through to Darwin, a group of English entertainers—The Tommy Trinder Show—decided to venture off the beaten track. Seven kilometres from the bitumen road, they felt they'd adventurously 'gone bush'. They demanded lunch, all 29 of them.

Where *was* Cookie? Too bad for me, Cookie had tired of any further kitchen duties that day and succumbed to the need for a little drink. She was stretched out dead drunk on the kitchen floor, wearing nothing more than a benign smile, entirely naked, one leg cast with happy abandon over the big breadbox.

My heart did a slow sink, about as low as it could go. I felt utterly abandoned. I dared not tell my mother, or Cookie would cop it later, when she would probably be in a fragile recovering state and not up to a verbal lashing. Anyway, Mother was busy in the bar with the show folk.

What to do? Should I roll Cookie into a corner and throw a couple of tea-towels over her? No! Complete removal was the best way to go. It wasn't hard to do: she was small, very slight, and quite easily dragged to Peterson's wood stacks outside the kitchen, safely within the environs of the 'no entry' zone.

Then out came cans of everything—vegetables, cream, fruit. I tried the steak cooked on the salt-strewn stovetop. There were no complaints; everyone seemed satisfied. It was quite good, actually. I could cook, I could cook!

Soon after, Cookie departed, happy with the thought that she'd taught me to cook and glad to escape from Mother's new regime with its uncompromising rules. My frenzied entreaties to Cookie's departing back—'Tell me again about the casserole, and the custard too!'—were ignored. She left with the kindly words, 'You good cook now, Jack-a-leen,' which couldn't have been further from the truth.

Then she was gone. I was on my own.

Ringers passing the wide, gauzed-in kitchen windows were well aware of the novice cook within, and of the rules of non-entry that applied. They would stop and, with noses pressed against the gauze, ask, 'How ya handlin' it, mate?' and offer snippets of advice on the finer points of bread-baking and damper-cooking, at which they were all skilled.

Through that window I learned how to prepare a yeast bottle for bread, how to render huge boilers of beef fat into dripping, and the trick of adding some sugar and a dash of vinegar to the water if the salted beef was old and dry. When I advanced to the heady level of cake-making and baked one I wasn't too ashamed of, I would hold it up to the window and be encouraged with a 'Good on yer mate, you're doin' good.'

⁓

We bought our beef from the cattle station just up the road. There was also a herd of perhaps a hundred hardy goats, which grazed out and about, unhindered by fences, and prospered however lean the pickings. A goat from the herd was regularly butchered, and no one in the dining room denied it when asked if it was New

Zealand lamb. Chickens roosted in trees in the backyard, their eggs fossicked out of the big woodpile and other ingenious places.

Every bush establishment had their goat herd, station, pub and store, sometimes with an Aboriginal goat shepherd. On cattle stations the shepherds were usually a couple of old lubras. After milking early in the morning, they'd leave to wander with the herd, collecting any newborn kids along the way and directing their charges back each evening to be yarded.

Our pub goats wandered the ridges without a shepherd, usually straggling back to their yard in the evening. However, when the south-east wind blew hard in the cold months, they nosed right into it and were gone at a fast clip, with no return in mind. After they spent a night away at the mercy of dingoes, someone was sent out on horseback to turn them back; their tracks were followed for about 30 kilometres, and they were found still doggedly trudging into the wind.

My father returned for a while to help with repairs and restoration. He built a new store, and his initials are still clearly etched into its cement floor. In a vintage Bedford truck he carried prodigious quantities of wood from the bush; a huge pile of neatly chopped wood was soon available to feed the iron monster in the kitchen. The chickens were removed from trees and housed in a new pen, and a big vegetable garden took shape.

No washing machine graced bush laundries in those days. Two regular laundry lubras spent wash days with tubs, copper boiler and ribbed washboards. Clothes were hung out to dry on lines stretched across the yard, and had to be cleared before the goats returned to munch on anything they could reach. Hunger had nothing to do with it: this was just what goats did, for everyone knows that they have an appetite for inedible things.

A small Lister generator provided the power for lights from sunset until closing time. We had no electrical appliances; refrigerators were all kerosene-fuelled. There were other inconveniences too numerous to mention, but pub life on the old stock route continued without too much complaint from anyone.

I learned to cope with the casserole, the custard, bread-making and much more; I learned that anyone can do anything—and the bush, with its scarcity of conveniences, was the best place to learn.

CHAPTER 25

# Go Bush, Young Man!

Late in 1948 a man just 21 years old stepped off the small plane that landed each week at Brunette Downs Station on the Barkly Tableland. With swag in hand, Giltrow Poley saddle on shoulder, Ken Hammar came as a horse breaker to Brunette.

He had come, he had seen and was totally conquered; he vowed he was there to stay. It was to be many years before he set foot outside the Territory again. In that time he travelled some long, hard roads into the furthermost outback country he could ever have imagined, and would pass off as incidents bush experiences that others might retell with the drama of high adventure.

To the Aboriginal people with whom he had close association for all his years in the bush, Ken was known as Kenhamer, Malbo, Maluka, Boss, Olman.

~

Ken was born in 1927, almost exactly between the two great wars. He spent his childhood in Brisbane, attending a private boys school. There were no horses, dogs or cattle mustering; his family lived in a stone mansion by the Brisbane River, built in 1852 with convict labour and long heritage listed.

In 1943 Ken started at Gatton Agricultural College, and graduated in 1945. Considering his all-consuming interest in country activities, his father expected he would study veterinary medicine, but any patience he may have possessed for prolonged study soon evaporated on receiving his Diploma of Animal Husbandry.

He'd always had great empathy for the Outback, and believed—as the Territory ringer did—that cattle- and horse-work was the only thing for a real man to do.

Already a natural and excellent horseman, with success in various rodeos and bullock-riding competitions, Ken was honoured with an invitation to ride at the Brisbane Exhibition. As a rough rider, he had great strength and balance, and was rarely thrown.

When breaking in horses on cattle stations, riding the newly broken horses was a popular bush entertainment, with spectacular spills and skilful horse-work. Often lubras came down to the yards to be part of the excitement, compare the riders and, of course, give loud-voiced opinions of them. 'That Kenhamer,' they called out, 'him proper, no more little bit.' From a bush Aboriginal, 'proper' was used to describe something admirable or astonishing.

In 1948 Brunette Downs covered about 5,600 square miles—quite a sizeable cattle property. It takes good cattlemen to manage properties of this size, and Brunette flourished under the management of Eric Barnes, a cattleman of the old school.

The cattle brand was BDT and the symbol brand 'Axe Head', the old 505 brand having gone with the years past.

In 1884 Brunette had run 2000 head of shorthorn cattle; by 1948 the herd had swelled to 54,000, with 600 working horses. Of these, 130 were taken out into the stock camp for the first round of mustering, which took about six weeks. Around 18,000 calves were branded each year, while five or six mobs of bullocks and spayed cows in mobs of 1500 were taken off to distant markets by drovers.

Twenty-five men worked the stock camp. Four or five were white men, including the cook, who killed a beast every second day to feed the camp, and every day baked eight or nine loaves of bread in long trenches of hot coals. The remaining stockmen were Aboriginal.

The weekly wage for a white stockman was 5 guineas; he supplied his own clothes and tobacco. The Aboriginal stockman received £1, as well as his clothes, tobacco and the complete upkeep of his entire family, from grandmas on down to numerous aunts and piccaninnies. They were all housed, fed and clothed, and received regular medical care.

Some Aboriginal women worked in the homestead, wore a uniform, waited on table and carried out general household duties, usually under the eagle eye of an older lubra with years of experience and a strong awareness of her authority.

Bindi, a small wizened Aboriginal man, bore the grand title of head gardener, although a good part of his day was spent curled up asleep in the wheelbarrow. He had seen the white man come into the country, emerging like debil-men out of the distant haze on the great vacant plain; he was always eager to tell of the fear, strangeness and curiosity of such a sight.

This is the environment in which Ken landed after leaving Brisbane. During his years on Brunette, Ken handled large herds of cattle and learned to contend with drought, fire and flood, death, disaster, and the eccentric men with whom the Outback was liberally supplied.

⁓

In 1952 the Barkly Tableland missed out on the annual monsoon rains that soak the country, and the stations lost large numbers of cattle. Brunette's losses were close to 30,000 head that year, and hundreds of dead cattle were dragged from around the water troughs on bores.

That was the year of a great bushfire; it started in bush near Mount Isa, then roared through stations on the Barkly and across the grass plains of the tablelands, where it was fought with graded fire-breaks, back burning and station trucks loaded with water tanks. It raged for weeks, on through Newcastle Waters, westward through the Murranji Track, with the dry season winds behind it, taking it into Western Australia.

In its wake it left some Tableland stations completely burned out. Cresswell Downs, with only three bores, was without stock feed for the season.

⁓

Out with the stock camp, Ken had the unique opportunity of holding 10,000 head of cattle on open country, something few Australian cattlemen would experience.

This came about in Brunette's 5000-square kilometre Lake Paddock, which held around 30,000 head. As the musterers regrouped, uniting their cattle into one mob, they found that due to the poor judgement of the head stockman they had gone too deep into the herd. Now they had in hand this enormous, almost unmanageable mob of around 10,000 head.

Thirty men watched the cattle through the night on the plain, the huge herd moving constantly like a giant amoeba. When the horses were exhausted, the men advanced on foot, rattling billy-cans filled with stones and drumming on tin cans to keep the mob under some control.

The next day, branding and castrating began as usual, but the sight of 10,000 head stretched across the open plain in one mobile mob was a sight to remember.

Bronco branding was the only method of branding in those days on Brunette. The most calves Ken had seen branded in one day were 740 head at Rocky 2 Bore in 1949.

~

On the Tableland stations, bores supplied much of the water and were overseen by men known as 'pumpers', one to each bore. Diesel engines pumped water into big turkey-nest dams, from where it was directed into troughs. At that time there were eight or nine pumpers on Brunette whose job was to start the engines and keep watch on the troughs—nothing more, as maintenance was done by station mechanics who did a bore run each week. Pumpers were mostly solitary older men, with pasts hazy or unknown; the lonely bush life suited them well.

There wasn't much a young ringer didn't experience on the old stations. When Pumper Mick was found in his swag, quite blue and very dead from alcohol poisoning, the responsibility for his burial fell to Ken. The weather was hot, so a hasty burial was necessary.

Mick was a big man with no friends nor kin anyone knew of. Sewn into his canvas swag cover like a body prepared for burial at sea, placed on a truck with two Aboriginal men, Pudden and Willie, to steady him on his last journey, Mick was driven to where his grave had already been dug; Eric Barnes, the station manager, went along as a witness.

Over the rough road, the body began to roll in its canvas shroud, which sent Pudden and Willie into a panic. They leaped off the truck and set off at high speed to put as much space as possible between themselves and the dead man.

With helpers gone, there was no way Mick could be gently lowered into such a deep hole. Eric looked over at Ken, raised an eyebrow, nodded toward the grave, and they rolled Mick in.

'God bless you, Mick,' from Eric.

A harsh burial perhaps, but Ken engraved Mick's name onto a large rock. Sixty years later, unlike many in the bush, he has the dignity of a marked grave.

Ken's second year on Brunette was shaping up to be dry, no rain, not a drop—until March. Then, with the usual feast or famine conditions of the Outback, it rained and rained, and then some, and the country was inundated. Lake Sylvester, Lake de Burgh and Corella Creek merged into one huge body of water, estimated from the air to be about 300 kilometres around.

The stock camp had 4000 head ready for the road, with drovers standing by to take delivery, but the water rose so rapidly that the cattle were released back into paddocks. All those weeks of work were for nothing.

In the course of a muster, the stock camp moved its site every few days as the men advanced with the round-up. When the rains came, the camp was settled close by the lake. A brand-new truck loaded with fresh provisions arrived that evening, but with the continuing rain and the heavy black soil, the truck, still fully loaded, was going nowhere.

It was imperative they move to higher ground, so they began carrying what they could up onto a stony ridge. Almost dark, the rain still pelting down, they prepared to unpack a tarpaulin from its bag—someone's big mistake: the bag contained only leather hobble straps, resulting in a miserable night, with soaking swags and little tucker.

Next morning the country, usually an expanse of waving dry grass, was an inland sea as far as the horizon; the truck and its load were 6 feet under. The men needed tucker fast, and it fell to Ken to dive down and retrieve something edible—the prizes were a bag of blue-boiler dried peas and a sack of flour.

As luck would have it, a valuable Aberdeen Angus bull from the stud of Anthony Lagoon Station had the misfortune to be taking refuge on the high ridge as well, which proved his undoing; he was quickly dispatched and cooked on the fire they'd managed to light. Even with everything soaked, a fire can always be lit in the bush; wax matches in small flat tins will light in any weather, and dead wood soon burns with sheets of iron shielding the flames.

The bull saved the day, along with the pre-soaked peas and flour, which was edible within a deep crust. Years before, in my father's day in the bush, a consignment of flour, usually in 20-kilogram calico bags, was immediately immersed in a waterhole and left until water had penetrated just far enough to form a hard crust that protected the inner flour from infestation by weevils.

As the water rose higher, my father and his stock camp could only return to the station. Crossing Corella Creek was full of problems: two horses drowned, and the cook was no swimmer and had to be dragged across, mostly under water, with three bronco ropes around his chest. The poor man nearly drowned, but with rough resuscitation he rallied; upon arrival at the station, he collected his gear and departed, swearing never to return.

For those on Brunette today, it may be of interest to know a dugout canoe was once paddled 50 kilometres from the station to Lake Bore on a rescue mission, then a further 30 kilometres to Corella Creek.

When the stock camp reached the station, their first priority was to rescue the pumpers. With only the rim of their dam above water, the forlorn pumpers had taken refuge on the highest, driest place available to them. One of these men was Jack Kidston, a quiet little Englishman who had forsaken city life to go bush.

Settled on the rim of his dam, Jack saw a buffalo way out in the water making straight for his small, dry patch of earth, already populated with a menagerie all bent on survival. Sharing his precarious hold on dry land with an irate buffalo wasn't a happy thought; Jack raised his rifle, took aim—no, it was too far, and he couldn't afford to miss with ammunition so low. He waited, as pale sunlight shimmering down through cloud created a hazy veil over the water. The buffalo came closer, moving slowly, low in the water. It had a huge horn span. Jack took aim again, was about to fire—when in the nick of time he realised he held in his sights a man, not a beast.

*My God!* It's Whiskers Harrington, looking for a spot of dry ground along with everything else in this watery wilderness.

Whiskers had a wide and bushy black beard, and his chest and shoulders were also well-endowed with a thick, woolly black pelt. Across his shoulders he carried a wide yoke with his possessions attached to each end; his bald head, right in the centre, set off the likeness to a swimming beast.

Whiskers was never to know how close to a dead buffalo floating away on the floodwaters he had come.

# CHAPTER 26

# And That Says It All

After a few years on Brunette, to use his own words, Ken tired of looking at the arse-end of Tableland cows. He broke in a brumby stallion that came into the station plant, made a packsaddle and a pair of greenhide pack bags, and jogged off across the plain.

A paddock he built on Brunette still bears his name—'Hammar's Paddock'—and is his contribution to posterity on the downs. Perhaps its origins are forgotten today, 60 years on.

He spent a few months' horse breaking on Cresswell Downs, where his wage was the equivalent of 14 dollars per week, plus two dollars per head to break and shoe the colts—good money back then!

Moving on in the time-honoured way of the old Territory bagman, Ken eventually rode into Newcastle Waters, where he appeared on my horizon for the first time. Six foot three, sociable and charming, he could ride anything (he would agree, with reservations). Tough, hard as nails ('sure'). Perhaps not truly handsome, but a touch of Gary Cooperishness there ('oh, puhlese!'). Definitely someone to keep well within view on any girl's horizon.

Or, in Ken's words:

*'North of the Ten Commandments*
*West of the Barkly Plain*
*There's a place called the Ridge*
*Where there's beer in the fridge*
*And oh what a beautiful dame.'*

*I was at the Brunette Downs race meeting when I heard this and thought I should take a look. After the races I mustered up my horses and headed west to Newcastle Waters.*

*About 400 kilometres later I got there and walked into the pub. And there she was. The publican's daughter, Jaqueline Sargeant.*

*Fifty-six years later I still look at her each day with wonder and appreciation.*

*And that says it all.*

# CHAPTER 27

# The Old Stockman of the Bush

To have known the old stockman of the Territory bush is, I feel, my greatest claim to pioneer status. With the receding sound of hoof beats and distant crack of stockwhip, he has ridden off into the pages of history books and adventure tales.

Find just one word to describe him? I can only come up with 'hard'. He lived and worked in inhospitable country, with complete indifference to loneliness and danger. He belonged in a culture that regarded fear as an insult, and the synonym for brave was 'mad', as in 'mad bastard'.

He ate hard, mostly dried salted beef from animals he had killed himself, and he looked damned hard too—rugged, lean and muscular. Roughened by the elements, he could have been any age: a boy barely into his teens, yet with years of bush life behind him, or a leathery old veteran of the cattle trails. He may have been a drover, a bushman out of the scrub, or even a cattle station owner.

Clumping about in spurs and leather leggings, a walk on the outer side of his feet gave him a bowlegged look, but he didn't do much walking, would mount his horse to go even the shortest distance. The elastic sides of his laughin' boots gaped with age. He wore his trousers low on his hipless frame—from some, an indrawn breath threatened total descent and could cause an onlooker to pause transfixed in expectation of such a calamity. His hat was a fixture, day and night. With stockwhip looped over his shoulder, he displayed an easy grace.

He could shoe a horse, break in a colt, handle wild cattle and cook a fair damper in the coals of a campfire. He had no use for a store-bought cigarette; he learned from necessity to roll his own, rubbing the loose tobacco in a contemplative way in the palm of his hand. A practised flip into rice-paper, a quick flick of tongue along its edge, then with cupped hands and squinting of eye, it was lit and remained adhered to lip.

There could be a needle wrapped in thread in the band of his hat, to mend a tear or stitch a wound. No cologne for him: he smelled of horses, sweat and tobacco. Surprisingly quite a pleasant combination of bush scents.

I never saw an old-time ringer wear gloves. He did all his stock work, fencing and yard-building with rock-hard, calloused bare hands. He was known as a ringer because he rode circling his cattle to keep them together. On an Australian cattle station, a cowboy was a mere rouseabout who worked at odd jobs.

The ringer's swag was his bedroll, carried on a packhorse that he drove before him; a couple of blankets were rolled in a waterproof canvas sheet, secured at each end with leather swag straps. Everything he owned he carried in his swag: spare trousers, shirt, sometimes a dog-eared collection of bush poems, maybe even Zane Grey or Louis L'Amour. His swag was his home, the place where he slept. An extremely thin swag could be jokingly referred to as a 'cigarette swag', while a large one was regarded with misgivings; perhaps its owner spent too much time comfortably lying about instead of up and working.

He had no need of a compass or watch; he looked to the Southern Cross and took his bearings from the stars. He knew the country he rode, however vast the area. He knew the water-holes and how they were holding; what to expect of the country, wet season or dry. His roof, the open sky in any weather.

There was no need for him to acquire a head for hard liquor—he was born with one. When he joined his mates to drink, now *they* were gargantuan 'booze ups' that could and did go on for days—usually at the end of a long hard year, or after dreary months of droving, when enough rum flowed down their parched throats to gladden the heart of any distiller. For days the exploits of the year were exchanged amid laughter and argument.

He was the epitome of the craggy, hard-drinking nomad, riding the cattle trails. 'What other kind is there?' he might ask, and the greatest compliment he could receive was that he was a good cattleman. He believed there was nothing else for a real man to do.

Indelibly in my memory, he sits on his haunches, leaning back on his high-heeled boots, elbows on knees in that inimitable, muscle-numbing pose he could hold for hours, his hat tipped back from a weathered face, brown as old saddle leather. This is how I will always see him.

Those who came later, after his time, were more prosaic; they lacked the colourful romantic aura of this man in the saddle, for he was unique, and he has burned his image into the pages of Territory history.

⁓

White women were in short supply in the Territory; young, unmarried white women rare creatures indeed. For quite some time I reigned as the only single white female within a thousand miles across the stock route to Western Australia, and it brought the attention one would expect.

My name was bestowed on quite a few fancy equines in horse plants along the track, and often these animals were paraded with pride for inspection and viewed with varying degrees of approval. One of the first big cattle-station transport trucks sailed forth with my name emblazoned like a figurehead. I can only hope it brought the good truckin' expected.

I wore trousers a good deal, and often ringers would ask my mother why Jack-a-leen couldn't wear a dress or skirt more often—a touch of femininity was unusual and special in their lives.

⁓

At Newcastle Waters, Ken joined the cattleman Elmore Lewis, who was preparing for a contract muster of Montejinni Station, an outstation of Victoria River Downs. They broke in twenty colts to join with Elmore's horse plant, recruited several Aboriginal stockmen from the local camp, and were ready to ride out.

Early next morning we heard them coming, the hooves of 60 shod horses clopping along the hard bare ground of the Ridge, the creak of worn leather tuned with the *plop-plop* of the horses' bellies as they jogged on by, the clink of spurs and bridle bits sharp and clear in the still air.

As they rode past the Junction Hotel, Ken, then Elmore, raised the handle of a shouldered stockwhip to hat in a silent bush farewell. In a short while they were enclosed in their own bubble of heavy dust, out onto the Murranji Track, with about 200 kilometres to Montejinni.

I was not to see Ken for another two years.

# CHAPTER 28

# A Time Long Gone

Rosie was very young—not more than sixteen, I would guess. She was married to an old man of the tribe who kept a very close eye on her. Rosie considered herself somewhat more sophisticated than the other women in camp; she'd been up the track some miles to Mataranka and thought herself much travelled. She worked for a time in the pub's kitchen and cleaned the bathrooms.

Our shopping was a haphazard affair, with parcel deliveries by bus often crushed in mailbags or affected by heat, so items such as cosmetics were rather treasured and made to last. I kept lipsticks in the bathroom; it was cooler there.

Then they started to disappear, one after another, and I felt I must have been careless and mislaid them. It did not at first occur to me that Rosie was the source of their disappearance.

Tribeswomen didn't know of face painting other than for corroboree, but Rosie it had to be.

I mentioned this to my father, who knew how to deal with most everything.

'Leave it to me,' he said.

Next morning, within Rosie's hearing, he announced with much seriousness, 'Lipstick bin gone, eh? Well, I hope lubra no more find un, s'pos'n she put um longa face, he kin make for proper sick, make im swell up.'

That was all.

That evening Rosie's husband brought her up to my mother, drooping like a faded flower over his supporting arm, groaning with pain, her face swollen, appearing quite ill; around her mouth was evidence of removed lipstick.

My father came to take a look at poor Rosie and said, 'Ay-na-yah, look like lipstick bin on that face, no good belong lubra that one!'

Rosie groaned and gazed up at him with the eyes of a dying spaniel.

He pondered awhile, then said, 'Might be that one kind special medicine can fix im. I'll tell Missus about it, *uwai*.'

An aspirin was carried out on a saucer and carefully transferred onto a spoon, with a glass of fizzy drink to wash it down. Rosie's cure was miraculous; the swelling went down fast.

From that day on, the bathroom lipsticks remained untouched to the extent that dust was quite thick around their base when all else was sparkling clean. For Rosie, they were to be avoided at all costs.

What brings Bindi to mind I cannot say, but here he is flitting into memories of a time long gone. This Bindi very different to our wizened gardener at Brunette.

In those days it was unusual to see an obese inland Aboriginal person; in the 1950s, the inland people remained lean, hard and hungry. However, my father had a devoted follower—not old, not young, somewhere between, and so enormously fat that his features were crowded out from his bones with puffy overlapping flesh. My mother ordered shirts for him from southern manufacturers: huge, voluminous, tent-like things—'giant size', they were marked.

He attached himself unbidden to my father, and forever swayed behind him like a mammoth shadow. He refused to retire to camp or even to sit in the shade to observe all that went on, but followed along, carrying my father's tools, mumbling and finding fault with the young Aboriginal boys, and loudly repeating the Boss's orders to workers, with great bossiness.

Upon a step or ladder, panic could set in, and Bindi's cries for rescue of 'Boss, Boss!' caused the piccaninnies to collapse with laughter and my father some annoyance, for Bindi was ordered not to undertake anything too ambitious in his workplace exertions.

I was with my father one day when we came upon Bindi sitting on the floor by the kitchen without a shirt, feasting on an entire roasted goat haunch, greasy fat dripping down his many chins onto his huge chest. We paused at this truly astonishing sight. 'Behold the Cannibal Chief,' said my father, with a dramatic sweep of his arm. Bindi smiled and chuckled happily over his feast; he took everything my father said to him as complimentary.

⌒

Christopher Morley once said that, 'No one appreciates the very special genius of your conversation as the dog does.'

The pup was born under Jimmy Roberts' wagon one day, way out on the Murranji Track. When Jimmy's cattle mob reached Newcastle Waters, he gave the tiny pup to my father. The pup grew into a big, bully-looking white dog with a clear brown spot right in the centre of his back, so his name was pre-ordained.

Spot was a companionable fellow, always close by his Boss, who was ever willing to exhibit his clever tricks boastfully to anyone who cared to spare a moment. This dog was eerily intelligent. When old men of the local tribe wandered down from the camp to sit in a circle and talk awhile with my father, Spot sat in on the conversation, so to speak. He had the unnerving habit of staring hard at each man as he spoke, with an air of understanding all that was said.

If my father hadn't drawn the old ones' attention to Spot's conversational alertness, all may have been well, but casually he said, 'No more gamen now, this dog him savvy allabout nah,' which translated to 'No kidding now, this dog understands all of what you say!' Uneasiness surfaced then, and although the words could never be spoken aloud, there came a foreboding, born of centuries of superstition, that possibly the old white dog wasn't quite what he appeared to be.

The Aboriginals gave thought to which departed member of the tribe may have chosen to return his shade in this guise. Rumour ran in whispers that a relative of blind Bella's it must be, for had not the white dog become properly *coola* (angry) when she was tormented by the piccaninnies? Ay-na-yah, everything pointed to Bella.

Bella was old and frail, her eyes two pure white marbles. She was led along by another old woman of the tribe, each holding opposite ends of a long stick, the usual method to lead the blind; in this way they progressed slowly and often to the store. The piccaninnies stole Bella's food and teased her cruelly, running around her, snatching at her clothes. She would lash out wildly and shout furious abuse at them. Spot would rush in barking and snapping at her tormentors—perhaps the angry voices upset or excited him, or maybe he just disliked children.

Well aware of the aura that hovered about him, the piccaninnies rushed off in fright and made wide detours to avoid where he slept in the sun. The house lubras ceased shushing him rudely from the kitchen door, and tasty titbits were surreptitiously placed where they could easily be sniffed out. If he settled on their blankets in the sun, as was his wont, they no longer said a word, and let him be.

Life was all good for the old white dog. He had a love interest in a bitch that lived down the road at the saddler Archie Rogers' place. When her litter arrived, Spot, trailing bullock guts from a recent kill, set off to Archie's house, a good half-mile away. Archie told us that Spot gently deposited his offering at her feet with all the panache of presenting a bunch of roses. This was certainly unusual behaviour for a domestic dog.

Spot's presence was unsettling for the old ones, and after much thought it was reluctantly decided that he be given to Ken to take bush and live in his stock camp. I last saw Spot heading off in good spirits with not a backward glance or any obvious thought of any tribal affiliations.

So from his birth in the pale dust of the Murranji, the old ghost dog journeyed to the lush tropical pandanus country of the wild Limmen River, where soon afterwards he was taken by a crocodile. One must ask: what knowledge could this relative of Bella's, this Mudburra man of a dry stony inland, possibly have of big water and the dangers it holds?

CHAPTER 29

# Hard Men Who Lived
# Hard Lives

The old Territory was a man's land; it was hard country, could be a cruel one too. Living there meant observing a lifestyle different to one you could encounter anywhere else. 'An education in human behaviour,' my mother said.

Most were cynics, but not insensitive. They were contemptuous of cowards and trod carefully with their equals. Unsophisticated but wise, they were philosophers every one. They thought it essential to find humour in the most serious situations. In adversity they laughed, as only they could laugh, at themselves. They told tales of disaster and appalling mishap with thigh-slapping hilarity, and you found yourself smiling too.

Perhaps this is why some of the funniest tales to come out of the bush involve sad or unfunny incidents. Told with a twist of humour, they make light of life's cruellest happenings. If a man can't laugh at himself, he has no sense of perspective—and life would be unendurable, I think, in a harsh country.

My mother was often asked: 'How do you cope out here, a woman alone with unruly men?' I was there too, of course, but I was just a young girl, not in a position of responsibility. Perhaps being alone was the reason Mother managed so well; women were scarce and treated with great respect in any situation. However, she was also expected to maintain that respect; one misplaced step of unladylike behaviour would have been a fall from the pedestal, respect lost forever.

Once when a twenty-man pub brawl was in full swing on the road outside the hotel, a body hurtled in through closed doors, landing in a shower of splintered wood. Mother calmly demanded, 'Eight pounds, please.' The fight faltered to a stop and the warriors dug deep, paid up.

One would assume the fight was over, but with a few angry words, the odd insult, and without so much as an 'After you, mate,' they hurled themselves back into battle. No western movie could have done it better.

⁓

Each year Slippery Prendergast and his brothers, all drovers, came through the Ridge. Slippery was a short, chunky fella with the booming voice of a bronchial bullfrog—the result of many years' bellowing in the dusty wake of his bullocks.

In camp, swags were unrolled as far from Slippery as possible, for he had a habit of whistling in his sleep—not an ordinary whistle, but that 'Move along bullocks' kind a drover uses through the teeth. This could be madly irritating to men camped with cattle at night, who sleep lightly, alert to every sound.

Mother always insisted that those drinkers still upright at closing time take responsibility for their fallen comrades—no bodies were to be left behind when the doors closed at 10 p.m.

But one night Slippery was overlooked and remained lying where he'd fallen, in a limp heap under a long table on the enclosed verandah. The doors were closed and he was locked inside, with only his loud snufflings and snortings leading us to where he lay. It proved too difficult to extricate him from under the permanently anchored table—his bulky frame was wedged tight. With the generator off, we had only torchlight. Mother said, 'Oh, leave him there,' and off we went to bed.

He gave his piercing whistle a few times. Then, just as we were falling asleep, a loud 'Whoa bullocks!' rent the air in that awful bullfrog voice and echoed throughout the iron building. All of this while he was in the deepest grog-induced sleep. Never were his mates allowed to leave him behind again.

⌒

To spend one's annual holiday camped under the miserly shade of a Bullwaddy bush on hard red gravelled ground, opposite the Newcastle Waters Pub might not be the ultimate holiday destination to everyone, but to Chungaree Crouch it was. Each year just before the wet closed bush roads Chungaree appeared over the horizon. Then, with all the anticipation of settling into a glamorous resort, he unrolled his swag, lit a camp fire and presented his annual wages cheque at the pub bar with a cheery, 'Tell me when it cuts out Missus' before he proceeded with a wholehearted spree, joined by any ringers who happened by.

Chungaree, a white man, had always been known as Chungaree ('mate' in tribal talk) and had worked on Wave Hill Station for 22 years. He never ventured further east than Newcastle Waters; beyond that was 'stranger' country. The bitumen road was his boundary line.

Someone once sold Chungaree a motorcycle. He rode it for only a short time, never really made friends with it, and referred to it in stockman's terms. Over rough ground it had him 'grabbin' for leather', as with a rough horse, and it could take the bit in its teeth and bolt too. Chungaree and the motorcycle were not compatible and it was disposed of early in their relationship.

Chungaree was getting on in years, and with good intentions the manager of Wave Hill arranged for him to settle in an aged persons' home in Katherine. Shortly after he moved into his new quarters the old fella returned home late one evening noisily drunk, reasoning that he was in town and that meant a night on the booze.

With two comely Aboriginal ladies, he loudly celebrated the beginnings of his new life of retirement. This behaviour was unheard of among the aged inmates in this establishment.

Chungaree had to go!

Next day, swag rolled, he was packed off on the first truck heading west back to Wave Hill—the country he knew best—to spend the rest of his days.

Dick Scobie of Hidden Valley Station was a regular drinker in the pub and a bit of a brawler sometimes too. A tall, fine-looking man, Dick once told me the tale of his only trip to a big city.

He'd been 'courting' an Adelaide girl of the Lutheran faith; many German immigrants had settled in South Australia and Lutheran churches proliferated there. His courtship had progressed to the stage where an introduction to his girlfriend's family was due, so off to Adelaide she took him.

The crowds were unbelievable, the traffic frightened him and he clutched at her skirt as she swiftly disappeared around street corners. Alone and lost in a department store, he found an elevated spot beside 'one of them gammon ladies with a dress on'—a plaster display mannequin—and gave his shrill bullocky whistle for rescue. In general, he found city life not to his taste: 'No place for a ringer—never did see so many people in one place before.'

Then, on Sunday, off to the Lutheran church to join in the service and give praise to her Lord. He'd never been in a church before, but he told me he sang as loud as everyone else and had a thoroughly good time there.

'Where did you ever learn any hymns, Dick?' I asked.

'Well mate, I didn't know any hymns, so I sang "505 is the Brunette brand" good and loud, and everyone thought I was a proper good fella, and they never chucked me out!'

Cammy Cleary was one of the Territory's best rough riders. A balance rider, loose and fluid in the saddle, he flowed with the motion of a horse. He was as dedicated a drinker at the pub on the Ridge as any other ringer.

Now Cammy had a dog called Whisky, who was pure white, very large and well known for his ferocity; any sudden movement toward his owner was strongly discouraged.

One night, after Cammy had spent hours at the bar, he staggered away, presumably to his camp across the road and into his swag to sleep it off.

Closing time came, drinkers dispersed into the night, doors were locked and Mother entered her bedroom, which was close to the bar—there to be confronted with two laughin' side boots protruding from under her bed.

Together we took a boot each and made to remove the limp body attached, when suddenly Whisky appeared from under the low-hanging bedcover, aggressively stiff-legged and snarling a warning, very much in protective mode. Boots hurriedly dropped, we rushed for the door, which we safely slammed shut just as the dog launched himself against it.

We removalists retired to ponder the problem, which needed careful thought. With Cammy in the bar for the past few days, I knew Whisky hadn't been fed in a while, so I suggested that a half-pound of raw liver attached to a broom handle might do the trick.

The bedroom doorknob was gently turned, the juicy, bloody liver carefully offered, a white nose appeared, and the lure was thrown far out onto the verandah, the famished dog close behind it. Mother and I made a speedy entry into the room, closed the door firmly, took up our grip on the boots again, then dragged the body laboriously out past the bar to the front door and quickly rolled it down a low step onto the gravel outside. Mission accomplished.

Next morning, sheepish and apologetic, Cammy felt he hadn't fared too badly at the hands of these determined removalists—and his dog had been fed.

~

In the cow-towns across the stock routes and at the pubs along the way were many Irishmen who rode by, drank hard and threw themselves into any fight, whether it concerned them or not. It was said that they never knew when they were beaten. They had a roguish, ribald humour; were loud, boisterous, irrepressible and dominated any company in their bawdy, charming Irish way.

Mick Cussens was such a man. He had a swagger, was loud and brash—and was enthusiastically drinking himself into an early grave. Mick and his brother Bill had been droving since they were boys with their father, Sam, a reliable and respected Boss. They came with packhorse plant through the Murranji.

Everyone knew Mick—old Wirra-Warra. He'd once been an active man, adept at all things expected of a good ringer. But years of heavy drinking had taken a toll: he was dirty, seldom quiet, shouted incoherently about the place, rarely ate, and was never sober.

Unbeknown to my mother, who had little sympathy in this direction, Prentice came quietly to tell me that Mick was collapsed by the woodheap. We went down and found him there, unshaven and filthy; within himself he was as completely alone as a man could be.

I tried to feed him a little soup with a spoon; he couldn't speak, looked right into my eyes and gave a barely perceptible shake of his head.

The three of us sat there together on the woodheap in that ugly, hot, stony yard with the crows nosily irritated by our presence, sharing whatever strengths we had to share. An Aboriginal leper, advanced in his disease; a dying alcoholic, too young for death; a young girl in a harsh place, on a misguided mercy mission, acknowledging her complete failure to improve the situation in any way.

Mick's brother took him away after laying him on his swag on the back of their truck. He died soon after in Camooweal, that haven of old drovers.

If a ghostly yelling and cursing in the night around the old pub is ever heard, it must surely be Mick reliving one of his wild binges.

~

And then there was Jack!

No one asked if you knew Jack Vitnell, or if you liked him; everyone knew him, and I never met anyone who disliked him. He wasn't memorable in a worthy or honourable sort of way, for he was always up to some mild roguery and was totally irresponsible—but he was charismatic, unusually handsome, and always laughing his abandoned, loud, fruity laugh, which made you want to laugh too.

Jack wore his wide-brimmed cattleman's hat at a rakish angle, and had that swaggering, crotch-hitching, just-rode-that-outlaw-bronc-that-couldn't-be-ridden air about him.

He was a remarkable athlete and as entirely without fear as anyone I have ever known. He could ride a wildly bucking colt with an easy, flowing grace; 'as if he wus sitten' on a rockin' horse', as someone remarked. Once he fought his way out of a bar in town, locked five policemen in a ladies' toilet and was a marked man ever after. (Truly, did the police have no sense of humour?)

Or was it entirely true that he'd done this? Perhaps it was just one of those tales that adhered to Jack—although he was certainly capable of it, and I know someone who swears they were an eye-witness.

Whenever a loud party was in progress, Jack was right in its midst. If you couldn't see him, you could hear him, and with his departure from the bar, y'know, the gaiety was strangely diminished.

The usual ringer was somewhat reserved with strangers, but not Jack! When the occasional tourists came through the Ridge, he would set out to charm the ladies, telling them outrageous stories of his exploits. They would take his photograph and depart quite smitten with this handsome 'cowboy'.

Late one night, long after the bar had closed, a party was in full swing out on the roadside. The grog supply had petered out and Jack proceeded with the unthinkable—to pound on the pub door and wake Mother in order to replenish their liquor stocks. That took a certain courage.

As Mother's bedroom was close to the bar, Jack's pounding woke her.

'Go away!' said she, to which he replied, 'Please, Missus, gissus a bottle a rum, will ya?'

Mother: 'No.'

Jack: 'You're a hard woman, Missus.'

Mother: 'It's men like you have made me hard.'

Jack: 'Just one bottle, Missus. Please.'

Mother: 'Not before the bar opens tomorrow morning.'

Jack: 'You should get married again, Missus. It would make you feel more kindly to us blokes when we're thirsty and perishin' for a drink.'

Mother: 'Married again! You don't put your finger in the lion's mouth twice, my boy.'

Jack: 'Umm-m.'

They kept it up through a sleepless night; Jack sitting on the pebbly ground outside the pub door, Mother inside in her bed.

Jack was used to getting whatever he wanted, and my mother was a very determined woman—and though they would never admit it, they enjoyed this repartee through the night. At exactly ten o'clock next morning, she opened the pub door and passed a bottle of rum to Jack. He was still sprawled on the ground outside, a little drunk and half-asleep, and had to admit defeat.

In the watering holes of the old Territory, Jack's talents were slowly wasting away. Still quite young, he was found in his camp, where desperation for a drink had compelled him to swallow some awful stuff that proved lethal. He died alone, this handsome man who loved company and conviviality. Where a drink had been fun and made life agreeable, it had become a necessity.

Many in this country suffered the grim tragedies of thirst and fever, but alcohol and suicide were responsible for the untimely end of so many others who lived a bushman's lonely life.

～

How sad to think of them all gone, now part of the past. Genteel society couldn't accept them as they were; the Outback enfolded them without a glance into their backgrounds. In a sterner society, they would be branded drunks, eccentrics, ratbags. In the Territory back then, they were permitted to be themselves, and nobody looked askance at whatever oddities of behaviour they exhibited.

I found them impish—ribald, perhaps, but always full of good will. It seems to me that now there is only a small gap between the respectably dull and the quite objectionable, with no room between for the quaint and unconventional.

An old bush rogue once said to me: 'To be classed as a true Territory ringer, you must have shot a crocodile, dodged [stolen] a mob of cattle and bunked down with a willing young *queie* [girl].' He failed to qualify, he said, as he was such a poor shot he'd never hit a crocodile.

My mother described these men, who came through with cattle or for an annual break from the big stations out west, as 'a race apart'.

There was no organised entertainment, no cinemas, no opportunities for sport; they carried no radios and had limited contact with outsiders. There was the occasional bush race-meeting to enjoy—Brunette, Nigri, VRD (our abbreviation for Victoria River

Downs)—although it wasn't always possible to attend at that time of year with cattle-work at its peak.

Theirs was a preoccupation with the ability to ride, drink, fight, know cattle and horse flesh—always wanting to do it better than the next man, risk something more dangerous. Limited though it may seem, these were the things that made up their lives, and to do them well were their credentials.

Their stories of reckless riders of the bush would fill a book.

'Remember when Cammy Cleary rode that buckjumper with a glass of rum in his hand—never spilt a drop, mate.'

'How about that time at Newcastle Waters when we was all on the grog. We put up that bit of a yard with a few saplings, down there in front of the pub, y'know, and we rode them unbroken horses, just for the hell of it. Old Bill got his arm broke but it weren't nothing. Good times we had, eh?'

'Were you there when Ken Hammar rode Folly at the Brunette rodeo? That was one wild ride, mate. They wouldn't give him the prize, reckoned it was an exhibition ride on the feature horse—but he got it, by God.'

One might ask them, 'Why do you do these things?'

They would chuckle, shake their heads at you. 'Don't you know?'

It must always have been so, wherever men and horses gather together, doing things just for the doing.

# CHAPTER 30

# Travellers on the Murranji Track

A part from drovers, cattlemen and stock inspectors, there was a steady and varied stream of travellers passing through the Murranji to and from the west in dry seasons of the 1950s. They included the Quilties; Rod and his brother Basil Underwood; and Des Leigh, who owned Inverway Station—he was a good friend and always settled in for a long chat.

Ted and Dave Fogarty visited too. Dave conducted a good part of his courtship with the woman who became his wife, Joyce, over the open galah session on the outback radio. The progress of their romance was followed with as much interest as a modern soap opera.

Bill Tapp, another visitor, was a young man working with Bill Crowson on Montejinni Station. Fellow Territorians, let me tell you, in those early days Bill was a teetotaller. Yes, it's true! He never touched a drop. Sometimes he'd sit at the bar with a lemonade, while he and my mother would endeavour to correct all the wrongs of the cattle industry, the 'native situation' and anything else of local interest. Bill soon became a successful cattleman who bought Killarney Station and made a fine Territory showplace of it.

Bill died too early. His wife June is another of those wonderfully worthy women of the Territory who has worked indefatigably for the less fortunate youth of Katherine town community, and has always taken a keen interest in the problems and successes of local endeavours. They have a large and handsome family, successful in the local cattle industry.

Not everyone who came out of the Murranji came by horseback or motor car.

One morning just on daylight, a strange sound filtered out towards the Ridge. Approaching sounds from that direction were usually of stockwhip and cattle, or heavy trucks ploughing through bulldust. But this time, from out of the Murranji, came of all things, a motorcycle, with two persons crouched low, and so coated with bulldust to be unrecognisable.

Everyone up and about gathered around full of curiosity.

Out of the wilderness they came, fleeing an irate and abandoned husband. They jolted to a stop outside the pub, no time to spare for a shower, or food. First some fuel, then a solid shot of rum was rushed out while they were still there on the road.

Then they were off in a flurry of Ridge gravel, like grand prix riders—to where, we did not ask. How they managed to plough through miles of deep bulldust with their small motorcycle we could not imagine, there was no time for questions.

All day we listened for their pursuers, and with shaded eyes stared up the track, our protective lies as to their arrival, departure and direction taken at the ready. But not one came and we assumed they had made a safe getaway.

'Well Goddamn!' my father said, 'I've seen everything come and go on that track, naked myalls with a fist full of spears, their lubras and dogs. A fella pushing a wheelbarrow heading west, for the gold; cattle, donkeys, horses and wagons, but never before have I seen an eloping couple on a motorcycle.'

Polly (the lady on the motorcycle) was a daughter of the Cole family, early pioneers of the Kimberley. She was sister to Sandy Cole who, with his partner Ginty Gorrie, sank a number of the Territory's bores—those lifesaving watering places throughout a dry country for stock and man alike.

Polly's father, Tom Cole (not to be confused with Tom Cole, Territory author), pioneered the Canning Stock Route in days when only Aboriginal people knew how to travel a dry country.

The Cole family grew up among the Aboriginal tribes of the Western desert, and Polly was expert at performing their dances and songs. I have never seen the 'Emu Dance' performed better or with as much flair and authentic skill by any Aboriginal dancer.

Her mother was Mabel Bridge, for whom Mabel Downs Station was named early in the Kimberley story.

In 1890 the Bridge family made a slow two-year journey west from Queensland with their two children. They travelled a thousand miles in a wagon, with another baby born on the road. Mrs Bridge was the first white woman to cross the Murranji. Her daughter, Mabel, a child at the time, toted her rifle and took turn to guard the camp.

The naked Aboriginal people of the region were hostile, and protective of their watering places, but they were entranced by these fearless children and befriended them as they made their way through the old Murranji country, took them to water, and were beguiled by the strangeness of them.

Their iron sheathed wagon wheels ground slowly on through the stony ridges of the West, and into the sun-seared splendour of the Kimberley. Mabel Bridge married Tom Cole. Polly and Sandy were two of their eight children.

Tom Cole was the first man to take cattle through the Canning Stock Route, many years before Wally Dowling took it on. Later still, in 1941, the Lannigan brothers came through with cattle; it was always a rugged track depending on wells to water their stock.

When Tom married Mabel, her father Joe Bridge, who owned Mabel Downs, gave them 500 bullocks as a wedding gift and in 1911 Tom took them through the Canning to Wiluna in Western Australia, a six-month droving trip. He found the bodies of Shoesmith and Thompson on the tracks, killed two weeks earlier by some Aboriginals. He buried seven men there: the two white men, a half-caste and three Aboriginal men. He enclosed their graves with timber rails.

The hardship endured by this pioneering family, and others like them, who came with so little and left so much of their spirit within those who followed, are, I feel, often overlooked by historians for the more flamboyant forerunner of the Outback—those who rode in behind great herds of cattle to take up vast areas of country, and were well supplied with funds to build comfortable homesteads to settle their families.

The Cole family is still flourishing out there among the ancient hills that will never be bled white by a scorching sun, but blaze a savage red under rain, fade to dusty ochre in the dry, and where distorted old Boab trees squat with age-old patience, reaching their skeletal leafless fingers high to vaguely clutch at skittishly fleeing Kimberley clouds.

These gnarled old debil trees have stood for silent centuries in this red land of the Aboriginal people where now gold, pearls and even diamonds flourish in a land of cattlemen.

My friend Sandra Berlowitz, Mabel's granddaughter and a niece of Polly's, is a wonderfully loyal daughter of the West and is ever willing to extol the wonders of her beloved Kimberley. Her daughter, Kylie, and grandchildren too, are very much fixtures of outback life and still steadfastly hold the fort of family traditions. May they ever prosper out there among the wicked red hills of old Kimberley.

Then there were visitors we didn't know personally, but who were prominent figures. Titled Englishmen came to view family properties and were expected to rough it like everyone else. Authors, artists and politicians of various merit came from faraway cities. The American author James Michener passed through to Victoria River Downs and wrote of those he met in the bush.

Cattle buyers, hawkers and government employees also paid visits—anthropologists, too. The latter came in their quest to learn more of the Aboriginal people, bringing out their tape measures to wrap around the heads of boys, who later waited in vain for their new hats to arrive.

When the anthropologists gathered the old men of local tribes together to record tribal names and skin groups, some of these old men weren't above having a little fun with these strangers. They gave names of private parts of their anatomy and uses these could be put to, finding this hilarious, a great joke on the *gubmint* (government) men. Perhaps there are still recorded names of skins and family that are viewed very seriously, but would make you blush if you knew the truth. My father never did tell, and the old men returned to camp chuckling in high glee.

Roy Edwards and Dinny Connors owned Newcastle Waters Station, some thousands of square kilometres in size. The Ridge township was settled within the station boundaries, and their homestead stood right on the edge of town, a short walk to the Junction Hotel.

Roy had no children, and his estranged wife was Ida Edwards (nee Ashburner), who had been a matron of the pre-war Darwin Hospital. She had been a friend of my mother's, so Roy presented himself occasionally, when in residence, to take afternoon tea with Mother.

Although a gentleman and a wealthy, much-travelled man, Roy, in the manner of the true Territory eccentric, came to tea in beautifully laundered white shirts, entirely without a back to them, their frayed edges starched to crisp perfection; shining white shoes without the toes; and, to support his trousers, a child's skipping rope, artfully knotted around the waist, wooden handles dangling.

Mother never raised an eyebrow; Roy, thus clad, elegantly took a formal afternoon tea.

Much later he remarried—hopefully his eccentricities were contained.

The Walkers came through, vacation-bound, every two years, and each time their arrival was an occasion. Joe Walker had managed Ord River Station since long before the town of Kununurra was born. We always had a late night, catching up on the news of the past two years.

For my benefit, Mrs Walker would array herself in her impressive diamond jewellery and, in the poor light of our old generator, show how it had glittered on the dance floor at the Negri race ball. I was delighted with this display and quite thrilled when I was permitted to bedeck myself and flutter about.

On one visit the Walkers told a harrowing tale about two of their Aboriginal workers. The couple were asleep on the back of their truck with their newborn baby tucked in between them. They awoke when the mother felt her infant slipping steadily away and down her leg. A huge python had its jaws clamped firmly around the baby's face and was moving off with its prize. They rescued their child, but tribal law forbade the snake be killed and it was set free.

The infant was brought in to Mrs Walker, who found that, apart from deep wounds to his face, he was none the worse for the experience of almost becoming a snake's dinner. It can never be said that life in the bush was without a variety of incident, and it was the women on the stations who dealt with much of it.

Joe was a first-class cattleman and loved the station where he spent so many years. He had a repertoire of bush poems and always gave a rendition of what he called the 'Ord' poem whenever he had an audience.

> O, Heavenly Father, if you please,
> We pray to Thee on bended knees
> That you and your blessed son, Our Lord
> Will keep the 'cockies' off the Ord.
> O paralyse the duffer's hand
> When he lifts up his flaming brand
> Keep poddy-dodgers from the glen
> For Jesus Christ's sake, Amen.
> Now, O God, forgive our sins,
> And may every cow on Ord have twins.

Noel Healey was a strong and heavy-set man with thick, unruly grey hair. His manner was gruff, his conversation alive with earthy language, with no thought to who was present. My mother found him uncouth and didn't like him, but my father had great respect for Noel.

They had been friends since the early 1920s, when my father had come to pick up a singed and dejected Noel by the side of the road. His brand-new truck, which he'd just proudly brought through town, had caught fire and was beyond repair. 'I saw a spark,' he told my father, 'and only had time to throw my swag off before the fuel drums on the back went up. Went up they did, with not a thing to salvage.' The two men remained friends all their lives.

Like most bushmen, Noel was a jack of many trades. He carried early loading over long, deserted tracks. Later he set up a roadhouse with a liquor licence on his Dunmarra Station, beside the main north–south road.

He also had two daughters, Patsy and Nancy, whom I'd known forever. Nancy was old-time Territory all the way through: a hard-case character with a heart of gold. She was generous, drank hard, swore imaginatively and cooked like a French chef.

Nancy's husband, Stewart Somerville, had owned and operated the Argent Hotel in Mount Isa during the war years. The elevated prices of liquor and the continuous stream of servicemen ensured that at war's end they had accumulated sizeable wealth, and they retired south to enjoy the good life. They took up residence in a grand hotel, attended theatres and big city race meetings, and generally lived like the millionaires they were reputed to be.

Together they bought a large, luxurious yacht and named it NESS, Nancy's initials. No shod foot was permitted on its pure white decks, not even that of the US vice president, who spent an evening aboard. One fine summer's day, the NESS set sail out of Sydney, bound for Nouméa, where a dinner party was scheduled to take place at the Australian consul's house on the night of their arrival. As they neared port, the French pilot came on board to guide them in through navigational hazards, as was the custom and the law. Soon after, without warning, the NESS foundered and went down in minutes—they were shipwrecked! No one was ever sure how this happened; there were those unkind enough to suggest its sinking wasn't entirely accidental.

They were rescued from the sea and taken straight to the consul's dinner party, still in their sodden clothes. It was reported that they did not appear unduly perturbed by the loss of their beautiful boat. But the pilot wasn't fully licensed—a simple thing, easy to overlook, but crucial in their quest for an insurance payout.

With funds much reduced, they had no choice but to abandon their lavish lifestyle and return to the Territory, where they ran Dunmarra Station and roadhouse. They remained there for years, and Dunmarra became an inviting oasis for travellers on that dusty road before bush motor cars were air-conditioned.

Nancy presided there, generous and popular as ever. She had no children and made much of all the young people around the bush, black and white. Her friends ranged from the scruffiest old tribesman wandering in from the bush to sit by her kitchen door, to high-profile southern visitors. Everyone loved her.

An Aboriginal girl who had grown up in Nancy's family came back to work in the Dunmarra house. Later she became pregnant and ignored repeated urgings to check into hospital. She insisted that Nancy deliver her baby in the bush fashion—not an appealing prospect for someone without skills in this direction.

When it came time to for them to leave Dunmarra, I was in my early twenties when I went up from the Ridge to say goodbye. Nancy had few clothes, little more than the trousers she was wearing. She pressed into my hand the remains of a Chanel No. 5 perfume bottle and, generous to the end, insisted I take this last luxury item.

Several years later I visited her in Townsville, where Stewart, who had always been a very dapper fellow, was reduced to running a pie cart. The Catholic nuns called in regularly to collect food donations for charity; Nancy always had a basket of good things she'd made for them—cakes, jams, et cetera. She decorated her basket with vegetables, all artistically carved into the shapes of little men, whose private appendages were very apparent and out of proportion. The nuns found it a great joke, enjoyed the art work and thought her extremely clever.

On one very hot day of our visit, the Catholic priest called. Nancy welcomed him in, saying, 'Come in, you old bastard, take that dog collar off and have a cold beer.' He often stopped by and, I feel, enjoyed these visits quite a bit more than the sedate afternoon teas of the genteel ladies of his parish.

Nancy Healey Somerville, Territory born and bred. All sorts came out of this country. These were just a few of the many people of the old Outback who passed through the dusty track of the Murranji into Newcastle Waters. They remain clearly and warmly in my memory.

At Newcastle Waters we were surprised to find that missionary, Charlie, had come among us and intended to stay awhile. He and his small group were well known both by praise and ridicule. Some thought his teachings might do good in such a godless settlement as the Ridge, but most found his group self-serving, with a Christianity pretty much tailored to their own taste. Charlie's beliefs were never clearly defined, but in them Charlie fervently believed.

He took up residence in a small house close by the Aboriginal camp, and before long became known locally as the White Stallion, for obvious and not very priestly reasons. He held odd little services, uniquely orchestrated by himself; he served Holy Communion of Sao biscuits straight from the packet, and red jelly-crystal liquid because of the ban on Aboriginals drinking. When the store ran short of jelly crystals, canned beetroot juice made a richly red substitute.

The piccaninnies came out of curiosity, and were encouraged to stay awhile for divinity lessons and to be read Bible stories. The ones that appealed dealt with gory sacrifice and desert people clashing about in ancient wars—they used spears too, didn't they? Moses parting the sea wasn't well received, for they couldn't envisage a sea; the local creek was the largest body of water in their world, and it need not be parted to cross, one could swim it easily.

They ate his Sao biscuits, and stole his jelly crystals and most anything else they could get their little hands on. 'Ungrateful lil bastids!' raged Charlie, and up on the Ridge smiles were suppressed as he raged and complained.

Advents of special importance on the Christian calendar brought forth Charlie's most devoutly eloquent sermons. I was told, by a person who was present, that on the eve before Good Friday a larger congregation than usual had gathered, and Charlie was inspired with special evangelical fervour. The Easter story and the religious drama of the crucifixion took hold, and he declared to his brethren in a loud, impassioned voice, 'I am Jesus, I am Jesus!'

A serious and concerned voice, one obviously familiar with the Easter story, spoke up from the congregation. 'You is in for a real bad weekend, Jesus.'

The novelty of Charlie's services soon faded for the Ridge Aboriginals; they realised they would receive nothing more than gifts for their souls. So Charlie departed, in search of someplace with a more receptive audience.

CHAPTER 31

# On the Wilton River

Although it was to be two years before I was to see Ken again after he rode out to muster with Elmore Lewis, he had a hard two years on an isolated cattle run on the Wilton and in the Limmen country.

The muster on Montejinni Station over, Elmore Lewis rode with the plant back to the Ridge and, with a cheque in his pocket, Ken Hammar did what most bush travellers did then and joined the convivial company in Katherine's two hotels. Tim O'Shea's Railway Hotel was a popular watering hole where one could find numerous cattlemen, bore drillers, miners and transport drivers, all exchanging the latest news and trying to find something to their advantage.

The Katherine River, in its pandanus-bordered splendour, swept through the town and on through the grandeur of the river gorge.

In 1862, McDouall Stuart named this river for Catherine, second daughter of James Chambers, a financial backer of his expedition. Catherine had sewn a flag for him to take on his travels, and he erected it in a tree by the great river he named in her honour. Over time, the first letter of her name changed.

In Katherine, Ken met Freddie Ogden, who had taken up the grazing licence of Urapunga Station. Freddie had flown Spitfires during the war in Britain; now he flew for a local bush airline. They agreed to each take a half share in Urapunga, while Ken would run the station. He then flew out to Roper River, where the police officer, Dan Sprig, drove him out through bush to the station.

A small iron shed with a bark meat-house out back was the homestead. Water was carried with yokes from the nearby Wilton River. The branded cattle weren't worth counting—the big camp of bush Aboriginals settled there saw that the numbers were kept down. Ken faced an altogether disheartening picture: it was a station in name only.

Ken put together a stock camp from among the encamped Aboriginals and they mustered for several months. Conditions were tough. He lived frugally out there, with little choice but to share the lives of the bush tribespeople. Soon food supplies tapered down to beef and bush tucker; boots wore out and they rode with spurs on the bare foot.

Down on the river, a rogue crocodile was on the prowl. The grey-green monster had roamed for some time and taken two horses when they came down to drink. At night it circled the meat-house with its tantalising smells of fresh beef. The wily old fella was a humbug wandering silently at night; he was a danger to the camp people too.

Ken thought it a good thing to be rid of him. Before leaving on the next muster, he gave old Mulldahowie, an ancient Aboriginal man, a .303 rifle and one bullet. His last words were delivered with emphasis: 'Get him!'

Days later, on Ken's return, Mulldahowie beamed him a toothless grin of victory. He had the big croc's hide pegged out, salted and drying—all 5 metres of him! He'd used his old donkey to help drag the croc up to the house for skinning. No doubt advanced age had endowed the beast with certain wisdom in evasive tactics, but he'd proved no match for old Mulldahowie and his one bullet.

That night the old man held them all spellbound around the campfire, telling the long and graphic story of his success as hunters do everywhere. He had tied his dog close to the water's edge, he said, and every now and then given its tail a painful twisting. Its yowls alerted the crocodile that an animal was in distress and perhaps a handy meal was close by.

When at last the crocodile came cautiously up the slippery bank, Mulldahowie was waiting. One last vicious twist of the tail, a final yelp, and he quickly picked up his rifle, took a courageous stand just several metres from the huge creature, and shot him right through the eye!

One day a stranger rode into Ken's mustering camp, an unusual occurrence: a big, barrel-chested bear of a man, with a great bush of luxuriant, wiry red whiskers. Les MacFarlane, known as Mac, was travelling a mob of about 500 bullocks from his station at Mataranka to Boulia in Queensland. Several of his Aboriginal stockmen had deserted. The police officer at Roper Bar had suggested he contact Ken with a view to recruiting replacements from the camp by the river.

Following a lengthy discussion with Ken, three men agreed to go with Mac. Two days later he was back; the new recruits had had a rethink about a long droving trip and disappeared in the night. After a long talk around the campfire, Ken offered to see him through as far as Borroloola.

In Mac's camp were Big Mouth Charlie; Don-Don, an Aboriginal boy; and a young white fella, Bill Morton of New South Wales, who'd come north seeking adventure—no doubt he found it on this trip.

Due to drought conditions on the Barkly Stock Route that year, Mac decided to take his cattle through the deserted, untravelled Old Coast Road. When they reached the Four Archers, a group of hills near the Limmen River, they ran into good mobs of wild cattle, the descendants of those lost by early drovers.

The Limmen was perhaps the first river in Australia to be named by Europeans. When the Dutch explorer Abel Tasman sailed the northern coast in the 1600s, he named this great river for his ship *Limmen*. Three hundred years after Tasman's voyage, few Europeans had sailed its waters or ventured off the Old Coast Road to travel the surrounding country. It is officially called the Limmen Bight River but most people just refer to it as the Limmen River.

All the country between the Roper and McArthur rivers was vacant Crown land, and the numbers of wild cattle there suggested it might well be worth mustering, so Mac and Ken decided to apply for a grazing licence. Their only map was an old taxation zoning chart; on that they drew their boundaries, a large rectangle taking in about 4000 square kilometres around the Limmen River.

They could no doubt have drawn their rectangle much larger, and of any shape, but 'one shilling per square mile per year' was about as far as their limited finances would stretch. They erected a rough fence of bush timber across an area known as O'Keefe Valley, and there they let their cattle go. Mac returned to Mataranka and registered their land claim, and their grazing licence—'Limmen Gate Pastoral Company'—was born.

With this unusual and uncomplicated formation of a huge cattle station, so began a friendship that endured after their business partnership ended, until Mac's death in the 1980s. The long years of their association were filled with much that was humorous, hazardous and sometimes downright unbelievable—to write about it would require another book.

~

Ken settled on the new station and worked their grazing licence. He built himself a paperbark dwelling on Eastern Creek of the Limmen, but it was a nomadic life covering this large tract of land with horse plant, working stock, and building yards and paddocks of bush timber that had to be cut down with axes and snigged along by horses, the holes dug with crowbar and shovel.

On a map the word 'UNSURVEYED' spread over the Limmen country; in those days it was uninhabited, isolated, un-get-at-able. Helicopters hadn't yet made an appearance and there were no roads. One imagines surveyors saying: 'Oh, let the Aboriginals and horsemen venture there first. We'll come in later.'

The only wanderers were coastal tribes, who occasionally came through on walkabout: long lines of men and women slowly advancing and spreading out, retrieving every lizard, mouse and snake—anything they could find on ground they had burned. Into the coolamon or dilly bag it went. For beef and tobacco they sometimes helped with building a yard, before moving on.

Two of these wanderers left a young boy behind, his European name Roy. He had his 'grow im up time' in Ken's camp and took the name Hammar.

There were only two other white men grazing cattle on the western side of the McArthur River: Jim Marshall at Bing Bong Station on the Coast, and Cecil Teece, who had a small place on Rosie Creek, bordering Ken's country.

Riding out one day, Ken stopped in his tracks, amazed to see a small bush home—with garden, chickens, dogs, children—settled about 15 kilometres inside his boundary. Cecil, his wife Lorna and their three children were happily settled within. But there was no argument about it: they maintained a good relationship and mustered along their boundary together.

Cecil and his family had a hard life out in that lonely, unforgiving country, and it eventually got the better of them. Early one wet season—with long months of isolation looming, no markets for their few cattle, no roads, and the worries for young children out bush—they decided to pack their belongings and leave before the rains set in. They set off on horseback with their children on the saddle before them. Months later, during the following dry, Cecil returned to his little house and retrieved a few belongings. That was the end of another bush enterprise, undertaken with high hopes but doomed to fail.

Cecil later wrote a very fine book, *Voice of the Wilderness*, about his time on Rosie Creek, and of the experiences he'd shared with Ken, his only white neighbour for hundreds of kilometres, when they'd mustered wild cattle on horseback through the remote country of the Limmen River.

Over the years I saw Ken whenever he made trips to Moroak Station, where he trapped horses for work on the Limmen; Moroak had thousands of brumbies.

On one of these trips, Ken persuaded Jack Gill to return with him for a season's muster. Gilly was a white man, a good cattleman and handy with horses. Together they set off back to the Limmen with 50 horses.

At Newcastle Waters I packed a small box of what would then in the bush have been considered luxury items: food, books and tobacco, and two long, fat cigars, each in its own aluminium cylinder.

The package was taken bush by an old fella who knew where Ken and Gilly were camped. It was unpacked with as much delight as a parcel from under the Christmas tree. The cigars were carefully squirrelled away for a time when tobacco ran low.

On another of Ken's visits to Newcastle Waters, Polly took it upon herself to organise a corroboree for me and him, specially choreographed around our association with each other. We were to be guests of honour, so to speak.

It was the wet, when violent storms can punctuate the humid nights with thunder, lightning and torrential rain, then be gone just as suddenly, leaving in their wake broken tree limbs and gushing streams of rainwater.

Ken and I set off early to the corroboree ground, which was quite a way through bush paddocks and fences. We arrived to find the principal dancer dressed in an arrangement of feathers and plaited grass, but also wearing a large toy aeroplane upon his head. I took this to be an allusion to Ken's arrival from distant places; although he had reached the Ridge by motor truck, the aeroplane was possibly too flamboyant a symbol of travel for the star to resist, so on it went—and very effective it was too, jiggling about in dance.

When the festivities were over, Ken and I left to walk back just as a storm was breaking. Rain came down in sheets, lightning flashed about us, the thunder was deafening and in minutes we were drenched. It was the blackest night I can remember and we had no sense of our whereabouts. I was wearing a seersucker dress that grew longer by the minute, gathering a load of heavy red mud.

The rain stopped. A log burning from a lightning strike revealed a paddock fence, and we got our bearings from that.

We continued on through several fences to reach the road, with my skirt spreading way behind with its burden.

'What in hell are you dragging?' said my father.

'The police tracker may have had to be called to find us,' I said, which thoroughly miffed both men.

'Tracked trickier tracks than you can make, my girl,' said my father.

Ken, with a bushman's sniff, said, 'Got you home through bush by the light of a burning log, didn't I?'

~

To Ken, money was some mythical stuff that other people had and was only given thought when rations had been 'beef only' for some time, or there was a dire need of necessary materials for station work.

It was hard to build up a herd, as mustered cows needed to be regularly sold and wild cattle weren't as plentiful as first thought. And horses died in large numbers from walkabout disease; Ken lost thirty in one year. Walkabout was found to be cirrhosis of the liver caused by eating *Crotalaria*, a weed with pretty bright yellow flowers that comes up prolifically after rain. With walkabout, a horse will wander in a hypnotic state, without eating, without drinking, grinding its teeth in pain. A slow terrible death—an awful disease.

The need for funds loomed. With a mixed mob of about 400 head, Ken, with Gilly and Roy, started 'on the road', droving south toward the Barkly Tableland.

He'd been offered a fair price for this mob before leaving the Limmen—but on his meeting with the buyer, the price took a dramatic plunge. With no competition at that time of year, the buyer expected there would be a certain desperation to sell, especially after the distance travelled; their only option without a sale might be a long return journey.

Ken's cattle were a good mob in fine condition—the amount offered by the buyer was paltry. He refused to take it and decided to battle on in the hope one of the stations along the stock route might buy.

Burkie Cant, manager of Anthony Lagoon Station, was a great friend to the bush battler; he had been one himself, up in the hills behind Alexandria Station years earlier. It was Burkie who came upon Ken and Gilly droving their cattle.

'Where are you off to, Ken?'

Ken: 'Travellin' to sell this mob. Want to buy? All in good condition.'

Burkie: 'Sorry, head office said no more to be bought this year. Anyhow, let's boil the billy, have a drink of tea.'

Ken: 'Got no tea.'

Burkie: 'Well, some damper maybe?'

Ken: 'Sorry, nothing.'

Burkie: 'Well, what have you got?'

Ken: 'Got some salt-beef.'

Burkie: 'What's in your pack-bags?'

Ken: 'Salt, hobbles, surcingles.'

Burkie: 'Send the boy into the station. I'll have the storeman fix you up with tucker.'

Ken: 'Can't pay.'

Burkie: 'Don't worry about it.'

Roy rode in and returned in high spirits with tucker, and even a shirt and trousers for everyone.

'What will you do?' asked Burkie.

Ken: 'Just keep travellin' till we make a sale—have to do that.'

Burkie: 'Could be a long trip, mate.'

With that, Burkie drove off. Next day he came out to meet them with the news that head office had approved the purchase—no doubt at his urging.

Burkie was a great raconteur: one of his oft-repeated stories was of meeting these two fellas riding behind their cattle. They were bearded, with ragged clothes, no boots, nothing in the packs, and nonchalantly smoking big fat cigars like bloody cattle barons.

~

The year 1957 came in without drama, until the rains began—a big wet, this one—and those living around coastal areas were unaware of what lay in store for them.

Ken took Roy, who was then about eighteen, and they rode the 200 kilometres into Borroloola to meet with Jim Marshall on Bing Bong Station, and plan a muster on the Limmen and along the Old Coast Road.

With rain pending, Ken cooked a big damper to see them through the next 65 kilometres. The horses were packed and they were about to leave, when the Aboriginal Welfare officer called into their camp: 'Will you detour 26 miles downriver to the jetty?'

Word had been received that the *Cora* would be some days late, and Mick Baker (a resident of Borroloola) was waiting there alone.

The small ship *Cora* sailed up the Queensland coast around Cape York, into the Gulf of Carpentaria, then about 20 kilometres up the McArthur River, there to unload at a rickety jetty. The bulk was for the Aboriginal Welfare Department; very little came for the other residents.

With an uneasy eye on the gathering storm clouds, Ken and Roy rode off to give Mick the news of the boat's delay. It began to rain, then to blow—the rain bucketed down, the wind grew to a fury. A cyclone was fast approaching.

They made it to Mick's small vehicle, but it was far from weatherproof. Soon they were marooned on a small triangular patch of land surrounded by floodwater. They lay in soaking swags; the big damper was their only food. For three days they sat it out while the cyclone of '57 raged around them.

The strong flow of water carrying logs and debris swept around the jetty, which threatened to leave its moorings. With a bronco rope they secured it ashore, but the flow was too strong and, with a creaking shriek of farewell, it swirled away and careered downstream, bronco rope and all.

Next day dawned with clear skies; the sun shone on the devastation. A whistle tooted—there was the *Cora*, slowly making way up the cluttered river.

'Where's the jetty?' the skipper called through a loudspeaker.

'You passed it downstream, trailing a bronco rope!'

All stores, apart from a few packages, were for the Aboriginal Welfare Settlement. 'Well!' said the skipper. 'Who's going to unload? No one to unload, we head right back—don't you want your stores?'

'Nothing for me on board,' Ken answered, 'but we'll get the load off.'

The fuel drums were lowered into the mud; the boat's hatch covers went on top. Between the three of them, 40 tons of loading were manhandled up the steep, slippery bank. Just as the last box was set down, a flotilla of Aboriginal canoes arrived with men ready to unload!

Twenty-five years later, Ken met Mick again, and with their reminiscences came thoughts of the cyclone. Mick remembered: 'As they lowered a sack of salt on your shoulders, Ken, you sank to your thighs in mud.' Some of our youthful years may have been misspent—but hey, we were strong!

CHAPTER 32

# Jackie's Gone
# a Drovin'

In 1957, seven years after her return to Newcastle Waters, my mother decided to sell the Junction Hotel.

We had stood by in admiration and awe as Kurt Johansson's first road-train came rattling in across Newcastle Creek and pulled up in an almost perfect circle. The swansong of droving was written all over it.

So, after 25 years of owning this old watering hole, Mother sold out and went to live in the gentler environs of the south. My mother was rich! And she deserved every hard-earned penny.

Old Territorians never really die: they just fade into history books, or evolve into larger-than-life characters when tales are told about them around campfires. My mother became that harder-than-granite Missus who'd controlled the wild men travelling cattle through the old Murranji Track.

She bought a great stone pile of a mansion on a Hamilton hillside, overlooking the Brisbane River. In place of cattle herds there were passenger liners, and sturdy little tugboats with fine brave names of *Fearless*, *Faithful* and *Forceful* chugged back and forth. Mother had her great house converted into six large apartments, and on that elite suburban hillside, among the elegant houses, she raised an ornate house sign with the name 'Murranji'.

'Moo-rang-gee,' her neighbours mispronounced it. 'What does that mean?'

'Bush frog,' she told them, which was a close enough translation for city folk. They retired in utter bewilderment—why would anyone name a fashionable city house 'frog'?

For the next 30 years, encumbered with multi-labelled trunks, hatboxes and dilly bags—never one to travel light—Mother journeyed all over the world, playing bridge on many of the great ocean liners. After long periods without sending me so much as a postcard, she would emerge out of countries I'd never heard of. Once she rode down from the hills of a distant place on a mule.

Between travels she drove into Brisbane for consultations with her long-suffering stockbroker, and to check on the diligence of the unfortunate bank manager in charge of her finances.

~

'Cattle drive' is an American term; here you go 'droving', 'on the road with cattle' or 'travellin' cattle'. And 'stampede' isn't in the drover's vocabulary; when cattle take wild, headlong, out-of-control flight, it's termed a 'rush'.

With the pub about to be sold, I decided I'd take on a season's droving.

'Droving!' my mother shrilled. 'You must be mad—months on the road, sleeping on the ground in the dirt and dust. You'll never see it through.'

I knew most of the drovers on the road and I decided to join Bill Sharpe's camp. I'd known Bill for many years. He was a gnarled old man who had been a packhorse drover for much of his working life. Now he owned a truck, although the pack-bags and the odd mule still ran with the plant—just in case! Bill didn't have a lot of confidence in his truck, or his driving skills.

We were to spend seventeen weeks on the road, travelling a little over 1000 kilometres, with 1500 head of Victoria River Downs' bullocks bound for Walgra Station in Queensland.

Wages were agreed upon. We met in Katherine to drive out to Victoria River Downs and take delivery. On the trip out, we camped one night on the road—Bill in the back of his truck, me on my swag out on the ground nearby.

In the morning, the ground around my swag was churned into a deep track of powdered dust, about half a metre wide and dense with the paw tracks of an unknown number of dingoes. They had clearly been padding dizzily around for a long time, deciding whether to eat the body within their circle. I've spent many nights on the ground with dingoes harmonising in groups beyond; that was the one time they checked me out at such close quarters and with such obvious intent.

Bill took delivery of his cattle at Victoria River Downs. Pleuro inoculations completed, contracts signed, and the bullocks were our responsibility. We would travel about 15 kilometres a day, depending on water. We made our first move forward—only about 1000 kilometres to go, but what is 1000 kilometres in a Territory so big?

In the mob was a big, pure white bullock, very lame, hobbling along on the tail end. 'Cut him out, leave him behind,' someone said. 'Oh, he'll drop out soon enough,' came the response, 'probably before we reach the boundary.'

There were six of us in camp. An Aboriginal man named Cloud, a known unreliable, rolled his swag and crept off in the night just a few days out, but the rest of us were still there nearly five months later.

It was essential to make a good delivery, because losses weren't paid for. Any bullock picked up along the way in good condition was a handy killer—no point killing one of your own.

The cattle were watched through the night by men on horseback. Each man took a watch of about two hours, singing as he rode around the mob. An Aboriginal man might chant corroboree, although he was more likely to have a wider store of memorised popular songs than anyone else in camp. Some men had good voices and a large repertoire; those with lesser talents might recite poetry in a loud voice, or only muster a monotonous repetition of a few words, interspersed with a whistle or two and a 'Yo bullocks!' thrown in here and there, just enough to calm the cattle and ensure they didn't take fright and rush.

Six o'clock sundown, this was drovers' time. Toward sundown our bullocks fed up close to camp and settled down for the night. Our campfire lay between us and the resting cattle, a barrier that would hopefully cause a panicking mob to veer away from camp in a rush—though hair-raising stories are told of night rushes that took off right over the fire and destroyed camps.

The horse-tailer readied horses for the night, saddling and tethering them, and he took first watch. The boss drover took the last, or daylight, watch; he then woke the horse-tailer, who went out and brought in the hobbled horses, ready for the day's work.

In stock camps where cattle are yarded at night, with no watch necessary, men might sit around the campfire to talk for a time; on the road they usually took to their swags early. But sometimes, when first-time drovers sat among flickering shadows, hats low over their eyes, tense and quiet, an old drover would tell of times past; of the unmarked graves that lie under the yellow dust of the track; of touchy, unsettled cattle, easily set off in heart-stopping flight. The crack of a twig, the clattering of stirrups and saddle flaps when a tethered horse shakes itself, loud sounds in a quiet night, and the cattle would be off in a sweeping whoosh, more vibration than sound, like rolling thunder blanketed by distance.

An old hand coming off watch would make straight for the warmth of the fire, create a shower of sparks as he pushed a burning log back on with the toe of his boot, and nestle the billy-can down among glowing coals. Catching the drift of uneasy talk, he'd give a bark of derisive laughter, but not without a glance out over the humped shapes of cattle in the starlight. He would yawn, stretch his arms wide as if to encompass the cattle and all the Territory beyond, then into his swag.

~

After leaving Top Springs of the Armstrong River, we headed into the Murranji Track. The drover and pastoralist Nat Buchanan had pioneered this route in the late nineteenth century, cutting off some hundreds of kilometres from the old cattle trail through Katherine, Willeroo and Victoria River Downs.

But the Murranji had been one of the most hazardous cattle trails anywhere in the world, an ill-famed dry stretch of a couple of hundred kilometres, with only two natural waterholes that receded to mud late in the season. It was strewn with the graves of travellers whose waterbag had run dry or who had been caught unawares by a tribesman's spear. At Murranji Waterhole there seemed to be eleven graves, although my father said more.

The scrub was impenetrable for miles. Bullwaddy, the namesake of my family's old friend, is an ugly grey bush that sprouts scraggy limbs from its base, interweaving with its neighbours to form a solid cat's-cradle hedge, referred to in old Territory journals as hedgerow or hedgewood. It was this dense, tight barrier of Bullwaddy—along with forests of Lancewood, which shatters into sharp bayonets under rushing cattle—that made progress so difficult for John McDouall Stuart's exploration parties.

Through this crisscrossed mess of scrub, the wind whines at night, a soft moaning sound that can gather to a shrill howl. When the bushes twisted and sighed, all the sinister tales of this old cattle trail would come to my mind.

In almost every written account of the Murranji Track, a well-known verse is set down. The poet is unknown, but was surely one who had travelled this lonely route, for the poem acknowledges the fortitude of old drovers and the illusory fears that came in the loneliness of the night—for if one were ever to be touched by the spookily romantic tales of old bushmen, this was the place for it.

> *Wild dogs howl and hedge-wood groans,*
> *A night wind whistles in semitones,*
> *And bower-birds play with human bones*
> *Under a vacant sky.*
> *The drover's mob is a cloud of dust,*
> *The drover's mob is a sacred trust*
> *Where the Devil says 'Can't!' and God says*
> *'Must!'*
> *Out on the Murran-ji.*
>
> *Hedge-wood writhes in the dark o' night,*
> *Ant-hills glimmer a ghostly white,*
> *The cattle are galloping mad with fright*
> *From where the dead men lie.*
> *The drover's mob is a fateful trust,*
> *The life of a ringer less than dust,*
> *When God says 'Can't!' and the Devil says*
> *'Must!'*
> *Out on the Murran-ji.*

Then in 1923, Syd Peacock sank the first bore on the track for the government, 30 kilometres west of Newcastle Waters. (Syd had a daughter, Lucy, and a son with the catchy name of Percy Peacock.) Twelve bores followed, each 30 kilometres apart; drilled and equipped with windmills and holding tanks, they stretched west across the Murranji to the Armstrong River. A wide track was burned and cleared through scrub. By the 1950s the route was no longer so hazardous, but it still had its problems.

When we came onto the Murranji at Top Springs, our cattle were fresh, restless on camp, quick to take fright, and this country was notorious for the drum-like echoing sound of the ground where there was underlying hollow limestone. Even in daylight a rush was possible here, so a good drover was ever alert and ready for the unexpected.

There was also the dust to contend with: since trucks had begun churning through, the track was ploughed into bulldust as soft and fine as face powder, a metre or so deep for long stretches. It was a hazard for cattle on trucks; many suffocated in the billowing clouds. I recall Charlie Schultz of Humbert River Station losing 30 head of big bullocks on trucks through Murranji dust.

⌒

At last we emerged into Newcastle Waters. For the first time I was enclosed in the dust cloud of incoming cattle, instead of a spectator on the hotel verandah. We travelled across Newcastle Creek, awash with memories of life in the old pub, then out onto the Number Seven bore to camp and dip the cattle for tick.

We were now on the stock route that stretched across the wide grassy plains of the Barkly Tableland without a tree in sight; out there, it's said, you can see the curve of the earth on the horizon. The nights were still and very cold, but with the sun came the south-east winds, blowing constant and hard.

Northern sunsets are spectacular and dazzling, but the coming of daylight on those great empty plains is something to remain forever in a drover's memory. In that magical moment before real dawn, a silvery light appears with the stars still in the sky, the left-over moon pale and unheeded—'piccaninny daylight', we called it in the bush. It stirred you to leave the warmth of your swag, to revive the dying coals, put the billy-can on and get the horses in.

Where distant earth met sky, a sliver of sun peeped over the curved edge of our world and hung there a moment, testing the safety of a westward journey. Then hard bright light burst forth with a suddenness you could almost hear, and the day was there before you.

CHAPTER 33

# Droving Across the Barkly Tableland

**M**uch has been written about droving. Lately it has become a popular undertaking to bring a mob of cattle through stock routes in order to mark some pioneering anniversary or another. Young horsemen, would-be drovers, take on a few days on the road, recite Banjo Paterson, sing rollicking songs around the campfire, tuck into damper cooked on the coals, and sleep in swags with quaint modern additions to the old Birkmyre and blanket, then wax lyrical about the joys of the open road.

While I think it's good for young Australians to experience something of old outback life, let me tell you, 'It ain't like that!' There is little romance in droving. A real droving trip is slow, dreary and dirty. Unlike in the movies, when you mount your horse before sunrise and move the cattle, there's no stirring background music to give that uplifting mood of glamourous adventure—there's no 'Yipee-ki-yay, move 'em along!' Don't believe a word of that.

On the open plains of the old Barkly Stock Route, the drover's horse trudged slowly into the fierce south-east wind that blew back the bulldust stirred by thousands of hooves. The cattle plodded forward; the weather was freezing, the pace slow; the drover crouched low in his heavy coat, hat over eyes, bandana across nose and mouth. He had the look of an old bushranger, his grin exposing teeth outlined in dust, his hair stiff as a bottlebrush.

A bath was a quick dip in a freezing turkey-nest dam, late at night—or there was no bath at all, as was most often the case. Some, I know for certain, completed the four-month-long trip without so much as a toe dipped in water.

In the dry cool months, what we call the 'morning glory' clouds sweep down from Cape York. The early morning sky of the Barkly Tableland fills with huge rolling cylinders of dense cloud that can be more than 1000 kilometres long, descend as low as 200 metres and soar 300 kilometres into the heavens, like giant, furiously tumbling and curling surf waves.

As the clouds pass over, the sky darkens and a cool, unnatural wind curls like a dervish around you. You catch your breath at the bizarre grandeur of it. Can such a wonder be seen anywhere else in the world? I feel rather sad for those who haven't experienced our morning glory. How it must have terrified the old Aboriginals of the plains.

As we progressed across the Barkly, the cattle grew quiet and at night settled closer to camp. Old Snow, our lame bullock, was still trailing the mob. He lay quite close to our fire, his big white body clearly visible in the light.

Behind us by a few days, another drover with Victoria River Downs cattle, Eric Rankin, had a packhorse plant. While his wife rode with the cattle, his two children were strapped into a pack-bag on either side of a quiet horse; their small freckled faces peered out as they were driven along to the next camp.

We had 35 horses with us, some with very distinctive personalities.

There was Little Peanut: a bit flighty on a cold morning, that one.

Old Fireman: a top night horse, he knew what was expected of him when cattle took off in a midnight rush.

Sweetheart and Jack: the thieves, terrible nuisances around camp and always alert for a camp oven of setting bread, which they devoured hurriedly with long streamers of elastic dough unravelling after them. Cold curry, custard, damper—all welcome fodder to those two. No bag of flour could be left out at night without two ghostly white-powdered faces peering from the darkness.

Big Tony: one of Bill's old packhorses. Sometimes with everyone in camp and not a tree or shrub in sight, I would mount Tony bareback for a ride out yonder to take a toilet break. A lot of careful thought and no end of suggestions were given to this situation by the men.

'Carry a little bush, Jack,' someone might suggest. 'We won't look.'

'I don't care to be silhouetted against the horizon like one of those Balinese shadow puppets,' I might answer, and Tony and I would clump off into the far distance like the last of the surviving explorers.

Right before the wet season, the cold, hard winds stop and the Barkly is enshrouded in searing heat. This country has had its share of men who've died of thirst. It's a pitiless place to ride when withering in scorching temperatures; both man and horse have little time to live without water. Vast lakes that lift the spirits and quicken the pace dissolve into the shimmering haze of a mirage.

Perishers have scratched final messages on billy-cans, leather, anything to hand. In 1893 David McKay perished within the 80-kilometre stretch between Alroy Downs and Brunette Downs stations, and left a tragic note of farewell to Hutton, the Brunette manager, which ended: 'Good-bye old friend, I am off.'

Out across the open plain, a shadowy smudge, far in the distance, gradually took the form of a grave, well-marked and enclosed with a rail. Boomerang Jack Brady lay there—his was not a death from thirst, though. Malaria was Jack's undoing. His grave was such a lonely thing: it stood stark and forlorn, silhouetted against the horizon. I sat beside it awhile and gave Jack some thought.

Riding out there, you were a small thing on the great empty plain; you became sick, dismounted, lay down on the dry, hard earth, with a frightened Aboriginal boy your only comfort and companion, and you simply died and remained forever—what more is there to say on it?

'What an awful place to die,' I said later to my father, who had known Jack.

'Oh, not so bad for an old bushman, with cattle passing, drovers making dinner camp close by—I'm sure quite where he would have chosen to be.'

Jack became a member of bush ghost-hood, as you would expect in such a desolate place. A few travellers swore they'd experienced spooky encounters, apparently without a single bottle of rum in the pack-bags.

Over the border into Queensland, past the town of Camooweal on the Georgina River, the Territory and the Barkly were behind us. By now it was hot in the middle of the day and the cattle were tonguing as they trudged along. When we splashed through a waterhole, dozens of fish floated to the surface; they had fat yellow bellies and tasted muddy, but were a welcome change from beef.

We reached Walgra Station—the end of the line for us. Our cattle delivered in good condition, a successful trip all round. Old Snow went slowly in through the gate, as quiet as any home-raised poddy-calf. A thousand kilometres for a big lame bullock was a fair effort. The thought that he would end his days on someone's dinner plate as a juicy beef steak was quite unsettling.

Our horses were to be paddocked at the station until the next year; they needed a spell from continuous work. Very early in the morning, Bill Sharpe's truck accompanied the horsemen out.

Horse shoes were removed, hobbles packed away, and we stood and watched them go through the gate into the vast paddock. We forgave Sweetheart and Jack, who would now be deprived of their bounty.

The first 34 horses went joyfully and cantered off out of sight. Black Leviticus was last. He stood for a moment, watching us over the fence—we could imagine this was a fond farewell, but more likely it was 'Thank God, that's over for another year,' then he was off at speed to join his mates.

With horses gone way out of sight, we prepared to leave, but the truck Bill had never trusted refused to start, and no amount of tinkering by amateur mechanics could ignite the slightest sign of life.

We had no water—first law of the bush broken—and the sun was high, a hot wind blowing. Everyone had been rushing around and sweating heavily. We broached the radiator, but the strong taste of petrol only made us drier.

We settled down under the truck to wait for rescue. When our saviours came out late that night, we were parched, our tongues thick. Thirstier than we'd ever been, we had some small idea of what the early perishers had endured.

We had lived closely together for months—closer, perhaps, than in ordinary family circumstances—and had come to know and accept one another's peculiarities. We'd slept close together in our swags, wakened whenever the watch changed, argued over trivial things when the winds blew hard and diminished our good spirits—become friends.

# CHAPTER 34

# An Invitation

In 1957, droving over, I returned to Brisbane. My mother was settled in her mansion by the Brisbane River, no doubt planning her travels.

I didn't live with my mother, instead joining my friend Kay, a girl I'd kept up a casual friendship with over the years. She had bought a large old house in the outer suburbs, and six of us took up residence there. As well as me and Kay, there was Lorna—a some-time secretary, most-time party girl; a serious young country dentist bent on success in the city, with little time for gaiety; and two attractive young men who had plenty of time for fun and rented a bedsitter. Sixty years ago, the term 'gay' wasn't yet applied to their life of togetherness.

It was a carefree time for me after the harsh life of droving and the years in the Junction Hotel. Apart from the budding dentist, we were all set on having as good a time as we could manage.

My father had a saying he'd borrowed from somewhere: 'Hard work never killed anyone, but why take the risk?' For the few months we lived there together, it was a life of no tomorrows. Looking back 60 years, the missed tomorrows were pretty mild: no drugs then, no wild nightlife in the city; even the old south coast, now the Gold Coast, had just one nightclub and two or three hotels.

Kay's sister had lived in Paris before the war, and gave us a beautiful—if fairly worn—black dress from the House of Worth. The three of us were all pretty much the same size, so it was shared, but only on special occasions: a Worth night had to be a significant date. For a young girl, nothing beat stepping out in a Parisian 'little black dress'. The only rule with the dress was that it had to be properly cleaned after use—and the cleaners were very expensive.

Our two young friends in the bedsit were great company. Their lifestyle was frowned upon then—in fact, was it even legal? It wouldn't have mattered to us anyway. We relied on their opinions of our clothes and makeup, and they took up escort duties for us whenever necessary. They were two darling guys who left me with good feelings toward people whose lifestyles differ from the mainstream, for which I am grateful to them.

Throughout this fun time, I kept in touch with my mother. She rang one day with an invitation to lunch. 'I've cooked a curry,' she said. This was an amazing announcement—stunning! I tried to imagine my mother in her beautiful kitchen with its river views.

I arrived, camera in hand, to Mother who said, 'Let's go out to lunch. I buried the curry under the lemon tree. It looked strange.'

In 1958 city life was beginning to pall when a telegram arrived on the doorstep from Ken, the first news I'd had of him in twelve months. It had been sent from Borroloola, which would have taken a two-day ride from the Limmen.

It said: *Come prepared packhorse trip.*

A summons no less, right out of the blue—not an invitation to cruise the Greek Isles, or 'bring your best threads, we'll go Orient Express across Europe'.

Such presumption!

Would I go? Of course! The tropical and uninhabited Limmen River country was a much more attractive prospect than the stark Barkly Tableland I'd trekked the year before; besides, I'd always had a yen to see Borroloola. And a combination of Ken and Borroloola seemed pretty exciting after the suburbs of Brisbane.

'B'r'loola,' they pronounced it, or 'the old B'r'loo' or just 'the 'Loo'.

Land of the 'no-boot men' was Borroloola; curious tales drifted out of there of men who'd cast off their clothes and 'gone native'. Isolated from the outside world, they were never seen again.

In the 1950s, few travelled the lonely unsealed road to Borroloola: a station hand or two, the odd government official. In the wet season, the road was impassable; in the dry you drove in a dust cloud, with little possibility of meeting another motorist.

It was a standing Territory joke that old ringers, tiring of work in the dry, harsh inland region of northern cattle country, dreamed fanciful dreams of settling down to the indolent life of a 'lotus eater' in camps among the pandanus and paperbark trees along the undisturbed banks of the river in Borroloola; spending their remaining days lazily spearing fish and diving for lily roots, sharing their tobacco—and themselves—among the comely coastal lubras.

The 'dreamy, hazy, lazy, tobaccofied life' of an old ringer's fantasy, as William Makepeace Thackeray would have put it.

These were the no-boot men of old B'r'loola.

⁓

In the 1880s Borroloola took its place on the Territory map when it became a construction material depot for work on the OT Line. Thousands of metal poles were brought in to replace the old wooden telegraph posts, and donkey and horse teams carried them on to worksites.

The country along the McArthur River was considered one of the most distant and lawless regions of Australia. The only law in Borroloola in 1886 was that of the Winchester rifle and the Colt revolver.

With the discovery of gold in Pine Creek and Western Australia came an endless stream of prospectors, adventurers and Chinese coolies—and outlaws, too. Dreaming of the golden rewards that were the promise of every digging, they came through Borroloola, then on along the Old Coast Road. They came on horseback or on foot; some pushed hand-made carts for hundreds of kilometres. They came to get rich—a damned good reason.

Many died of fever; more than were ever recorded were killed by tribesmen.

My father had come to know some of these old trailblazers, and heard them tell of a feverish dash to stake a claim on the diggings, but for the most part their stories died with them.

All this lawlessness was now past. Borroloola had settled into a lonely outpost town of few Europeans; the Old Coast Road, once bustling with travellers, was deserted, overgrown, its lonely graves unmarked.

~

Now I was to see Borroloola—tales were told of its legendary past, but few had actually seen it. Into a swag went my battered riding clothes, survivors of last year's droving. With this my only luggage, I flew from Brisbane to Mount Isa, then took my seat in a four-seater plane surrounded by mailbags and packages for cattle stations on the regular mail run.

Course set north, we landed on dusty unsealed airstrips, then flew on over endless, empty land that aeons ago had been a vast sea, now with nothing to show of it but ancient, sun-bleached shells in unlikely places.

Through the haze of distance, the silver tinsel ribbon of the McArthur River snaked into view; we lost height and the river, lush with pandanus palms, its waters teaming with crocodiles, loomed larger, wider; and we came down on a bumpy strip, scattering wallabies and galahs feeding in the late afternoon sunlight.

Close to the strip stood a rambling house of old Territory style: sharply gabled roof, and wide verandahs enclosed with gauze to keep out the swarms of flies by day and clouds of mosquitoes by night. But not another building, not a person to be seen. Was this Borroloola?

I soon learned that the gabled house was the home of Ted Harvey, the Aboriginal Welfare officer, and his wife, Nettie. Built in the 1880s as a police station when one was sorely needed, its small cell, barred and sturdy, was still quite ready for occupancy if necessary.

⁓

Six months earlier, when the cyclone had marooned him on the banks of the McArthur and interrupted his ride to the coast, Ken had been on his way to Bing Bong to arrange with Jim Marshall a muster of the Limmen River country. Now it was time to put the plant together and head bush.

Along a bush track down through Rocky Creek, Ken and Jim had set up camp under spreading mango trees, giant relics of the fine vegetable garden grown by Chinese in the lively days past.

Jim was tall and rangy, toughened by years of bush work; a capable cattleman whose life held few comforts on his small station on the coast, where he lived with his Aboriginal wife, Bessie, and six-month-old son Colin.

As a sixteen-year-old in the merchant navy during the Second World War, he'd had two ships blasted from under him by German submarines. The hours he spent awaiting rescue were all the more perilous because he couldn't swim a stroke. After the war he forsook the sea and made for the bush.

He and Ken had ridden in from the coast to stock up provisions for an extensive muster that would take them through country not travelled since pioneer cattlemen brought the first bullocks along the Old Coast Road.

In Ken's camp was the ever-present Roy, as well as Jackinabox and his lubra, Dinah. Jack was a wiry, jockey-sized Aboriginal man from Arnhem Land. Intelligent and steadfast, he raised his hat to any Missus he met, and was devoted to Ken. Jack had suffered much as the victim of the grisly tribal practice of removing the kidney fat of an enemy; he forever bore the scars on his small, sinewy body. Like many Aboriginals who lived among us, he had acquired his 'white-man name' as a child around the stock camps. Though now middle-aged, he still had the brisk and lively manner of his namesake.

⁓

There were few white people in Borroloola, while the Aboriginal population was large. Many bore the aquiline features of the Malays, who years earlier had sailed the coast in their proas gathering sea cucumbers, better known in the Malay world as trepang, to be sold in Timor.

These early fishermen had set up temporary camps to boil, sun-dry and smoke their catch, and in the 1950s one could still come across enormous iron boilers, like giant witches' cauldrons, rusting on isolated beaches. Other evidence of their visits are the majestic tamarind trees that grow prolifically along the coast. Fiery sauces were carried in hollowed bamboo; discarded seeds took root.

Of course, many of the local Aboriginals were also descended from Europeans. All of the unmarried white men in Borroloola had Aboriginal partners; with few white women in the bush, it was natural for men to form amiable, lasting relationships with lubras from local tribes, although at that time it was against the law for a white man to cohabit with an Aboriginal woman. If he was charged and found guilty, the sentence was a mandatory six months' gaol term. It was possible to apply for permission to marry, but not encouraged.

Men who ran off to live illegally with a bush woman were referred to as Lochinvars, alluding to Sir Walter Scott's poem: young Lochinvar came out of the west and rode off with a lady on his trusty steed. Actually, on some occasions this is exactly what happened—a girl would hide in a prearranged place in the bush at night, and the Lochinvar would ride out silently in the darkness to take her up behind him and gallop off, hoping the law and the tribesman to whom she was promised wouldn't appear on the scene too soon.

CHAPTER 35

# The Townsfolk
# of Borroloola

In its heyday Borroloola basked in the fame of its fine library. With no newspapers or periodicals coming in, it was a boon for miles around. But as the town's importance waned, the books were removed. Some were stored in the old gaol, where the white ants attacked with their usual ferocity. The old tomes were soon reduced to dust, with not so much as a bookmark left for second helpings.

Borroloola also had two pubs in its early days. A rather grand hotel by bush standards had been built with Chinese labour around the same time as the police station, but hadn't fared so well over the years: through neglect and help from white ants, it had gradually fallen apart, until the final blow was dealt by a cyclone. Its timbers had been hauled off and used for firewood, which required less effort from the easy-going locals than gathering fuel in the bush.

When Ken and I wandered through the ruins, we found evidence of fine old furniture in jumbled heaps, bedheads of brass and painted ceramics. The shattered decorative china of rum and whisky barrels lay in the shambles of what had been the bar room. What joy these things would bring to an antique dealer today.

This hotel, or what was left of it, was now owned by Tim O'Shea, that popular Irish publican in Katherine, and Jack Mulholland was the keeper of the ruins. In fact, much of the deterioration had taken place during his somewhat dilatory tenure. He was one of O'Shea's Irish imports, and rumour persisted that a connection with the outlawed IRA had caused his hasty exit abroad.

In keeping with local practice, Mulholland was married to an Aboriginal woman called Andrea. With their children they lived a carefree life among the wreckage of the old pub, in a dwelling put together from odd bits of the ruins.

In this hut Mulholland sold a few grocery items and a little liquor from the sparse stores that came into Borroloola from the *Cora*. Mull would empty everything in a heap on the floor and take the labels off, so it was a lucky dip of shopping; the shape and size of a can might give clues to its contents—however, what you hoped was a can of peaches might turn out to be green beans. He would sell you a bottle of rum if you were quick about it, as stocks tended not to last.

Mull also collected and distributed mail from what had been the small meat-house behind the pub. On taking delivery of the mailbag from the fortnightly plane, he would upend it onto the slatted floor. Sometimes a letter slipped through unchecked to the delight of his goats, ever hopeful for the windfall from above. Many a long-awaited cheque was chomped up, and one's excuse for not acknowledging a business letter was, 'So sorry, the post office goats must have eaten it,' which was sure to cause some interest in a faraway city office.

Although Mull wasn't inclined to labour, and was somewhat taciturn to boot, I liked him: he was very amusing in a gruff sort of way. Over the years we often sat together on boxes under the tamarind trees and shared a pannikin of tea.

But Mull had a poor opinion of women generally, and once told me, in his thick Irish brogue, 'They are all lyin', deceitful creatures.'

'You have no time for women at all?' I asked.

'Well now,' he said thoughtfully, 'I wouldn't say *that* exactly.'

No doubt the numerous children tumbling about him in the dust attested to some small fondness.

Mull once told Ken he thought me the only 'worthwhile' woman he knew. High praise from a confirmed misogynist!

~

Another long-time resident was Roger Jose. He and Ken had been friends for years, so now he was to be my friend too. Although he was a white man, Roger had lived long under a tropic sun and was burned almost as black as any Aboriginal. Sometimes it was thought that he was one.

He rarely spoke of his past in the bush and it was considered bad form to enquire if personal information wasn't offered. In the Territory bush a man's origins were of little consequence.

Roger shared a jolly lifestyle among the ruins of the old pub with Jack Mulholland. On the rare occasion Ken had ridden into Borroloola from the Limmen, Roger had extended a hospitable hand and invited him to roll out his swag by his hut. Ken always brought along a bag of salted beef and Roger hung each piece on hooks around the outside of his hut to dry in the sun, which gave it the appearance of a German butcher's shop.

When the cyclone that finished off the old pub raged through the town, Roger's little hut whirled off with it. He gathered sheets of iron from the debris, erected another basic dwelling and cyclone-proofed it by encircling it with a barrier of fuel drums filled with earth. But when fears of another cyclone spread, Roger moved the pub's 20,000-litre corrugated-iron water tank on to a rise of ground some way off, and he and his Aboriginal wife, Biddy, settled their home within. She had succeeded her sister as Roger's wife, and was well aware of her exalted station as chatelaine of the tank on the hill.

A doorway was cut into their tank, covered with a flap of hessian, but there were no windows. Roger and Biddy were deathly afraid of spirits and the debil-debils that lurked in darkness—the less access they had to the home, the better.

Over the years Ken and I came to know Roger well, probably better than anyone else did. Apart from his unusual home, he was an ordinary man of the old bush. But an aura born of his lifestyle grew up about him and drew the attention of tourists, who were always alert to the unusual. The few travellers who ventured to Borroloola were directed Roger's way, to have a chat and see his novel homestead for themselves.

After a lifetime of exposure to true Territory eccentrics, I didn't find Roger so bizarre. He enjoyed his chats with the travellers, and could hold his own in any company and conversation; he was well read and had opinions on everything.

He'd once spent time in the Alice Springs gaol for supplying liquor to an Aboriginal man. He quite enjoyed his stay there and found the cooler climate a nice change; however, he was less impressed with the paucity of the tobacco ration and felt a greater generosity in that direction would have rounded off an otherwise enjoyable break from his humdrum bush life. When time came for him to depart, he regretted leaving the care of his vegetable garden to someone else.

Years before, another reclusive resident of the local bush Albert Morcom had been a busy Territory hawker, continuously travelling as he sold his usual array of country goods. Then he'd been seduced by the prospect of joining the lazy lifestyle of Borroloola, and settled down in a little iron shack, close by the river. He did a little dealing with the local Aboriginals, exchanging tobacco and sugar for fish and bush tucker.

Albert was an educated man. He spent much of his time writing to people all over the world, sending off specimens of dried bush flowers and presenting himself as living a much more exalted lifestyle than he actually did. In mango season, Albert's largesse knew no bounds. He would send someone off to collect mangoes from trees in the old Chinese gardens, and large, heavy boxes of fruit were sent off to his Australian pen friends, who received huge bills for airfreight on stringy mangoes that they could happily have done without.

Albert was a fund of tales from the past, with racy snippets from the lives of some of our most respected elder citizens, not to be recounted here. His memories were also dotted with wistful reminiscences of his conquests of ladies long gone.

He would have had me believe that the name Borroloola came about when the wild men of the past rode into town and demanded to borrow Lulu. All quite untrue, of course: Borroloola means 'place of paperbark tree', and indeed they do abound there, reaching great height and girth along the springs and waterways.

Albert supported a heavy build-up of grime on his person, which to my eyes seemed to grow alarmingly fast for someone who spent his days doing nothing. He would just sit in his reclining chair outside his little hut, where he kept a watchful eye on the few who passed by, with special attention to the groups of giggling young lubras who were well aware of his interest.

Every couple of years when boredom set in, or he felt the need of a little attention, Albert took to his bed with a vague illness. The medical plane was summoned to take him to Darwin Hospital, where the unfortunate nurses were required to give him his very first bath since his last visit and shave his matted beard—and, on one visit, cut off his flannel vest because hair had grown through and become a permanent armour.

He returned after these hospital visits physically refurbished, and in the best of spirits settled back into his old routine of observing his small world from the rickety chair outside his humble home.

Blind Paddy was another notable resident. He was the most Irish of men, with an accent still as heavily flavoured with auld Ireland as it had been all those years before, when he'd stepped forth from a ship onto Territory soil while en route to somewhere else and never returned on board.

Very old and perpetually bad tempered, Paddy was a genuine hermit who had seen it all, every aspect of Territory life—although by the time I met him, unfortunately he could barely see at all. But his old reputation as a pub brawler still hovered about him; when he was drunk, his sight wasn't so bad that a well-aimed bottle wouldn't connect with an unsuspecting victim.

It seems the Territory was always well-supplied with wild Irishmen. Someone got it right when he said, 'God gave the Irish whisky to prevent them ruling the world.'

Close by our camp, in dense scrub, was a small corrugated-iron shed. This was the home of Mervyn Pattemore the missionary, his wife, Leanne—one of the two white women in town, as I was travelling there, not a resident then—and their three fair, angelic-looking children, delivered into this world of isolation by Mervyn himself. They lived a frugal life and the local wallabies regularly turned up on their dinner table.

Their religious group was small, so Mervyn had restricted funds to educate children from the Aboriginal camp. It was an uphill battle to maintain regular attendance; I gave the project little hope for success, although Mervyn would never entertain such negativity. He was a good man, God-fearing and selfless, always kind and hospitable, and totally alien to and quietly disapproving of Borroloola's unconventional and un-Christian scene of that time.

Mervyn was inclined to quote scriptures and give eternal thanks to the Almighty for his harsh and frugal existence. Nobody, it seems, ever received credit for anything they gave to him: whether cash, food or something else, it was always a special gift from God—hallelujah!

I've read of these men that they gathered together to argue the merits of English literature and air their talents as poets. This could hardly be true. Roger and Mulholland were friends, but they both disliked Albert; Paddy disliked most everyone, and wouldn't have sat discussing the merits of anything. They were all wary of Mervyn and his fervent Christian teachings.

But it's true that although they were aloof with strangers, once you were accepted into their special fold these men were entertaining company, with incredible tales to tell of the Territory's boisterous past. To sit with Roger and share his boiled wallaby certainly beat taking lunch in a smart city restaurant.

CHAPTER 36

# Under a Wide
# and Starry Sky

The journey was only about 60 kilometres from Borroloola, but it took us two days' riding with horse plant to reach the coast where Jim and Bessie lived on his small station. Their house was a rough shed in the grassy dunes above the beach, with a wood-fired kitchen stove, a greenhide bed and not much else. No one I ever met knew how the station acquired the name Bing Bong; maybe, as was often the case, a mispronounced Aboriginal name became permanent.

Dinah, myself, Jackinabox, Roy and Ken settled our camp some way off; we slept in the usual fashion in our swags by the open fire. Although days were always hot, the coastal nights were quite cold. At that time of year it almost never rains, but daylight comes blanketed in dense fogs that leave moisture dripping from the trees. Rivulets ran into the folds of our canvas swag covers; you could awaken with a very damp head unless, turtle-like, you stayed completely under.

Because of the heavy screen of fog in the dimness of early morning, the horse-tailer relied on the horse bells to muster. But the bells would have to come off as we progressed into the wilderness; we would be mustering wild cleanskin cattle and the sound of bells can be heard for miles on still night air.

Preparations took close to two weeks before departure. Horses needed to be broken in and shod, gear repaired, and greenhide (untanned cattle skin) hobbles and ropes made; several of our pack-bags were also made from greenhide, as it was cheap, durable and in constant supply. There were four working horses for each person and eight pack mules loaded with everything: branding irons, axes, shovels, shoeing gear and rolls of hessian for temporary yards.

Certainly we weren't overloaded with tucker, as we killed our own beef, so we just needed coarse salt for preserving meat, a few potatoes and onions that would need careful rationing, a little rice, flour and dried hops to make yeast for bread-making. We rendered our own fat in the camp oven for cooking. Overall, we considered ourselves well provisioned.

～

At the height of all this activity, Ken had the misfortune to become poisoned—how, no one knew. His condition deteriorated alarmingly and we feared he would die. With no motor vehicle or radio we had to rely on our own limited medical resources, with 'limited' being a generous assessment.

Jim possessed an ancient bush medical book with a sketchy diagram of how to assemble an emergency stomach pump, and he searched through his work shed for suitable bits and pieces. He came up with some tubing and an old-fashioned stirrup pump that had served time spraying weed killer and cattle tick. With light from a kerosene lantern flickering in the wind, we assembled our equipment on the ground beside the patient, who was rolling about in terrible pain.

Dinah, superstitious woman that she was, disappeared into the bush to be well away, fearing a death was imminent. Bessie and the boys sat silently around the fire, watching us.

I had a bad feeling about this. 'Suppose the tube should enter a lung instead of his stomach?' I asked.

'I've drenched plenty of horses,' Jim answered, flourishing his apparatus about authoritatively. 'It'll be right.'

He seemed confident and I was in dire need of a confident associate right then, especially as I was to operate the stirrup pump.

'We'd better let him know what to expect,' I said, and tried to get Ken's attention with a brief explanation.

'You're going to *what?*' he croaked between groans and retching.

'Pump your stomach, make you feel better,' I replied.

His eyes opened wide as realisation dawned; he drew his knees up to his chest and rolled away from us and off his swag. 'Like hell you are,' he moaned, before attempting a feeble escape on hands and knees.

'Better leave it,' I said.

Jim was reluctant to disassemble his creation and seemed disappointed; he had given the whole thing a lot of thought.

Soon after, some uncanny sense of averted disaster brought Dinah back to sit by the fire.

As for the patient, I think fear of the treatment shocked him into an early recovery, although he was a bit weak and shaky for a few days. He wasn't as appreciative of our medical efforts as I thought we deserved. 'You should be grateful,' I told him huffily. 'We were trying to save your life.'

                        ⌒

Preparations were progressing well and there wasn't a great deal to do in camp, so I took a four-pronged fish spear and went down alone to the beach, hoping to provide a change in our dinner menu of beef and more beef.

I struck fishy gold in no time with a pile of fat mud crabs, so many my bag overflowed. I took off my trousers, tied a knot in each ankle and stuffed them with the remaining crabs, then drew the belt at the waist tight, making a neat bag.

Flushed with success, I decided to try for a fish as the tide was starting to turn, so went into the water with all the confidence of an expert spearman. Tides sweep in fast there; although I was still in shallow water, I soon found myself with a deep, fast-running channel cutting me off from shore and, to set the scene, a not-so-small shark cruised lazily along its length.

I felt a prickle of fear. I was stranded in the sea, my only companion a shark, and soon the sun would set. I imagined everyone at the camp coming up with a different theory of my disappearance. Would they search for me before or after feasting on the crabs? The crabs! If I didn't get back to shore soon, the incoming tide would wash them clean away—an entire afternoon's effort lost.

Holding my spear in what I imagined to be an iron grip, I took the plunge at the extreme end of the sandbar on which I was stranded. I made a diagonal approach to shore, going with the flow of the channel.

The water was neck-deep, flowing fast. I forgot about the shark. If I'd had to swim I'd have been swept out for sure, but strong legs, the spear for an anchor and a will born of panic took me almost the length of the beach to reach rocks at the far end, just as light faded.

I sat cold and shivering on the rocks, looking out to sea. The shark had gone; only the white ruffles of choppy waves flickered in the poor light. I walked back to camp and sat dripping by the fire; the men hadn't yet returned.

Later one of the stock boys rode down to collect my crabs. He returned at full gallop, empty-handed and very agitated, with a disturbing tale of a body lying on the beach: 'Must be dead man, proper dead, might be drowneded, leg bin stand up proper stiff pulla.' My trouser legs, of course, were filled with crabs.

No one was particularly interested in my daring swim, especially not with 40 mud crabs for dinner.

Here the heart wasn't so much bent on adventure as it was on the economic rewards from a successful cattle muster—but there was an element of adventure, as there must surely be in such an undertaking.

On the day of departure, the newly broken horses were inclined to play up and gave bucking shows in the yard before settling down. Not a lot of time was spent breaking in a horse in this situation; these men had complete confidence in their ability to handle any horse, and knew it would settle with work. The wild cattle would be more difficult to handle, so we were driving twenty coachers—quiet bullocks—to steady them as they were mustered.

There seemed no limit to the country we could muster; to the west and north-west was vacant Crown land, thousands of square kilometres of it, scattered throughout with cattle that had never set eyes on humans. No fences, no roads, no man-made bores or wells, but numerous springs among the river systems of the Roper and Limmen.

Each day we were up before daybreak for a quick breakfast of corned beef, left-over curry or fresh beef if we'd recently killed. The horse-tailer mustered the horses and mules that had been hobbled out to feed the night before. The men would then pack the mules with the heavy gear, saddle their horses and let the cattle out of the yard—a touchy business with cattle mustered the previous day, as a beast might break out and cause general panic. It took time before they would settle and move forward. And if hessian was used for a yard, it needed to be taken down, rolled up and packed, a bulky item to balance on top of a packhorse.

While the letting-out was in progress, Bessie, Dinah and I finished packing and mounted our horses, then held the spare horses and packed mules back. When the cattle settled and the men were moving them off, we drove the horses forward and followed, keeping some distance in the rear.

When wild cattle were spotted they were rounded into the coachers. This usually entailed a wild gallop, with breakaways pursued and thrown, the usual procedure with wild cattle. Galloping up close to a beast, the rider left his horse, hit the ground running and grasped the tail; the beast then turned to challenge, but with a sharp sideways pull on his tail, he lost balance and fell to the ground. The upper hind leg was jerked up to ensure he lay flat, then his hind legs were crossed and bound together with a wide leather strap, usually all in one smooth motion.

These straps were generally carried around the waist. Some strapped them around the thigh, or even bandolier-fashion across the chest, although there was danger there: a horn could become entangled in a chest strap.

Sometimes fresh horses, unused to their rider leaving the saddle at a gallop to throw a beast, would bolt off in fright. Jim devised an anchoring method whereby two short, lead-filled pipes were carried on either side of the horse's withers in leather pouches and attached by a third leather rein to the bit, then released as the rider left the saddle.

There was no shortage of scrub bulls—huge, defiant old beasts with enormous heads and wide, hairless circles around their eyes where flies had feasted and tormented them, adding to their fearsome appearance. As they turned and trotted out to do battle in the hard sunlight, the dust rose in sharp, flame-like puffs from their great backs.

When thrown, the thick, sweeping horns of these wild old warriors were sawn off—with a short saw, carried on the saddle—and the cavities packed with teased rope steeped in tar, called oakum. This kept flies away, and acted as a disinfectant and healer. The bull was then castrated on the spot.

Here he was then, blood from the dehorning streaking his wild-eyed, dusty face, snorting froth and long tendrils of saliva from the heat of the chase, waiting for the coachers to be brought up; then, hurriedly unstrapped, he joined the mob, often furiously rampaging throughout, charging and attacking all in his path.

If this kept up he was thrown again and knee-strung: the ligaments above the knee severed by a knife. This didn't hamper walking or even trotting, but a gallop was out of the question. Sometimes repeated defiance wasn't worth the trouble and the beast was let go, hopefully to be picked up in a later muster and sold as a stag or big bullock.

Treatment was certainly harsh, but a matter of survival for man and beast.

There was no market for bull meat then—that was to come in the 1960s with the American demand for hamburger beef. Throughout the Territory, thousands of these old scrub bulls were simply shot to control numbers. On Victoria River Downs Station alone, 5000 bulls were shot just the year before the bull-meat market came into operation.

It took a lot of skill and practice, not to mention guts, to face up to and throw a ton of sharp-horned, belligerent feral bulls. Galloping over hard, pot-holed ground in sharp limestone country, leaping off a speeding horse, the men took their lives in their hands every day. Just one misjudgement could mean instant death or, worse, a bad goring in isolated country with no help at all. A good horse was sometimes lost, disembowelled by a vicious horn, and there was poor reward. Cattle prices were low, markets scarce, but this was our life out there. It was a dangerous life too.

'It's a fine day to-day, A good day to die!' This cheerful observation is attributed to the American Plains Indian riding out to battle.

Perhaps I was a romantic, but probably just pessimistic, for in the misty light of early morning, when I saw those two stern, hard-faced men ride out, silent and straight in the saddle, their men-at-arms behind them, or when a man left the saddle at a gallop to throw a huge bull thrusting his horns in fury, I held my breath and thought of gloomy consequences.

They would have laughed at such extravagant imaginings, and toward the end of our time out there, in spite of some heart-stopping incidents, I pretty much disregarded mishaps between man and beast, as did everyone else.

In country like this, cattle yards could be made of posts and rails, with the fresh hide of an old bull cut into strips to tie them in place. Greenhide tightened as it dried and became hard as iron, so yards like this could stand for years. But when camping in the right area, yards could also be walled by natural stone, with cliffs forming a pocket that need only a few rails across a narrow entrance.

Among the escarpments, ridges and valleys of the Limmen run these rock walls, high and straight as though cleanly sliced with a giant's knife. In a place known as the Lost City, a perfect ball of stone, shaped through centuries of winds, balances loosely atop tall pillars, and low arches link stone chambers together.

While exploring caves in the Limmen, Ken once came upon bleached human skulls and masses of bones—an ancient burial site, or something more sinister? His Aboriginal companions refused to venture too close to where they believed prowling spirits of the dead hovered.

One of the most remarkable stone yards is the Limmen Gate, located on the western side of the river. A natural pass, it opens onto good grasses and springs in a perfect circular yard. Its narrow entrance could be barricaded to hold a mob of 3000. The old bush people, like Dinah, were restless there and avoided its silent interior. Slanting through rocks, the late afternoon sunlight made it seem haunted.

# CHAPTER 37

# Graveyards in
# the Grasses

'The earth his bed, the sky his canopy,' wrote William Dampier of the Australian Aboriginal, and so it was with us out there on the Limmen.

We were travelling the Old Coast Road in the footsteps of prospectors, cattle drovers and adventurers who had journeyed through here in the last two decades of the nineteenth century. We rode past lonely, overgrown graves of long-forgotten men, just a few moss-covered stones sunk deep in the earth. If there had ever been a name to these graves, they were long gone.

Men lay there who had sweated and plodded along this very track. With great plans and high hopes of a rich gold strike or successful settlement, they'd died without help or comfort, succumbing to fever or speared by Aboriginals. This was as far as they'd come with their dreams.

The stars that had guided men for centuries were still there to guide us. On the cold, crystal-clear nights of the dry season, it shone so brightly in the glittering, crowded sky that it pointed direction and marked the march of time. At night a cattleman would say, 'When that star moves across to there, call me for my watch.'

A long time ago, the local Aboriginal people believed that when each new moon appeared, it was newborn and hungry. It ate its way so ravenously across the night sky that its stomach swelled full and round, and it lit the country bright as daylight. Then, as it continued along its starry pathway, there was no more food to be found. Slowly it starved, grew ever smaller, then died, only to be replaced with another moon, ready to repeat this mythical journey, dodging stars as it moved across the heavens.

To the old Aboriginal of that area, dinner time was midday, so when referring to midnight it was naturally: 'Dinner time belon'ta moon.'

~

We welcomed the few days' break planned for the next camp. Horses needed attention; a beast had to be killed and salted down; there was laundry to be done. This last was simple—everything went into a bucket made from a flour drum, flakes shaved from a bar of homemade caustic soap were added, the whole lot boiled on the campfire, then rinsed and draped over low bushes to dry.

This area is known as Albinjula, which means 'Valley of Springs'. Seventy years earlier, the abundance of water had so appealed to John Costello, a member of the pioneering Durack family, that he'd decided to form a station there. He brought in stock, built his homestead and settled his family.

The project was a failure, doomed from the very beginning. Although water was plentiful, the area was poor cattle country. And the Aboriginal tribes were hostile: fences were no sooner erected than they were torn down, the wire used to make spears— more than one man in the bush has taken a spearing from a weapon made from his own fence. Costello and other cattlemen of that time left coils of wire beside their newly erected fences, hoping this would discourage tribesmen from dismantling them with their tools. Not a chance of that: they ignored the coils and continued to hack patiently away with their stone axes.

They also devoured Costello's horses and cattle, and raided his vegetable garden; on one raid they got off with a season's entire potato crop. At last he gave up, moved to take up Lake Nash Station and built the first homestead there.

In the silence of this abandoned place, flowering shrubs planted 70 years earlier still grew among the grasses. An enormous tamarind tree cast shade; perhaps Mrs Costello had envisioned sitting beneath it in years to come, her family about her. I filled my hat with tamarind fruit and rode on out of that deserted place.

Throughout the months of our muster I carried one of these tamarind seeds in my pocket. Later, at Borroloola, I germinated it in a jam tin. It travelled with me wherever I could take it, graduating into larger tins. Finally I planted it with the same hopes for its future as that pioneering lady of long ago.

We grew fond of some of our animals. My favourite riding horse was Blue Eyes, named for her one cloudy eye. She was a sleek chestnut mare, her good looks marred by long, deep scars down each side of her rump where a crocodile had raked her with its claws as she scrambled away up the bank of a creek.

Dinah's two hunting dogs trotted behind her horse. Big nondescript hounds, they were useful for tracking down special treats for her dinner, including goanna. Placed whole on the fire to cook, the skin is pulled back and guts removed. They are greasy—the fat tastes not unlike chicken. The Aboriginal people I knew really relished a good feed of goanna and always kept a keen lookout for the lizards.

Along the way, one dog produced a litter of pups. Each morning before mounting her horse, Dinah settled the pups inside her shirt; there they travelled all day, joining their mother for a feed at midday dinner camp. If the day was hot, Dinah dunked them in a waterhole, then back into her shirt went the wet pups.

Throughout the muster, Bessie carried her baby Colin—six months old when we'd set off—on a small cushion in front of her saddle. If a bull came charging out, we rode for our lives, sometimes with a sharp horn uncomfortably close to our horses' tails, threatening to add further scars to Blue Eyes' rump. On these wild rides, Colin bobbed about, his little sou'wester hat, with its pattern of yellow ducks, flying in the wind. I can't recall ever hearing him cry while on horseback; I think he quite enjoyed the noise and activity.

Dinah—always one to avoid risky situations—usually managed to be out of harm's way. She employed the strategy that it wasn't the bull she need outrun but the other riders, so she'd try to keep us between her and immediate danger. Dinah was no fool!

Bessie and I, with Colin, were on foot one day when an exceptionally large and irate bull came snorting and charging out of the cattle mob, straight for us. Our only refuge was a tangled clump of thorny konkerberry bushes—hardly protection from an angry scrub bull, but it was all to be had. We dived into it, oblivious to the sharp thorns raking our faces.

We huddled there with Colin between us, the bull stamping his feet, his massive head almost within reach, blowing hot frothy breath at us in snorting puffs. He swept his horns through our fragile shelter—first in a wide arc, then with an upward toss of his head that brought a glaring red eye so close it seemed unnaturally huge. The sharp, shiny tips of his horns were surrounded with frayed, ragged fringes, the result of rubbing on trees to ensure a lethal edge. I thought of the times I'd seen such a horn pierce deep into another beast with one thrust.

We were totally silent, numb with fear. We held our breath and leaned away from him, almost atop each other. Not a sound from Colin, just wide-eyed interest. I hoped there was a god up there and tried to think of a quick prayer. The Hail Mary? The Ten Commandments! I had never coveted my neighbour's wife (eh! husband), nor his oxen (well, maybe), but never had I bowed down to a graven image (really, not ever). A timely memory lapse here, for the times in Convent School spent kneeling before statues of the Virgin, and numerous saints, to ingratiate ourselves into their good graces.

Then horses galloped up—whips cracking, men shouting, a flurry of hoof-beats, and he was driven back to join the mob in hand.

We emerged from our konkerberry fortress on shaky legs, covered with bleeding scratches. I don't know how long we'd huddled there. Only Colin was unfazed, grinning happily from beneath his yellow duck hat, which was balanced at a rakish angle from the frantic manoeuvring among prickly branches.

I can't think how I lived to tell this tale. Why didn't the big bull charge straight in at us? Perhaps the thorny tangle proved some restraint, perhaps our terrified silence helped, or was it just good luck? To say it was a trifle unsettling to a person of my delicate temperament is to put it mildly.

If the big bull could think such thoughts he may have reasoned with some relish, three humans pieced to their fundaments with his spear tipped horns would be just revenge for all bulls of the bush who had fallen to man's rapaciousness, and he came very close. Still, one cannot begrudge him his moment!

Of course it provided some amusement for the stock boys: 'Told ya, Jack, ya gotta be quick or they'll go ya.'

Looking back, a fleeting thought crosses my mind of the movie-screen hero rescuing his heroine from certain death, then clasping her to his chest in spite of vile villains in close pursuit. We, on the other hand, standing scratched and dejected, were severely reprimanded for being in the wrong place on foot.

CHAPTER 38

# Naming
# Butterfly Spring

We were moving south, away from the coast, and mustering part of the grazing licence Ken shared with Les MacFarlane. Mac had sent George Lewis, Elmore's brother, with some stock boys to meet up with our camp and claim his share of the cattle mustered: those bearing the NNT brand. They followed the fires we lit to burn off rank grass as we passed; smoke spiralling high is visible for miles.

George was one of a passing breed, a fine old cattleman who knew no other life. He was getting on in years, taking a fraction longer to mount his horse in the early morning. He and his two brothers had been droving and working cattle from childhood; they were real nomads of the cattle trails. They could neither read nor write and George believed this a good thing; it kept his mind clear of unnecessary clutter, he said.

George's arrival was quite an event for us: he brought news from outside and the extra men were welcome in camp.

Several years earlier, George and Ken, with Aboriginal stockmen, had travelled 600 head of bullocks from Mac's Moroak Station for sale in Queensland. Late one night they settled the cattle well back in a stone yard. Instead of erecting a barrier across the entrance, which was about 30 metres wide, they made camp there. Night horses were tethered in readiness and a campfire burned brightly; the men unrolled their swags and settled.

George's eyesight was poor and he wore glasses. When he got into his swag, he placed them on his hat beside him as usual.

During the night, the cattle rushed, set off in fright by a sudden sound among the surrounding rocks. They tore through the yard's narrow entrance in panicked flight, sweeping the night horses away.

At the first movement from the yard, the younger, more active men managed a quick getaway up into the rocks—but George, almost blind without glasses, floundered a moment.

Edric, one of the stockmen, took hold of him just as the mob was upon them and threw him behind a slim sapling, the only barrier available. Grasping George by the shoulders, Edric swung him left then right to avoid the slashing horns visible in the pale starlight.

A couple of thousand hooves careering through a 30-metre space left barely an inch of ground untouched—except, as was discovered in the morning, George's hat and glasses. They were exactly as he had left them, thickly powdered with dust but without a scratch.

⁓

Before moving on from camp in the morning, we'd get the bread started in the camp oven, tie the lid down and pack it firmly on top of the load, preferably on one of the more docile mules; a couple of our mules were only recently broken in and devils to catch.

As well as being hardy and seemingly impervious to sickness, mules are notoriously fractious and stubborn animals that could try the patience of the most even-tempered handler. Ken, not a patient man at the best of times, once took out his pistol and shot dead a fully packed, uncooperative mule in utter exasperation late one evening in the bush.

Some years before this muster, Ken and Jim had lost a saddled riding mule out bush. In the miles of surrounding unfenced country, it was six months before he was found. Still saddled, he had weathered an entire wet season; the girth strap had chafed deep and skin had grown over in part, saddle cloth and reins had gone, but otherwise he was lively and in good condition.

When watching a mule jog along with bread dough in its camp oven on top of the load, it wasn't unusual to see the rising dough overflowing its lid and cascading in heavy elastic streamers down the sides of the mule. What to do? Catch the mule, if it was in a mood to be caught. If not, then run about after a crazy bucking animal with dough flying like snowflakes, unload, knead the dough, repack, move on to catch up with the cattle, cook the bread at the evening camp. If the day was hectic and bread not set, a damper was quickly cooked.

Flour, water, cream of tartar, carb-soda—this mixture can be made into small, flat scones cooked directly on hot ashes; johnnycakes, they were called. Carried loose in a pack-bag for days, they became as hard as stone; dunking in tea was the only way a tooth could pierce them.

When there was no rising medium, these small scones were made with just flour and water, and derisively called 'mission johnnycakes'.

~

A waterlily-covered billabong provided additions to the menu. Lily roots—their bush name *guneyas*—were dug out of the mud and roasted or boiled in corned-beef water; Aboriginals had traditionally pounded them into flour. The fat seedpods in the centre of the flower have a pleasant, nutty taste, raw or cooked; the long, moist stems, though tasteless, are useful to chew for their moisture.

At water's edge, pandanus palms produce a big pineapple-shaped cone, bright orange when ripe, with small tasty nuts that are hard to extract. Other bush tucker includes yams, konkerberries, bush plums and currants, all seasonal. Best of all, as any bush kid knows, is sugarbag or wild honey. The small black native bees are more like flies and do not sting; they're drawn to a sweaty shirt on the back of a horse-rider and cluster there for the moisture.

We had been two months out in wild country when one evening we made camp early, some ways from a creek dense with the round green leaves and huge blue flowers of waterlilies.

I decided to take a swim before the cattle were yarded and the men returned to camp. I splashed about, collecting a few *guneyas* to cook with our dinner.

As I emerged naked from the water, trailing my purple lilies, I glanced up to be confronted with two white men standing on the high bank. For a few moments we stood as absolutely still as statues, staring at each other, our mutual shock inspiring total silence. Then, without a word, they turned together and disappeared over the bank, and I made swift departure to camp.

That evening, with the din of cattle camp echoing around the ridges, two men approached our camp. They were part of a national mapping team, travelling the bush in a Jeep, working as they went.

After joining us around the fire for their first meal of fresh meat for quite some time, they described their total shock to see a young white woman, naked, rising silently from the water with a bouquet of flowers in her hand. They told how they'd just as silently gone back to their vehicle, produced a treasured, hoarded bottle and had a hefty shot of rum, then returned to the waterhole and gazed down on the silent, deathly still water.

Naked? Carrying a bunch of flowers? Been in the bush too long, mate.

~

Country around the Limmen varies: black soil flats close to the river, long valleys, numerous springs and a wide variety of tall trees.

By the river grows our old coolabah tree, whose qualities are eulogised in poems and bush ballads such as the famous 'Waltzing Matilda'.

Carbeens, straight as marble pillars, have pure silver-white trunks, cool and silky, on which to press one's cheek after a scorching day of riding in bush. On the plains at night they catch the glint of moonlight, which earned them the sobriquet 'ghost gums'.

The skeletal kapok trees cluster on dry, stony ridges; their velvety, brilliant-yellow flowers can be eaten if one is desperate enough.

In or close to water, the melaleuca or paperbark tree grows to great height and girth. Its hundreds of layers of tissue-fine, waterproof, papery bark are used for everything: rafts, coolamons, waterproofing dwellings, and to wrap meat for cooking in a *mongoo* or ground oven. Its thin trails of drooping, willow-like branches sweep across the water in a breeze—the long, thin beards of the old men that these great trees really are—while the silver needles of its disintegrating, honey-scented bottlebrush flowers thickly coat the water's surface.

The bloodwood, another stalwart of the plains, takes its name from the dark red sap that runs in clumped, jelly-like cascades down the rough bark of its thick trunk. At that time of year in the dry season, bloodwood are heavy with creamy flowers, the branches alive with flocks of parrots—their raucous voices deafening as they argue while feasting on the honey-rich blossoms.

Then there are messmate trees, the stately broad-leafed Leichhardt pine, the pandanus palm, and the poisonous, round-leafed ironwood.

Of all the trees, snappy gum was the preferred firewood in camp. It burns with a fierce heat and produces the kind of glowing coals best for bread-making in a bush camp oven.

One day we came onto a large, serenely beautiful spring. It was set, partly shaded, beneath a high rocky outcrop and fed with a waterfall.

The air above the water was thick with thousands of yellow butterflies, providing a dense cloud of hovering wings. Displaying a singular lack of imagination, I bestowed it with the name Butterfly Spring—well, it could hardly have been called anything else.

The cartographers entered this name on the map and it remains today.

Toward the north, a spiral of feathery smoke on the horizon gave rise to much speculation. Who could be riding out in this country? We kept a close watch and waited.

Two days later an old Aboriginal man and two lubras—one young, the other quite a bit older—rode up to our camp, driving their packhorses ahead. The man's name was Undai. He lived on a coastal mission station and made this trip every couple of years with a view to doing a little business in the bride trade.

He unpacked, settled his camp nearby and came over to see our Aboriginal boys. He displayed his wares, our boys showed some interest, but the price was high and Undai wasn't about to waste time on insolvent wishful thinkers. Nothing doing in our camp, so next morning he moved on down along the river.

News later filtered through to us that he'd sold both women and made a nice profit of a horse and other sundry items. The older of the two went to Tom Hume, a well-known part-Aboriginal man; his father had been a white teamster in the old days and Tom was born beside a wagon on the road to Borroloola.

It could be said that Tom and his bride lived quite happily ever after. Tom's son Percy, who was close to being a full-blood Aboriginal, took the younger one and didn't do so well in the deal. She proved to be a regular virago, making his life quite miserable before running off to greener pastures.

CHAPTER 39

# My 'Get Up and Go' Had Got Up and Gone

After four months' mustering along the Limmen, and with several hundred head of mixed cattle in hand, we decided to call a halt.

Jim was anxious to return to work on Bing Bong, while Ken had been working with a wooden stake deep in his hand, becoming more painful each day. Removing it would entail heavy bush surgery, which temporarily would do even more to restrict his ability to throw cattle and hold the reins, so there the splinter remained. Gloves were unknown out bush—if skin became dry, rendered beef fat was rubbed in; for a cut or injury, tar was applied.

Jim had a contract to supply the Aboriginal Welfare Department in Borroloola with fresh beef and a delivery was about due, so it was decided that Ken and I would take six fat cows into town, while Jim with the stock camp and cattle would return to Bing Bong.

We put together our riding horses, exchanged our mules for two packhorses, said our goodbyes, and the camp split up. The pups now made a dog pack, trotting with lolling tongues behind Dinah's horse. Colin was still perched before Bessie's saddle, but the duck-patterned hat was long gone. The stock boys were happy to be heading back and waved cheerily to us as we made off in different directions.

Our clothes were ragged and, with the men's heavy beards and pistols low on their hips, we looked like an outlaw family group on a wanted poster of old bushranger days. Some were without boots. In fact, Ken often rode and threw bulls over the roughest country barefoot, as there were no replacements for worn-out shoes, so the soles of his feet were as calloused as any bush blackfella—he could strike a match on them!

Borroloola was a six-day journey from our present camp. Ken and I took Jim's big packhorse, Sputnik, who was an equine disaster—sway-backed, with a large and ugly head, ears flopping every which way. Ken found something disparaging to say whenever he set eyes on him, mumbling insults along the lines of 'He belongs in a dog-food can.'

But worse was to be revealed: Sputnik was entire! It seemed unbelievable that he'd been left a stallion. Most likely Jim had trapped him with brumbies and somehow he'd been overlooked, his manhood remaining intact before he was hastily broken in to carry packs. At least Sputnik was strong, carrying our swags and all our tucker bags—and anyway, we were stuck with the poor old fellow.

After a couple of days, Ken and I came out onto the main Anthony's Lagoon–Borroloola road. From here we had the use of small, permanent bush yards. Each night we hobbled out our horses and made camp.

Just on sundown one evening, the familiar jingle of hobble chains carried around the necks of travelling horses drifted towards us on the still evening air. Hurtle Lewis, brother to Elmore and George, rode up, on his way to Borroloola. He managed Tanumbirini Station, a lonely back-of-beyond place in those days. As was usual when meeting someone after a long period of isolation, we sat around the fire well into the night.

Although he was a white man, Hurtle was sun-burned a deep mahogany. Unlike George, whose hair was silvery white, Hurtle was dark and surprisingly sprouted a thick, bushy, dark red beard. He was perhaps 50 years old, but I don't believe he was sure just how old he was.

Hurtle looked out from his insular, illiterate world with limited knowledge and understanding. His conversation was sprinkled with malapropisms, and he had an odd and humorous way with words. Around the fire one night, when our talk drifted to war in foreign parts—jungle fighting with guerrillas attacking unarmed villagers—Hurtle's heated rejoinder was: 'Gorillas, eh? Well, what did they expect givin' them big monkeys guns?'

When his attention was drawn to a word he hadn't heard before, Hurtle was impatient to use it himself, often quite out of context. Some of his quaint words have taken permanence in our family vocabulary, and an odd look comes our way at times when we refer to polar bears as polo bears, drakes as grakes, a flop-eared spaniel as a water Spaniard, and so it goes on.

One of Hurtle's favourite words to throw into conversations was 'superstitious' when the appropriate word was 'suspicious'—and, indeed, Hurtle was ever suspicious of people's motives, especially in horse-trading and cattle-dealing. If he received a letter or an account, which he rarely did, he would ask you to read it for him, then slyly take it to someone else. It would secretly make the rounds of the camp until he was satisfied he'd learned its true contents.

Hurtle's affairs were handled for him by a Darwin solicitor, Brough Newell, but Hurtle had it firmly in mind that the man's name was 'Bluff Mules'. When someone said, 'No Hurtle, his name is Brough Newell,' Hurtle would testily reply, 'That's what I said—Bluff Mules.'

Hurtle was a keen racing man and usually brought a good horse to bush meetings. On this trip he had among his horses a fine thoroughbred mare, Maggie Jane, of which he was very proud; she was his most successful racehorse to date.

When we moved off camp next morning, driving all our horses together, Hurtle's eye fell upon Sputnik—who, in spite of his heavy load, had developed a spring in his step. His floppy old ears were making a valiant effort to prick and his woolly neck was arching quite youthfully in the direction of Maggie Jane.

'Jeeze Cris, he's a stallion!' Hurtle bellowed, and for the remainder of the trip he travelled with his horses well apart from ours, with a watchful eye on Maggie Jane. He feared that for all her aristocratic breeding, she wasn't averse to a bit of rough trade, as they say—but his chaperoning paid off and Maggie Jane's virtue remained unsullied.

One night, after setting up camp, we realised that from here on into Borroloola there would be no place to yard the cows, so we decided to make a long day of it and avoid a night watch.

After leaving around three the next morning, we reached Borroloola that afternoon. We delivered our cows, then dropped by with bags of salted beef for Roger and Co, as it must have made a welcome change from fish and wallaby. Afterwards we settled our camp once more under the mango trees.

It had been a long hard day, the last day of a hard four months.

Although the muster was a success as far as cattle numbers went, there would be no sale until the following year. It was already August; the first storms would come soon. The cows would be kept as breeders, while the bullocks would have to be walked about 300 kilometres up to Anthony Lagoon on the Barkly Stock Route, where two or three buyers came through each year in the dry season.

This was the only market for us—you either sold them, or walked right back and held them for another twelve months. There was, of course, some collusion among these buyers. You could be sure that if you refused the first buyer's offer, any subsequent offer would be lower. Little wonder some gave up and simply walked off their grazing country.

I was sitting on my tightly rolled swag, which had just been unpacked from Sputnik, when Hurtle, spurs clanking, led his horse into camp. 'What's up girl?' he asked me. 'Where's your get up and go, eh?'

My 'get up and go' had long got up and gone. I was thin as a starving whippet. My clothes were threadbare and I was burned black as any bush lubra.

'Consider your looks, avoid the sun,' the good books and our mothers warned us—how quaint! Four months with only a hat between you and the sky, and your complexion is the last thing to consider. Anyway, we had no mirror.

In camp I sat gazing into the fire. I had seen Borroloola, travelled the Old Coast Road, ridden the wild Limmen country. I'd come for the adventure and now I was all set to return to a touch of civilised living. I would fly out on the first plane, go south, eat 'proper' food, wear 'girl's clothes', lie on the beach in a snappy bathing costume and get used to a roof over my head. That all takes some doing after months of waking at night to an expanse of sky aglitter with stars that were now as familiar as the ceiling decoration of a city bedroom.

CHAPTER 40

# 'With All My Worldly Goods I Thee Endow'

It must have occurred to Ken that if I left on the plane, I would likely never return.

The fortune and cattle-baron status he'd deemed essential before he took on the responsibilities of married life had not yet eventuated, and his future was bleak financially, and he wasn't a man of the pencilled-moustache, 'come with me to the Casbah' type, so his marriage proposal went thus:

'I reckon we should get married right now. What do you say?'

'Umm . . .' I replied.

'You might show a little more enthusiasm,' he huffed, and with that went off to see Mervyn the missionary.

So ended any daydreams of snappy bathing costumes and a lazy life on southern beaches.

It was Mervyn's first marriage service and he took care to see that everything proceeded in an orderly fashion. 'You must have a witness,' he said, 'and I'll apply to have a licence sent down from Darwin—so remember, stand by when the mail is sorted and make sure Mull's goats don't eat it!'

~

'With all my worldly goods I thee endow.' A couple of saddles, pack-bags, the odd mule and some horses were the sum total of worldly goods in this union.

The bride wore red—a blinding red dirndl skirt, patterned with large, vivid yellow trumpets, the fabric purchased from Jack Bailey's little store. Jack was a good-looking, silver-haired man whose age was a little north of 50, as they say in the bush. During our absence from Borroloola, he had opened a bush store with a small stock of sweets, drinks, fishing lines, fabrics, et cetera. It proved a popular gathering place for the local Aboriginals, and promised to be a successful venture.

My skirt was made from the least dazzling fabric of his stock at '1 and 6' (15 cents) a yard. You may wonder that if this was the least dazzling, what dazzle the remaining stock offered—considerable, I can assure you! And any lubra will tell you she'd take any colour as long as it was red.

I had a shirt less ragged than the rest, which would do, but footwear posed a problem—riding boots with a skirt was definitely not on, and as the happy era of the sixties had not yet happened, bare feet and bare elsewhere weren't yet the order of the day for women. Ken solved this problem by placing my foot on the leather flap of a mule pack and cutting around the outline; straps from a camera made thongs.

Duly shod and gowned, I was for better or worse.

Ken and I had known each other for eight years. Although we'd spent little time together, we'd expected that one day we would marry, but those were hard times for cattlemen in that country. Grazing properties were larger, but the sale of store shorthorn cattle wasn't a profitable business. Most could only battle on from year to year, gradually building up their herd and hoping for eventual prosperity.

~

At 8 p.m. on 14 August 1958 we collected Roger and Biddy from their tank home. It was a courageous effort on Roger's part to venture out at night on our behalf, as over the years he'd absorbed the Aboriginal fear of what darkness held, but the desire to support bride and bridegroom, and Biddy waddling along in the rear, secured his presence as witness/best man to this little ceremony. Biddy was to be my attendant: huge and as black as the night outside the shed where Mervyn lived, a wad of chewing tobacco bulging her cheek.

Mervyn was standing by, his wife's wedding ring to be borrowed for the occasion. A night breeze fluttered over the bridegroom's tattered trousers and bare feet; glinted over Roger's long grey beard. He appeared gravely imposing, standing supported by a stout wooden staff. With his sandals of greenhide and clothes he had sewn himself, he appeared to have stepped out of a biblical illustration—a splendid patriarch leading his people through the wilderness.

All went well after a fairly nervous beginning, and Mervyn was close to concluding the service when Roger, ever mindful of his duties as supporter and witness, held up his hand and called 'Halt!' He and Mervyn then entered into a long theological discussion that threatened to stray, in a casual conversational way, into areas other than the subject at hand.

'Are we married yet?' I whispered.

'Shh, getting there,' said Ken.

Bearing in mind why he was there, and satisfied that all was understood and in order, Roger, with a wave of his hand, gave an authoritative: 'Proceed.'

With a grand flourish, Mervyn pronounced us wed. Biddy grinned and spat a stream of tobacco juice on the earthen floor, then I returned the ring. There was a glass of cordial for all, followed by an entertaining hour of picture slides, and Ken and I began married life in the Outback of the Outback.

We collected every last penny of cash we had, which amounted to a grand total of three pounds, and presented it to Mervyn for his services; although he asked for nothing, his need was certainly greater than ours. We had then truly joined the bush brotherhood of old Borroloola. It was a common adage that if the residents were all upended and shaken, not a penny would fall from their pockets.

After delivering Roger and Biddy back to their tank, and ensuring they were well secured against the darkness, we walked hand in hand back to camp, where we woke up Hurtle, who was unprepared for such happenings as weddings in the night. He rattled about preparing a billy-can of tea, and we sat around the fire until late in the night.

Next morning I gave my eye-blinding skirt to a camp lubra, who was delighted with it. Roger presented us with a double-sized mosquito net as a wedding gift, very practical and well received—the mosquitoes were voracious by the river and came buzzing in their thousands late in the afternoon, just before dark. I've seen them land so thick on a man's back that a slap would leave a blood-stained handprint on his shirt.

That morning Ken and I borrowed a native dugout canoe—a long, hollowed-out trunk of a Leichhardt pine tree—and spent the day paddling miles down the lonely deserted McArthur River.

Depending on the skill of the paddler, a dugout can be hard to balance. In crocodile-infested waters, great care has to be taken not to initiate a roll. Ken's years among the coastal Aboriginals had honed his paddling skills, so I merely sat quite still with a good grip and an eye peeled to the distant bank in case we had to swim for it. The big saltwater crocodile plays a cunning, silent waiting game, ready to attack anything careless enough to venture into his territory.

We returned just before nightfall. The glare off the water had left me with a headache of rock-splitting ferocity, and I sported a heavy coating of sand-fly bites. The honeymoon was over.

When our families eventually received news of our bush nuptials, they celebrated with champagne and a fine dinner at a grand city hotel—certainly a contrast to our corned beef and billy-can of tea.

There's an old adage in the Territory: 'If you wish to taste your own beef, go dine with your neighbour.' With no money due from cattle sales until the following year, we had to consider our options. Food was no problem—there was an abundance of fish, and we killed our own beef (or someone's beef). There would be cattle work after the wet, but that was six months away.

We were giving thought to what we should do, when one day a dusty Land Rover pulled into camp. It was Jack Travers, a well-known and popular stock inspector. He had news that Bill Sharpe, my old boss drover, had 1500 bullocks in hand on the way into Queensland.

Ken was due to ride out to help brand and paddock our cattle at Bing Bong, so in a rash moment I decided to take a lift with Jack and maybe a job with Bill for a few weeks, which would make enough money to tide us over the wet.

So that's exactly what I did. Two days after I was married, I was on the road droving again.

After Jack had dropped me off and he was leaving, his Land Rover pulled up beside me and he gave me a book with heavenly pictures of palm-fringed beaches, a nostalgic reminder of an idyllic past; I remember its title as being *Life and Love among the South Sea Islands*. What was I, a Pisces, a water-sign creature, doing in this parched, sun-baked desert of a place?

Bill was short-handed this late in the season and the country was very dry. I rode with the cattle all day, there was no friendly camp work with the company of a friendly cook and horse-tailer, and there wasn't the camaraderie of the year before.

One night the cattle rushed; next day everyone was edgy and tired, and we had to navigate a careful track around an irritable cook.

I crouched down behind a wind-break of corrugated iron sheets that protected the fire from the strong winds tearing across the plain. The light, deep ash from the burned gidgee logs was pale grey, almost white and light as mist, and covered clothes and hair, settling in every crevice of skin. There I sat to avoid the howling wind, tears streaking through the ash powdering my cheeks—a dejected modern-day Cinderella. What was worse, my parents were unaware their only child was married. My spirits reached rock bottom. I thought of my father's admonition never to indulge in self-pity, but I did anyway.

It wasn't an auspicious start to a marriage and I could only hope life and circumstances would improve. Perhaps it can be said that: 'Greater love hath no woman than she takes on droving through the Territory's harsh outback stock routes for her man.'

⌒

After a few weeks' riding in clouds of dust in the rear of the bullocks, we crossed the border into Queensland, over the Georgina River and into the town of Camooweal. In spite of the nearby river, this little cow-town had baked through too many summers to achieve any feature pleasing to the eye. It had a few tired, dust-shrouded trees, a smattering of small houses, a couple of pubs and stores, and mountains of discarded liquor bottles, along with herds of goats on its outskirts.

I left camp here and was looking forward to a hot bath and clean hair. I wondered how I'd handle the claustrophobic feeling of sleeping indoors for the first time in five months. I'd barely set foot inside my room at the pub when the bar erupted in a free-for-all brawl, with men crashing through passageways. My closed door flew inwards and hung off its hinges almost at my feet.

I sat on my bed, knees up under my chin, less than happy. It was quite like old times: the usual booze-induced brawl that was part of the local scene.

I was offered a lift to Mount Isa, so I picked up my swag and departed hot on the heels of my arrival, hopefully for more peaceful climes. I arrived in Mount Isa to find there were no hotel rooms available in town. At the last hotel I approached, they told me there were no rooms, but there were four beds on a verandah upstairs. Would I care to take one of these?

Would I? You bet I would. I moved right in, after a long session in the public bathroom. The bathrooms of bush pubs in those days rarely bore Gentlemen, Ladies, Boys, Girls, Guys, Dolls or other quaint signs of gender direction—the twain met, or hopefully didn't meet, under the sign 'BATHROOM'. The prospect of sharing with a wild bunch of ringers in town on a spree raised a number of questions, some too grim to contemplate.

After scrubbing off a long accumulation of grime and bulldust, I chose my bed and retired early, clad only in minimal underwear. There hadn't been any nightgowns in my life for quite a while, and as a lone woman in camp I'd slept in shirt and trousers.

Early next morning I woke, stretched flat on my front, and took in the sight of a pair of large, well-worn, ornately tooled riding boots. With a cautious turn of head, I saw there were more boots under that bed. Other evidence of the bed's occupation arose in the form of two big bare feet, one attached to a long hairy leg protruding well past the end of the bed, establishing that its owner was very tall.

The beds were all occupied and within arm's reach of one another. It's a well-known fact that ringers weren't given to the sissy conventions of underwear and generally slept naked in their swags.

'Mornin', G'day, Hi ya,' from all.

We all lay still and expectant, no one moving. I had an unnerving vision of three naked ringers, one very tall and hairy of leg, and myself in pink panties, all making our dignified exit along the verandah together.

I made the first move, a ballet-like twirl that draped my body in a sheet, and departed alone, pink panties visible from the rear only.

After a few days of shopping for clothes and other necessities, I was ready to head back to Borroloola and married life. Boarding the same small plane I'd flown in earlier in the year, I was once again a lone passenger buried among mailbags and packages. This time I was going home as a genuine resident of Borroloola, even if the residence was only a swag under the stars.

Ted Harvey, the Aboriginal Affairs Officer, and his wife Nettie invited us to stay with them. They had a big house, no children, a dog and a large household staff. The prospect of moving in with them was very appealing—but we'd decided to make adobe bricks and build a small one-room house to shelter us over the wet, which wasn't far off.

We settled our camp near the spring and started work, carrying countless buckets of water to make a puddle of termite-nest mud and spinifex grass. Ken made a wooden mould to set one brick at a time. It took weeks, but it was quite encouraging to see the growing pile of bricks drying in the sun.

We became friends with Ted and Nettie, and were regular visitors during their years there. Ted had been a wartime pilot, one of the daring young men who flew great, lumbering, often overloaded cargo planes over the dangerous mountain ranges of New Guinea. He was a keen fisherman and there was no better fishing in Australia than on the McArthur. Nettie was a city girl, and I think not one for the great outdoors.

One night while Ted was fishing on the river in their small boat, accompanied by Nettie, he shot a crocodile. As it died, it reared up on its tail and vomited a partly digested dingo onto the boat's occupants, at the same time as knocking over their lantern. In their frail craft, in the darkness of the wide river, the little enthusiasm Nettie had for fishing died in its infancy.

# CHAPTER 41

# Missus Ken

Jack Bailey had become so enthusiastic about his little store-keeping venture that he'd decided to make a trip to the distant wholesale houses in Mount Isa. Because Mervyn's sermons had implanted the notion of Christmas in the more receptive of his Aboriginal flock, Jack planned to promote the festive season and boost business. Nothing too fancy, he told us, but with Christmas not far off, he'd leave before the wet set in and add a few frivolous odds and ends to his stock.

We gathered at the store to see him depart in his truck.

Jack made it to Mount Isa, bought everything he wanted and set off home.

He was found beside his truck in the middle of the road at Top Crossing of the McArthur River. He was on his knees, bent over, his head to the ground as if in prayer to a foreign god—and quite dead, possibly of a heart attack.

Jack was buried right where he died and the road took a sweeping curve around his grave. We bush travellers gave him a salute whenever we drove by.

So it was that, just as it had been gathering momentum, Borroloola's general store died.

~

The Aboriginal tribes living around town received government rations brought in from the *Cora*. On certain days of the week they came across the river in their canoes and congregated in the huge, hangar-like storeroom at the welfare centre, where supplies were brought and stored.

There was clothing of every description, blankets, all kinds of canned and dried food, wholemeal flour, sugar, tea, baby foods and milks. To us, living on beef and bread, the big sacks of shelled almonds put a seal on our envy.

Fresh vegetables from the huge welfare garden, fresh beef supplied under contract by Jim Marshall, and unlimited fish, dugong and turtle. In 1958, the local Aboriginals were supplied with a more nutritious diet than most well-off people in city suburbia. These rations had been carefully compiled by nutritionists and dieticians to ensure they received all that was necessary for their good health.

But what they received and what they wanted differed entirely. They wanted white flour, lots of white sugar and plenty of tobacco. They spent hours sifting wholemeal flour through wire gauze to eliminate the meal, refine the texture and make it as close to white flour as possible. Much of their canned goods were exchanged with Albert Morcom for extra sugar and tobacco.

The cans of baby food weren't popular—their recipients often threw them into the long grass of the roadside on their way back to camp. On one occasion I made quite a haul collecting the discards in their wake.

Apart from tea, sugar and flour, beef was what they asked for. Everything else, in whatever quantities, was accessory—not 'proper' food. No matter what delicious tucker was offered, if there was no beef three times daily, it was a case of: 'That's nice, now where's dinner?'

Ken once asked an old blackfella working for new chums in the country if the tucker was good in his camp.

'No,' he replied, 'no good. We get piggy-piggy mornin' time, Chinaman dinner time, only blackfella night time.' This meant porridge for breakfast, rice and vegetables for lunch, and beef at night: not the way to go food-wise, as far as any bush Aboriginal of those days was concerned.

There's an advantage to not having a home or responsibilities or bills to pay; if you don't like a place, roll your swag, mount your horse and ride on.

In those pre-wet season months, we lived in the bush surrounding Borroloola and had little knowledge of what the future held in store for us.

We hadn't begun to assemble our mud bricks into any sort of dwelling and the wet was fast approaching. The short, sudden 'knock 'em down' storms that flatten tall grass had already come crashing through as they do just before the proper wet, warning you to be prepared. These come at the end of the wet too.

I had metamorphosed after our marriage. I was no longer Jack-a-leen as far as the Aboriginals were concerned—I was Missus Ken.

The jetty that had floated off in the cyclone hadn't been replaced and the *Cora* was soon due with the all-important wet season supplies. The captain had sent word: 'No jetty, no unloading Borroloola stores.' Instead he would turn around and head straight back downriver.

With a view to improving their bank balance and to ensure the town received its supplies, Ken and Jim contracted to build a new jetty. It was to be a quick and simple job, with bush timber, basic tools, shovel, crowbar, axe and saw all they had to work with.

Jim, a non-swimmer, was stationed on the high bank with his rifle as lookout for crocodiles, while Ken went under water to shovel out holes in the mud for carbeen-trunk pylons, each sharpened at one end to ease them in. Log decking was assembled for the finishing touch.

In ten days the jetty was complete, just in time for the *Cora's* arrival. The unloading went well, the captain was happy and the jetty was approved by all. And, thankfully, Jim and Ken were both £250 richer.

Bill Sharpe had offered us the loan of his truck to use just before and during the wet: an offer not to be ignored. With our improved financial situation we were able to fly to Mount Isa and buy a kerosene refrigerator, a wood-fired stove and some building iron. After loading it all onto Bill's truck, we returned to

Borroloola, intending to finish our brick house and feeling rather pleased that it would have an iron roof.

~

However, the *Cora*'s arrival had not been an entirely pleasant experience for Ken.

When the small ship arrived at the jetty, it was a time of high activity around Borroloola. A flotilla of small watercraft, native dugout canoes and dinghies of all sizes headed downstream, all bent either on ferrying loading back to town or just sharing in the general excitement of the arrival.

Ken hitched a ride to the jetty with Mervyn, whose small, open-cabin truck—untrustworthy at the best of times—chugged down a road boggy from recent rains and criss-crossed by streams of clay-coloured stormwater. Slow travelling broke up the drying mud-crust and left the road in an even poorer condition.

With their few stores packed, the men started back along the track and came to a jolting stop in bog-hole after bog-hole. In the sweltering, steamy heat it fell to Ken to do the digging and pushing, while Mervyn manned the controls.

With flagging energy and patience, Ken ventured to suggest it might be wiser to avoid the boggy sections, take a detour where possible. However, Mervyn, good Christian missionary that he was, placed trust in the Almighty to bring them successfully over the road He'd provided, and would hear no argument as he drove steadily forward into whatever lay ahead. After dealing with each hazard there was a pause for a short prayer of thanks, then they'd be off again, straight down the centre of the road into yet another disaster.

Perhaps hoping to maintain some reserves of energy in his digger, Mervyn called a break for lunch: the sharing of a small tin of sardines. Ken had his head back and mouth open in anticipation of the meagre offering, when Mervyn called an indignant halt—grace hadn't been said.

For Ken, grace was not on. He wasn't an ungrateful man but was loath to give thanks for two sardines to an uninterested Almighty, whom he felt was responsible for their miserable situation anyway.

Mervyn was convinced their problems along the road were God's will and lay blame fully on Ken for the troubles they were encountering.

'Hardly my fault,' Ken said, 'you're driving!'

'It's your fault, Ken, because the Almighty has taken offence at your blaspheming and bad language.'

So the long, slow trip continued, Ken wondering why he hadn't taken a canoe downriver like everyone else.

As they came onto the outskirts of Borroloola in the dark, covered with mud, the ancient truck gave up and, with a shuddering gasp, settled down on its threadbare tyres like a tired old packhorse onto its haunches at the end of a hard day. An uninterested Almighty had belatedly taken the time to heed Mervyn's prayers and the fuel had held out to within a short walk of home.

⌒

Ken and I came often to visit Roger. Once while I was fussily attempting to rearrange the box on which I was sitting, he cautioned me not to upset the clusters of red-back spiders beneath.

I could only assume his attitude to red-backs was: leave them alone and they will do the same for you.

One hot afternoon we were sitting with Roger outside his tank home when a horseman rode into view, heading our way. On spotting him, Roger hurried inside for his shotgun, which he referred to as his 'fowling piece', and without a word began blasting away.

The rider was Jack Shadforth: a big man, very fat, and not given to moving fast. He'd just swung his leg over the saddle to dismount when he came under Roger's fire. The speed with which he regained his seat was remarkable for such a heavy man—then he was away toward the trees, riding hands and heels. Our last glimpse was of his bug-eyed, terror-stricken face peering over his shoulder.

With a final volley for good measure, Roger sat down with a satisfied air.

'What was that all about?' Ken asked.

'I sold that bastard a mosquito net and he told someone it had holes in it—can't abide a liar.'

Another time, Roger was unusually withdrawn and preoccupied.

'What's the trouble, Rog?' Ken asked.

'Well, you know,' he answered, in the grave, thoughtful way he had, 'the other night I had a little drink before I went to bed and things haven't been the same since.'

'What was in the drink?' asked Ken.

'Oh, a little White Lady, rum, some other stuff. And do you know, I had this remarkable dream. I was in an Eastern harem, and—'

'Say no more,' said Ken, 'I get the picture.'

'Well now,' said Rog, 'ever since I've been trying to replicate this mixture and I just can't get it right. I've been having terrible nightmares.'

'Try giving it a break,' Ken suggested. 'No drinks for a few nights and the nightmares will go, you'll see.'

And they did, but sadly for Rog, asleep in his upturned tank in the bush, the frolics in the harem were gone forever too!

Whenever invited to share Roger's lunch, I found a quick peek into the pot simmering on his campfire necessary before taking on the contents, which could be any animal or vegetable one could imagine—I remember a completely uncut pumpkin bobbing among unfamiliar chunks of meat.

'What's that thing with a tail?' I asked with studied nonchalance.

Roger came over to stand by his bubbling pot, regarding the contents with interest. 'It's a goanna,' he decided.

'It's small,' I replied.

'It's a different kind, never tried it before.'

I thought I detected some uncertainty as to its edibility. 'I'll just try some pumpkin today.'

⁓

I can't think why I should have been so faddy about Roger's offering on that occasion, as I've eaten my way through the goanna and bird world.

Weeks spent on a steady diet of dugong, when we lived with coastal Aboriginals while we were travelling through their country, left me ready to grow flippers. Dugong is very good to eat, its flesh streaked with layers of fat rather like bacon. The Aboriginal hunters speared it from their dugout canoes and shared their catch with us in exchange for beef. They used dugong oil on their skin and hair too.

Add to this mare's milk, pandanus nuts, waterlily, goose, crocodile and turtle eggs, and buffalo and camel meat, all consumed with varying degrees of enjoyment—and once, in Singapore, well-prepared frog legs and snails. (My father, in his buffalo-shooting camp in Arnhem Land, had his cook make cake with crocodile egg.) But I never could take to crocodile flesh: the decaying carcasses of skinned crocodiles left too memorable a stench for me.

Ken can add flying fox, porcupine—and budgerigars.

He and some Aboriginal boys out bush without food resorted to a meal of the small birds. With a hungry night looming, they armed themselves with strips of fencing wire and waited in bushes by a waterhole. When a dense flock of budgerigars made a graceful wide swoop to water, Ken and the boys hurled their wire strips into the flock in the manner of throwing sticks. Placed whole on hot coals, feathers and guts removed, the birds made quite an acceptable fowl.

Speaking of fowl—we once came upon two eagles having a fiery tug of war with a magpie goose, and joined the battle. They didn't give up easily and were inclined to join forces against us. The prize was a goose stew for dinner.

# PART III

'Far better is it to dare mighty things, to win
glorious triumphs, even though chequered by
failure . . . than to rank with those poor spirits who
neither enjoy nor suffer much, because they live in
a grey twilight that knows not victory nor defeat.'

TEDDY ROOSEVELT

'Over and above all is a splendid
almost prodigal hospitality.'

J. MURY, 1897

# CHAPTER 42

# Managing McArthur River Station

'Whither thou goest, I will go.' So sayeth Ruth and so wenteth I, out onto the wild McArthur side, as the poem written by a jackeroo goes:

The Big McArthur Side

*Out on the big McArthur run,*
*Out where there's action, thrill and fun,*
*Out where the monthly mail comes through*
*From Camooweal to the distant 'Loo,*
*By the big McArthur side.*

*Out where there is no strife or fuss,*
*Where the outside world don't trouble us,*

*We ride to muster, draft and brand,*
*And stick to jobs we understand*
*By the quiet McArthur side.*

Not long after the *Cora's* departure, Frank McMahon—who managed Cresswell Downs Station—took his last trip for the year, before the wet made the road impassable, to McArthur River Station, one of the earliest settled stations in that part of the Territory. This was the only road to McArthur and Borroloola, unsealed and lonely.

McArthur has quite a romantic history. It was formed by an infamous old cattle thief, Harry Redford, for the McCansh family in the late 1880s, when the entire area was at its most wild and lawless. It was named in honour of the famous John Macarthur family, the first Merino breeders in New South Wales.

When Frank offered Ken the job of managing McArthur River Station at the grand wage of £12 per week, we were delighted at the idea of a haven for the wet season and set about moving there as soon as possible.

We loaded our worldly possessions onto our borrowed truck, turned our backs on the mud bricks that had taken so long to put together, and went off in the best of spirits to take up residence in the station homestead. It was slow travelling over a road deeply rutted with dried tracks after recent storms.

It was almost dark when we reached the river crossing, then onto a road that led to where the homestead had stood for the last 70 years.

Vague and shadowy movements on the roadside caught our attention. The truck's lights swept over a large herd of the most extraordinary huge goats, their strange cat's eyes flashing in our lights. They made no move to rush away but clustered close together, horns clacking, obviously resentful of this intrusion into their untended lives. Too many had the long beards of billy goats. They were clearly the station's herd turned feral, and should have been a warning that all was not as it should be.

The night fell down around us as it does in the bush. We unrolled our swag to camp in the middle of the road, the goats still inquisitively standing their ground close by.

At daybreak, intending to settle into our first home together, we drove on to the homestead, but there *was* no homestead. What a shock that was for us homeless newlyweds. Exactly like the Borroloola pub, the house had collapsed into a huge termite-riddled heap. It never took long for hungry white ants to gnaw their way through timber uprights, and these ones had been of Oregon pine, shipped at great expense from the south years before—perfect fodder.

We stumbled on through the debris in a disbelieving haze and came upon a lean-to of sorts where part-Aboriginals had earlier set up camp. A kerosene refrigerator stood there—that was promising!

We opened the door and staggered back from the stench of rotting beef. The refrigerator had been carefully stacked as full as possible with raw beef weeks before, probably just after a recent kill. The burner hadn't been lit; obviously someone believed that closing the door was all that was necessary to render it cold, so count this fridge out.

As if in compensation for this unnerving find, dangling incongruously on a cord from a beam was a plump pink leg of ham: smoked, dried, encased in cotton gauze, the only old-fashioned kind found in the bush then.

We stared at it. Such a luxury! Everything is relative, you know, and for us it was like finding gold on a rubbish tip. Who'd brought it there and how long it had dangled, unmolested by man or beast, remained a mystery. My guess is that no one there knew what it was or what to do with it. We decided to keep it as a treat for Christmas.

Making our way through the sad remains of this famous old homestead, we discovered a small roofed section that was rickety but erect. It provided a faint flicker of hope that we might find something useful in its dark, shuttered interior—anything would do.

In near darkness we pushed the door open on its rusted hinges and brushed away its decorations of thick hanging cobwebs. We carefully stepped inside, feeling rather like intrepid adventurers entering the lost tomb!

We knocked open the old propped windows for some light, which set off a soft, papery rustling. Gentle and whispery at first, it increased to a frenzy of movement—the floor was carpeted with thousands of fat brown cockroaches that crunched under foot and scuttled up our legs.

On a rod along the wall hung a row of army overcoats, each on its own hanger. An attempt to lift one down began a domino effect of disintegration.

On a shelf beneath the coats, in a neat row, were a number of good-quality riding boots, but on inspection they all proved to be for the left foot. No one knew of a one-legged stockman, so they remained a mystery too.

Standing in splendid isolation on a shelf were a dozen cans of army-issue butter concentrate, their carton dissolved into dust around them. Along with the ham, this was all we salvaged in the way of stores, but we felt quite fortunate; they were luxuries as far as we were concerned. When had we ever had a ham and butter in our pack-bags? We carried off our spoils with great good cheer.

As we wandered about the old place, we had the gradual awareness of an unusual bush silence and soon realised there was a total absence of birdlife.

'There's not even a bloody crow around here,' Ken said.

Somehow you don't much notice these sounds until they aren't there, then the silence settles about you, and you pause and wonder about it.

This mystery was solved when Ned, an old bush Aboriginal man, wandered in hoping for a handout of beef, and explained that the piccaninnies had kept up such a barrage of stones and shanghais on anything with wings that the survivors had given the place a wide birth ever since.

'All gone,' he said, with a wide sweep of his arm, in that theatrical way of the old bushman when announcing a calamity. 'Bird all gone, nuddaplace.'

~

So there we were. Ken was manager of a 15,000-square-kilometre cattle station that ran right down to the Gulf of Carpentaria, with the great river running within its boundaries.

No longer was it the 55,000 square kilometres of pioneer Ernest Favenc's day. How the mighty had fallen, and what a discouraging outlook for the new manager. No paddocks remained, so at season's end horses were let go at Goose Lagoon and got a scatter on during the wet. No branded cattle were held on McArthur: those mustered were walked up to Cresswell Downs on the Barkly Tableland. There was no station vehicle, a scattered plant, and very few supplies to tide us over the wet, which was nearly upon us.

The stock camp residents were Aboriginals from Borroloola: Yellow Fred, Bruce, Big Tom, Johnny Ah One (who was part-Chinese), and several others. They were all excellent stockmen.

⁓

It was imperative we have some sort of roof over us, and pretty soon too.

To avoid having to cross the river in flood, Ken decided to settle on the opposite side to the ruined homestead. He built a small one-roomed shed with bush timber uprights, corrugated-iron walls and roof, and an earthen floor; he also constructed a kitchen workbench from a packing case covered with flat iron, and a roomy bed from a frame of ti-tree saplings laced across with greenhide. We rolled our swag out and our first home was complete the day before Christmas.

In the early daylight of Christmas morning, I woke to the clattering of pots and pans, and sat up to take in the vision of a broad backside encased in a vivid pattern of bright red flowers, its owner bent over to light the woodstove in the corner of the room.

'Who's that?' I asked.

'Well, me H'Alice, ain't it,' came the reply, in a who-would-you-think-it-was tone. 'I work for you, Missus Ken.' It wasn't a question, but a statement; I had been told, and that was that.

Alice was Big Tom's wife. She kept up a bossy clattering among the dishes and made tea, and this she continued to do for the next twenty years.

The ham leg was to feature prominently at our Christmas lunch. The outside boiler was lit early, and everything prepared for its cooking. But alas, tragedy had struck and there was to be no ham that year. It hadn't been hung high enough in a tree, so the dingoes and wild dogs had fossicked it out during the night and chewed it to the bone. We made do with corned beef and vowed we'd do better the following year.

# CHAPTER 43

# Our First Wet Season

After Christmas the proper wet set in and the rain was continuous, so there was no chance of moving out and less of anyone coming in. Our shed was as hot as hell under the iron roof, but we were thankful for a dry camp.

With no radio, we had no idea what was happening elsewhere in the world.

When it got too boggy to ride out to kill, we shot a goat from the herd that from long habit still gathered each night on the old station road.

A rival team of feral donkeys, dozens of them, would materialise silently out of the bush just on sundown, and gather opposite the goats. They were the descendants of the old donkey teams that had once hauled heavily loaded wagons. They stood quite still when we passed, their long furry ears twitching at every sound as they stared brazenly back at us with their big shiny, knowing eyes.

Johnny Ah One decided against leaving for Borroloola in the monsoon rains. One morning after a night of torrential rain, Ken went down to see how Johnny had fared through the downpour.

Sleepless in pitch darkness, with light only from the many matches he'd struck, Johnny had spent most of the night dispatching big centipedes of the yellow and black kind, which were intent on sharing his swag. He had gathered about thirty of them and lined them up trophy fashion. His vigilance had paid off: he'd made it through without having to endure a poisonous bite.

It was necessary to send mail away, and we decided a few supplies wouldn't go amiss, so Ken, Johnny and I prepared to ride the 70 kilometres into Borroloola. I was given the best horse—a big grey, a good goer, with lots of heart. Though unnamed, he was valued in the stock camp for his stamina, as he wasn't one to adopt that reluctant, martyred air when a little extra was asked of him.

The rain had let up for a bit, but it was fiercely hot, with the temperature hovering around the 50-degree mark. The humid air seemed too heavy to breathe. There was bog everywhere, the road just parallel tracks of yellow muddy water; added to this, clouds of flies kept settling on our sweating bodies and in our eyes.

We made our way around the worst bog, the horses placing each foot gingerly in front of the other—one could have sunk to its belly. Then we followed along the Abner Range, taking high ground over ridges and hills where possible.

In the late afternoon we rode into Borroloola, my horse still gamely striding out. Heavy with sweat, his hide had changed from light grey to dark gun-metal, his tail swishing and skin quivering to discourage settling flies. The bush belief is that grey horses have a peculiar and very bad smell when they sweat. Perhaps they do, but on that day the great old horse could have smelled just as bad as possible—I was just happy to have him there in those conditions. My shirt was like a second skin; it could have just come out of a washtub. My hair was plastered to my head.

We unsaddled at the welfare house, with Ted and Nettie as pleased with our unexpected company at that time of year as we were to see them. Of course a bath was offered: outback Territory of the past must surely have been the only place in the world where it was customary to offer visitors a bath or shower along with afternoon tea.

It took a painful session under Nettie's shower for me to separate myself from my trousers. The sweat pouring down my spine had set up a raw, oozing chafing, and the seat of my pants had set stiff and hard as plaster against my skin.

We spent an enjoyable day with Nettie and Ted. Although it was tempting to stay longer, rain was pending and conditions could only get worse on the road.

Early next morning Johnny came up from the Aboriginal camp, then we collected our mail and rode on back to our lonely little home on the banks of the McArthur. Seventy kilometres through heat and bog can seem endless.

Heavy monsoonal rain always brings to mind my father juggling eggs in the kitchen at Newcastle Waters, pretending they were his rain stones and claiming success for the torrential downpour pounding on the iron roof. These antics always had the kitchen girls falling about with gales of laughter.

~

Cresswell Downs gave us a truck for station use—a huge Dodge of advanced age and decrepitude. It would chug along in forward gear well enough, but a screwdriver was needed to remove the gearbox cover and rearrange the gears if you wanted to reverse, and then to travel forward again.

Ken, Johnny Ah One and I took delivery of a full load of 200-litre drums of petrol and numerous 45-kilogram bags of coarse salt at Cresswell, and then left to return to McArthur. Travel was slow, the weather hot with the steamy feel of impending rain. The old truck protested its load with every rise in the road, and we protested whenever the gearbox rearrangement was called for.

In the late afternoon, just as the first fat drops of rain splattered onto the dusty road, we drove down into the dry creek bed of Top Crossing. The steep opposite bank proved too much to ask of the heavily loaded vehicle, while the rain settled into a steady downpour. Under our repeated efforts to climb it, the bank became slippery as a slide and the radiator, attached to the cab with stays, slid backward onto the fan blade, which chopped out a great chunk.

A steady rivulet of water began snaking down the creek bed, under the truck and over our feet. If the rain continued, the creek would rise fast. The only way out, if we weren't to lose everything, was to unload as quickly as possible, which was easier said than done.

The drums of fuel came off first and we had to roll them up the steep, slippery bank. Next was the salt, soaked through and tremendously heavy, which had to be manhandled off the truck and stacked high on the bank.

While the two men battled with the load, I struggled back and forth: with hands and toes dug deep into mud, I clawed up the bank and slithered back down, carrying rocks to form a paving to give the truck traction on its way up.

When the last of the load came off, we were sloshing about in the dark of the very early morning in deep, swiftly rising water—it was time to get out fast.

Johnny and I waited on the bank. With rushing water well up the old truck's sides, Ken coaxed it inch by inch over my stony paving. We held our breath as we watched the slow-turning wheels. Then the truck groaned with effort as it crawled up onto the road, just as day was breaking. Mud covered, soaking wet, hands and shoulders rubbed raw, we boiled the billy and had something to eat.

Next we faced the reloading of rain-soaked salt bags and mud-slippery fuel drums. We cut a couple of saplings to make a ramp for the drums, then the salt went on, and finally we were ready to move out. The crossing was swirling with muddy water. Another escape that was due to hard work rather than luck.

Driving past poor Jack Bailey's lonely, rain-soaked roadside grave, we felt more fortunate than him.

We travelled slowly, stopping frequently to fill the damaged radiator. As luck would have it, we found Fred Ellis, who owned

Tawallah Station, camped by the roadside. Fred's old truck, with its greenhide tray, was hardly in better condition than ours, but he always travelled with two big drums filled with every conceivable spare part. We used all the solder he could dig out to patch our radiator.

We were back at McArthur that night.

CHAPTER 44

# End of the Wet

Time drifted on in our isolated world, until one day there was a loud yackering from the Aboriginals' camp—'Motor car, motor car coming!'—and we knew the road was open, the wet was over.

Frank McMahon and Bill Taylor, the Anthony Lagoon policeman, made it through—the first of the few who travelled this road throughout the year. We sat around and talked with them till well into the night, catching up on the news of the past five months.

All the while Frank made heavy inroads into my cache of homemade beer, which packed quite a punch. The beer brought out Frank's generous side and, happily on the way to total inebriation, he decided airily that I should be on my own wage—£14 a week, no less.

Next morning as they were preparing to leave, there was no mention of the previous night's offer, so I hastened to remind Frank of my great worth to the running of the station. I received my wage even though it was £2 more than Ken was getting as manager.

~

With the wet over, mustering began in the surrounding harsh, unattractive country, where a wild ride through rough coral limestone took some courage.

At the beginning of the muster we decided to abandon our iron shed by the river to be closer to where we'd be working. We loaded our woodstove and kerosene refrigerator, and moved to a small two-room timber house on McArthur's southern boundary. Built on high wooden supports, it was located right on the bank of a limestone creek called Top Springs—not to be confused with Top Springs of the Armstrong River at the western end of the Murranji.

No one had lived in this house for years, and snakes of all kinds and sizes, centipedes and other creatures had proliferated undisturbed.

File snakes lived under water in the mud—big ropey creatures, they weren't poisonous. The Aboriginals felt for them with their feet, finding them good tucker; after one hard bite on the head from strong teeth, the snake was curled around with its tail placed in its mouth, and set to cook on the coals of a campfire.

Huge pythons sunned themselves on the rocks by the water, while the highly venomous king brown or mulga snake took to frequenting our makeshift kitchen under the house.

Ken's method of killing any snake, if necessary, was a grip on the tail, a swing around the head, then a sharp whip crack. Charlie Schultz of Humbert River Station was the only other person I knew who used this method. It took skill and agility, and a man must be good with a whip—Ken *was* skilled and could always draw an audience; he had a personal whip crack he called 'The Western Castrator': the whip tossed from one hand to the other, finishing with a sharp crack deep between the legs that was guaranteed to extract from every man watching an involuntary tightening of the lower abdominal muscles.

Protection of native snakes in the wild is all very well, but a 3-metre king brown—as thick as a man's arm, with the fierce glitter-eyed look peculiar to this deadliest of serpents—rearing up out of the onion box called for harsh, permanent measures. If bitten by a king brown in the bush, death was a certainty.

So while Ken was away in camp, which was most of the time, out would come my trusty .410 shotgun, a gift to keep snakes from under the bed and crows from the vegetable garden. Long gone were the days when a birthday gift was something along more feminine lines.

Then there was the black-headed python: a menacing-looking snake with its long, thick, striped body and jet-black head, although it wasn't venomous. The Aboriginal people believed very seriously that bad luck would befall anyone who harmed it, so it had free access to the best rocks by the creek to bask in the sun. I once saw a black-headed python killed, and the very next day the killer broke his leg in camp; no bush Aboriginal of that time would have put that down to chance.

Our lubras were afraid of snakes. There'd be fearful shouts of 'Schnake, schnake, me prighten for schnake!' from a safe distance, then they would excitedly offer conflicting suggestions as to how Missus should proceed with its extermination. When they were sure it was dead—quite sure, after much prodding with long sticks—it was carried off for all to admire. 'Look, look, Mighus bin killum schnake. Im proper cheeky pulla long schnake that un, Mighus'—which meant they believed I was unafraid of snakes, which was far from true.

I was a vigilant watcher for snakes and other dangerous wildlife, including centipedes and spiders, which is probably why I'm still living the life of a vigilant watcher and haven't fallen prey.

I planted a big vegetable garden on the bank of the creek to supply us all with vegetables in the cooler months. From April to September was good gardening weather; after that nothing would flourish in the extreme dry heat, except the perennial sweet potato and a few hardy vines.

The creek bank was high above water; with no pump, serious thought had to be given to the problem of watering this ambitious project. The regular practice of two buckets on a yoke carried up by the Aboriginal workers each morning was hopelessly inadequate, barely enough for the kitchen.

Ken, ingenious as ever, constructed a shadoof—an age-old watering system used by the Ancient Egyptians, and a couple of thousand years later it worked just as well for us. The water was levered up by a bucket-like scoop attached to a long pole with a counterweight on the other end, and emptied into channels that ran between the raised beds. Our garden flourished.

⁓

It was that time of year again. The creek was drying back and the vegetable garden withering under the hot sun.

Christmas wasn't far off. We wanted to improve on the previous year's corned-beef dinner, so we made out a list and posted an order for fresh fruit and other appropriate Christmas fare to a grocer in Mount Isa. This was due to arrive with the mail plane at Borroloola. We drove to Borroloola in the old truck with the wonky gearbox and no doors on the cab—a slow, hot trip.

Early storms had made the country around Borroloola very wet and boggy. The 'six-mile' was a regular wet season hazard, but we had come to know the tricky detours along the hard ridges. Even when the country was a sea of rainwater, we could weave our way around the bad patches.

For some reason the mail plane was delayed, so we settled down beside the airstrip to wait. Storm clouds were building. Hours passed. We knew that if rain set in, the road would be a quagmire and another trip before Christmas would be out of the question, so we decided to wait another half-hour.

Just as we were about to leave empty-handed and disappointed, we heard the plane's faint engine and there it was, a silver speck against a backdrop of black storm clouds.

Hurriedly we loaded, leaving just as the rain began in earnest. We cleared the six-mile, then set off along a dirt road that was disappearing fast under water. We kept carefully on the road—a fraction either side and we would have sunk in deep mud. We ploughed on, the water washing into the open cab.

Then Ken made a violent swing to the left and off the road. Down we went, sinking quickly, until the truck's tray settled flat on the mud. In the fading light and looking across the floodwaters, Ken had realised at the last moment that the swirling whirlpool ahead was a deep creek crossing the submerged road. Without doubt we would have been swept away if he'd continued.

It was just on dark. We camped on the tray of the truck, surrounded by water, mud and mosquitoes. In the morning digging began.

Three days later, Ken's hard work paid off. With a track of saplings and bushes under the wheels, the truck crawled slowly, slowly out. By this time Ken had worn the seat out of two pairs of trousers, while the Christmas tucker had all been eaten, right down to the last apple and the final nut.

⌒

Soon after Christmas, Ken made a horseback trip to Cresswell Downs for some wet season supplies. Rain set in with a steady downpour.

On New Year's Eve I was woken in the night from a vivid dream of being attacked with red-hot pincers to find an outsized yellow and black centipede attached to my upper arm.

Next morning, with a mammoth throbbing arm and a raging headache, I consoled myself with the thought that there were probably a good many people around the country this New Year's Day with as bad a headache as mine, but happily for them for much more cheerful, festive and less painful reasons.

Ken arrived back in torrential rain. I heard the familiar clink of spurs, the pad of hooves and soft snort of horses I was always alert to. I acquired an unerring ear for this sound over the years; when men were overdue or stock boys hadn't shown up, this was the sound to await, and it could infiltrate my deepest sleep.

Ken had left Cresswell at 4 a.m. and arrived at 2 the following morning. Travelling alone, he'd ridden about 130 kilometres straight through, in continuous heavy rain, over deep bog and creeks all up, with two riding horses and two pack mules loaded with two 30-kilogram bags of sugar, four 20-kilogram bags of flour, swag and sundry items. Not a bad effort by anyone's reasoning.

Soon after his return from Cresswell, Ken took off alone through bush for Eastern Creek on the Limmen River to meet up with Aboriginal stock boys mustering our Limmen property.

Wet season work out bush was pretty near impossible by motor vehicle and damned hard work on horseback. Ken departed with two riding horses, two bull-catching dogs and his big pack mules, Quid and Barramundi. It was slow travelling, scorching heat, oppressive humidity and long stretches of deep bog.

It wasn't too long before the dogs were unable to keep going, so he strapped them on top of the loaded mules, which were soon down belly-deep. Toiling back and forth in thigh-deep mud, he unpacked the mules, cut long saplings to help lever them out, then moved on through swampy ti-tree flats and further problems.

This is one of the many memories that surface years later, when you're settled in a dry camp and look out onto the wet saturating the country into mud.

CHAPTER 45

# New Additions

At Top Springs we acquired our first real pet together, a brolga chick.

The brolga is of the crane family, with the crane's long supple neck and awkward legs, and has the most beautiful sliver-grey plumage. Known in the bush as 'the native companion', the brolga is as loyal a pet as any dog. He dances most elegantly at mating time, with his great wings outstretched and long neck bowed in a graceful pas de deux with his partner.

As a small child I had a brolga as a pet, who was a bit of a nuisance, in my father's tool shed. One day he swallowed a small shiny spanner, which had to be removed by working the obvious bulge back up along the length of his swan-like neck.

At McArthur River, our brolga chick was brought in by the Aboriginals and presented with some ceremony. I made no enquiries as to how they had acquired him—sometimes these things were best left unasked. He was instantly a devoted pet and had free run of the station, settling in as to the homestead-born.

We just called him Brolga. He would settle down beside me with contented chortlings and trills. If I moved away, he moved too, unfolding his long legs, laboriously and awkwardly rising, then following along in his stiff strutting gait. Lying in a swag, I would open my eyes to find his long beak inches away. Satisfied I was aware of him, he'd fluff his feathers and gently settle on my chest, quite content to be part of the gathered company, even if it was asleep.

He was an avid gardener's mate, bossily striding about while plucking out plants he thought best removed and neatly laying them down by their beds. The removal of a long bed of tomato seedlings, which he tidily placed in a line, was his undoing—he was banished from the garden.

When the lubras and I were gardening, he would glide over with his great wings spread—landing gear at the ready—and hover for a moment, just to tease, then plop down outside the fence and stride furiously up and down, head bent, clucking angrily to himself. He looked exactly like an irate schoolmaster striding about with his hands behind his back. The lubras would say, 'Him proper *coola* that un, him swearin' belong to we.'

Brolga particularly liked settling down in a water dish, such as the dogs' drinking bowl, in which he regularly washed his food, swishing it around and leaving bits to float about. He also liked to sit his big body in the basin that held soaking leather.

Every day he went with the lubras to the waterhole and fluffed his feathers in the shallows. On the walk back they draped their towels across his back and he strode along trilling happily to himself.

He was king of our animal realm—no dog dared defy him.

My first pregnancy was a period of prolonged misery. It was during the hottest time of year; temperatures were in the 40 degrees without a fan or even a cool breeze to enjoy. We had no generator, only carbide light, but we did have our kerosene-operated refrigerator, for which I was especially grateful.

Morning sickness became an all-day condition and so I was rarely vertical, my nose everlastingly buried in an old enamel basin; even today I recall the pattern on its chipped interior. Cresswell Downs was generous with station supplies and we had a well-stocked storeroom of canned goods, but there was little I could manage to eat.

Ken became quite desperate about my inability to keep food down. After some discussion and thought—reluctant, as food wasn't my favourite topic then—I told him that I could maybe eat an orange.

Ken left for Mount Isa to purchase a case of oranges, involving a round trip of some 2000 kilometres, most of it on dirt roads. It was one hell of a trek for oranges, but they got me through long, hot months of continuing illness.

I never did get to see a doctor. Around eight months into the pregnancy, I thought I'd better track south or Alice would be sharpening her bush knife for the big event—or, even worse, Ken's veterinary skills would be called upon.

At the height of a sweltering wet season, clutching strong paper bags and a water bottle, I boarded the mail plane at Mallapunyah airstrip and flew off in a haze of biliousness, little caring if the plane got there or not.

It didn't! Engine trouble forced us down at Borroloola, and I staggered off and sat in the shade of a tree at the edge of the airstrip.

After some time I was told, 'Sorry, no plane till tomorrow. You're staying overnight with the Festings.'

Tas and Pat Festing had taken over the Aboriginal Welfare post from Ted and Nettie Harvey, and they made me welcome for the night. In years to come, Pat became a very good friend. She had six children and never suffered a moment's indisposition in their production; in fact, she breezily told me that with the birth of her last baby, she'd walked back from the labour ward smoking a cigarette—now *that* was fortitude way beyond any effort I was able to muster.

Next day I headed down to the big city hospital in Brisbane. Ken arrived later, just prior to the baby's arrival. In those days a man wasn't permitted in the delivery room, his presence considered bothersome, so he remained at home or in a hospital waiting room.

I have never held with the penchant of women writers who give intimately detailed descriptions of their obstetrical ventures. I cannot think this makes riveting reading, however vividly presented. Suffice it to say, after 36 hours in a labour ward, I emerged with both a daughter and the enduring belief that when a medical person tells you 'birth is a perfectly natural procedure, nothing to it' they are wilfully lying and are absolutely not to be believed.

Our daughter Dominique arrived with everything in its right place, all in good working order, perfect in every way. Her father announced to all those interested—or otherwise—that he had a filly foal, and in true male fashion took full credit for the whole thing.

~

When the stock camp was in, the Aboriginal boys and lubras went bush for a day to bag a goanna or kangaroo and keep their hunting skills honed.

Our dog Murphy—the end product of many bloodlines, with bulldog predominating—was sometimes taken along to assist in the hunt. Murphy wasn't fast, but with prey well in hand he was a killer: almost anything within his great jaws was dispatched with a few shakes of his bulldog head.

One Sunday Big Tom returned home early, in high excitement, to tell me the tale of Murphy's unfortunate involvement with a big wallaroo. The dog had taken the scent and, master hunter that he was, headed off with as much speed as a bulldog can muster.

The wallaroo made straight for the waterhole and Murphy splashed in bravely after him. They met in midstream, where the old dog was promptly enfolded in the wallaroo's strong embrace and nonchalantly held under water. There was no question of the outcome without assistance. Killer of many kangaroos, the old fella had bitten into more than he had a hope of chewing.

Big Tom, seeing his main hunting offsider was going down fast, and no doubt mindful of the explaining he'd have to do to the dog's owner in the event of a lone return, leaped to the rescue and brought Murphy to the creek bank. Tom's explanation to me went thus: 'Poor bugger Murpie, he bin jus bout nearly pinish. I bin proper prighten for that old pulla dog, that big kunghru he bin jus nearly drownded im. I bin fetch im art, pump-im, pump-im, water bin come art long time.' Murphy had been saved to hunt another day.

With his crumpled old bulldog face drooping miserably, Murphy stood by, damp and dejected, listening to this unflattering dissertation of his hunting misjudgement.

In one of her sometimes misguided acts of generosity, my mother presented us with a borzoi—a Russian wolfhound—believing its reputation as a killer of wolves would make it a perfect bush dog. Nothing like the borzoi had ever been seen in that part of Australia.

The dog was narrower than a greyhound and she stood higher than my waist. We didn't give her a real name—she was just 'the Russian'. Aloof and elegant, she would have been more at home gracing the pages of *Vogue* magazine with an equally haughty fashion model than scruffing about in a stock camp. Nevertheless, her flowing, silky coat soon roughed up, and she became a regular bush dog, well able to hold her own in confrontation with the less noble canines.

On the opposite side of the world, the Russian's ancestors would have followed Cossack horsemen across the snowy steppes. This heritage prevailed, as she found it no effort to lope steadily along for miles behind Ken's horse.

It soon became apparent, however, that a Cossack's dog wouldn't have been required to swim in the icy waters of Russia. The Russian couldn't swim an inch, but in hot weather she splashed fearlessly into our deep waterhole to cool off—then came the slow sink, her hind legs going first, the rest gradually following until her long sharp nose and splashing paws were all that was visible.

With no sign of panic, she re-enacted her drowning on a regular basis; possibly she considered near-drowning the hazard of going for a cool swim. Luckily one of the lubras was always around to rescue this 'proper myall dog'.

Aboriginals passing through would ask our lubras about that 'different kine dog you got here', and she would be paraded in a possessive kind of way while her attributes were lauded. The finishing touch of, 'E can't swim, this kine dog, you know,' would bring forth exclamations of awe and disbelief. All the while the Russian stood by coolly with her usual superior attitude.

CHAPTER 46

# Heading Bush

After Les MacFarlane relinquished his share in the Limmen grazing licence and settled into working Moroak, his station out from Mataranka town, we became the sole proprietors of the Limmen River Pastoral Company and decided it was time to move out there.

We bought a Chevrolet Blitz truck from army disposals, stocked up on building materials and whatever else our limited resources would allow, and prepared to head out bush.

Those who heard just where we were going thought us quite mad, and Ken heard from all sides, 'You can't take a woman and baby out there,' but we were ready, packed and set to go.

After final preparations we left very early on a sweltering hot morning, just before the start of the wet season. We headed into

Limmen River country where we would make our home for the next 30 years.

Loaded beyond the hilt as usual, we drove slowly out of Borroloola and into dense bush—from there we had to clear our own road. Jackinabox was sent ahead on horseback to blaze trees, marking out a navigable track for us through country without so much as a horse pad to follow. He had no experience with motor vehicles, so he blazed his trees up stony hills littered with large rocks and down through impassable creeks, setting a track where only a horse could travel.

Ken had to ignore much of his marked track, set off on foot to find a suitable route through this tangle of virgin scrub, sometimes cut down trees to widen our road, then return and drive on. It was a snail's pace journey; the sun beat relentlessly down on the unlined metal cab of our cumbersome army relic. There were no doors on the cab, which wasn't such a bad thing, as it allowed us whatever breezes the slow progress created.

Dominique came to look forward to her frequent showers, from a billy-can of water poured over her head.

The big Blitz wheels laboured up over rocky outcrops, then lurched and crashed down the other side, often delivering a hard blow to the head on the cab's steel roof, or causing the steering wheel to whip around out of hand and deliver a jarring crack to the arm of the driver. We lost count of the number of times the wallaby-jack was unloaded to deal with yet another puncture of the huge tyres.

It took several days to negotiate the final 200 kilometres to Grasshopper Plain, a wide black-soil plain stretching out from the banks of the Limmen. It was bordered by rugged hills interspersed with permanent waterholes, fed from springs that bubbled up through sandstone on the plateau above then cascaded down to cool shaded pools. On Grasshopper you could swim beneath a waterfall and say to yourself, 'I am the first white woman ever to be in this place.'

The name Grasshopper is a bastardised version of an Aboriginal name long disappeared with the old bushmen, so Grasshopper it remained.

We unloaded by a creek and made camp, then set up Dominique's cot. This had been built to our own design: high enough for her to stand, wide enough for her to roam a little and fully enclosed with wire gauze, a safe haven from mosquitoes and all else that crawled or flew.

That first night camped by the creek, a violent storm saturated much of our stores and I gave an uneasy thought to the approaching wet season, but we had reached the end of our road and I was relieved we'd made it thus far without too many setbacks.

Our first need was permanent shelter. We cut ironwood posts, as no termite could put a mandible through them, and in our loading we had corrugated roofing iron. A floor of flattened ant-bed went down, then the kerosene refrigerator, woodstove and a bed of saplings laced with a greenhide base—but no clock or watch, as we worked on sundown and daylight. We hadn't thought to bring a calendar, so time and dates became muddled as the year progressed.

At night we still had no electricity, just carbide light: a cylinder containing lumps of carbide is fitted into a jug-like metal container, about 30 centimetres high, filled with water to create a gas, then lit from a burner on top.

It gave a good flame, but on occasion an ominous bubble erupted due to a gas build-up, and the cylinder could shoot skyward like a rocket. At first bubble I would rush outside, my nightgown flying, to deposit the whole contraption on the ground and await the explosion. Although I never did experience the rocket act, I'd heard so many frightening stories that it scared the wits out of me!

I had always read late into the night. To enjoy stress-free lighting, I gave up on the carbide lamp and took to lying on the floor close by the light from the burner of our kerosene refrigerator, which was not without some discomfort.

A nearby area of smooth flat stones seemed a likely place to settle our laundry; tubs and copper boiler were moved in, all set for wash day.

Sometime later, when our household was well settled, Tom Hume, an old part-Aboriginal man who knew this country well, revealed that our laundry stones covered the grave of a long-ago traveller, a white man whose bush journey had ended right there on the bank of the creek. How he'd died, no one remembered, but those travelling with him had done the best they could with his grave.

He lay there undisturbed through the years, until he became part of our household and shared wash days with Dinah. Endowed with an Aboriginal's fear of those departed, she would certainly have been wary of sharing space with a dead man, however long gone. We decided not to tell her and wash days rolled on without anything of a debil-debilish nature taking place.

I wondered sometimes about the white man who lay under the hard earth just a step outside my kitchen door. I had good feelings toward him and the fanciful idea he welcomed this family who'd come to relieve his loneliness. In his lifetime, our very existence in this place would have been impossible.

⁓

When our house was completed, Ken built a horse paddock with help from the stock boys. Much of the barbed wire came from old fences on Brunette Downs Station, exchanged for posts of cajuput, a broad-leafed ti-tree, cut on the Limmen and carried down on the Blitz.

Tools were still basic: the old cross-cut saw, crowbar, axes, adze, brace and bit, and that was about it. What Ken could have done with a chainsaw!

Forty head of our horses were paddocked at Cresswell Downs Station on the Barkly Tableland. Roy and two Borroloola boys, Jack William and Larry Boy, mustered them and walked them 300 kilometres back to Grasshopper.

This all meant that just before the monsoon set in, Ken had yards, paddocks and working horses—and out there stretched hundreds of kilometres of country with wild cleanskin cattle to be mustered and branded with our new brand LTK.

⁓

The Aboriginals had settled their camp beside a big billabong. All through the night, millions of frogs croaked so deafeningly the air seemed to vibrate with the monotonous sound. While the other workers prepared to leave for walkabout during the wet, Jackinabox and Dinah decided to stay.

They were used to sleeping on the ground as bush people had always done; now they had swags and a tent fly, but it can be an uncomfortable night in the rainy season even under canvas, so we gave them the good bed and mattress that we had brought in to replace our own greenhide bed.

Calling at their camp early one morning, Ken found the two of them camped on the ground in their swags, their four dogs comfortably settled on the bed with its fine mattress. They never did use it—old habits die hard!

~

When Dominique was born, I had serious misgivings about how I would cope with a baby out bush. In fact, the responsibility of caring for a baby in any situation daunted me.

Dr Benjamin Spock was the baby doctor of the day, and to mothers of that period his was the last word—and you listened, my dear. His book was on every nursery shelf, so I purchased one and bowed to his words of wisdom.

Dr Spock was very straightforward, his advice covered every imaginable crisis and—the best thing for me—his words usually came with a consoling air: everything is manageable, there's nothing that can't be cured, never worry. I loved him! I became so reliant on his advice—or was it his authoritative reassurance I sought?—that I turned the dog-eared pages of his little book for advice on every ill and treated every one accordingly.

At the end of that first year, when all the stock boys left with Ken in the Blitz for walkabout, I was left alone with eighteen-month-old Dominique. Before they'd gone, I'd cut my hand on barbed wire, so Ken was going to bring back some sulfa tablets, which were early days on the antibiotic scene.

While he was away, the infection became worse, with a red line running arm's length and a swelling in my armpit—all indications of serious poisoning.

I was very sick and turned the pages of dear old Dr Spock for his usual comforting advice. No comfort was forthcoming this time, however: all he had to say was, 'If this occurs, go see a doctor, even if you must travel all night.'

No way could I travel anywhere and there was no hospital nurse here to chattily ask me, 'Who is your next of kin, my dear?' Ken was possibly bogged in black soil a hundred kilometres out; Dominique was sitting imperturbable in her cot; my mother was abroad somewhere—perhaps in Europe, maybe Asia; my father could have been anywhere. Such were the conditions of an outback life of isolation.

I bathed and fed Dominique, and placed her in her cot with several bottles of water, for I knew Ken wouldn't be more than a day or two even if he had to walk.

I groggily fossicked about in storage boxes, found a nice skirt and blouse I hadn't seen in months, tidied my hair, applied lipstick, and lay down to await the outcome. No way was I going to be found untidily expired in unattractive clothes.

I lay in the dark silence of a bush night while fireflies darted excitedly about, flickering their little tail-lights. Without the Aboriginals there was no familiar sound of corroboree down by the creek, only the clicking of the gecko and the desolate cry of the curlew—a sound that does nothing to lift your spirits when you're alone at night.

If the lubras had been there, they would likely have run off; it was no place for a bush woman to be close by someone who might die. But they'd have taken Dominique for safe-keeping. Such thoughts raced through my mind all night; perhaps they were dreams that the white cockatoo dream-bird of Aboriginal myth carried on fluttering wings.

Next day Ken returned with the sulfa drugs, and after a time tried and true bush nursing worked its magic and tragedy was averted. Although this little tale was made light of—as is usual in the way of the bush—it was a serious situation to be in. I'm sure if Ken had been delayed further, there would be no story to tell—or no one to tell it, anyway.

Did you know King Solomon's horse was named Monsoon? Monsoon is an Arabic word meaning season.

The rains came early during our first year on the Limmen, and the blue-black soil turned to heavy gluey mud, a nightmare to traverse in any way at all. It sucked at bare feet and built up on boots in gluggy lumps that made it impossible to move any distance. No road out of Grasshopper was passable, so we just had to sit it out. Sitting out the wet was to become an annual exercise in our lives, as it was in the lives of all those in the far Outback of northern Australia.

Fresh, ordinary vegetables became a memory. We cooked pigweed, which could dissolve into a jelly-like mush if overdone—not the most delicious of plants. Later we made do with leaves of the sweet potato vine, or even the new shoots of pumpkin vines; neither would rate a mention in *Epicure* magazine.

Christmas came! It was too boggy to take a horse with pack-bags out to kill for fresh beef, so Ken, with rifle in hand and a bag over his shoulder, went barefoot through the mud, hoping to bag a plain's turkey for Christmas dinner.

Hours later he trudged back, layered with a heavy coating of grey mud, with a fine big turkey in his pack-bag, plucked clean, right down to the last pin feather.

I found this surprising because Ken always had a strong dislike of plucking a bird—any bird—so it fell to the lubras to prepare anything caught in the line of fowl. Still, I stuffed and cooked the bird without comment. It made a delectable and festive sight on our lunch table, surrounded by gum leaves and a few gumnuts I'd painted a brilliant red, as a substitute for holly berries, using the dregs of an old nail polish bottle.

It wasn't, perhaps, the best turkey we'd ever eaten, but was well received in the present situation. Dominique munched happily along the length of an outsize drumstick. A wild bird was nothing to complain about when the alternative was dried corned beef that, in the heat and humidity, was infested with small beetles. It took quite some time soaking the dry beef in water to remove them, and to plump up the salted meat that had hung for a time outside in the beef-house.

At this time of year, brolgas frolicked about the wetlands in large numbers, dancing their dainty pas de deux and, with their long pliable necks stretched skyward, loudly serenading in their rackety, strident voices. Of all the bush birds, the brolga was my favourite.

After Christmas, when it was still too wet to ride out for beef, Ken said he might have to shoot a brolga.

'Shoot a brolga?' I said. '*Never!* Not a brolga.'

'Well, you had one for Christmas dinner!' he retorted, and right away I had a flashback of that cleanly plucked bird and Dominique munching a mammoth drumstick.

⁓

Stores had dwindled over the wet, cattle mustering was soon to start, and we needed to post an order for supplies pretty soon to catch the *Cora* before she set sail on her northern run.

While Jackinabox mustered the horses for a trip into town, I settled down with forms and price lists to make out an order that would see us through the mustering season. Only absolute essentials: flour, tea, sugar, hops, potatoes and onions, and horse shoes, nails, leather and the like. Coarse salt, an essential on a station then, was available from salt pans on the coast.

Add all this up—costs far too high! Well now, cut this out, we'll get it next year. Could I slip in a few kilos of dried fruit? Barley was listed at 10 cents a pound, so we could afford a sack of barley and cancel the rice. It would be curry with barley this year—all good tucker!

Must have tobacco—no Aboriginal stockman would work without his tobacco. I've seen a man ride miles in bush to retrieve a plug of tobacco he'd hidden, or smoke dried tea leaves, paw-paw leaves or other foliage you wouldn't imagine smokeable. White stockmen hungering for a smoke did the same.

Mail was wrapped in waterproof oiled silk, the forerunner of plastic wrap, and Jackinabox left for Borroloola, driving the packhorses ahead of him. It would take him six days to reach the town, perhaps longer if creeks were running high and he had to swim the horses. After a few days socialising with the local tribespeople, he would make tracks for the trip back home.

Rudyard Kipling wrote that, 'The God who Looks after Small Things had caused the visitor that day to receive two weeks' delayed mails in one.' Make that twelve weeks' delayed mail.

As mail arrivals could be weeks or even months apart, we'd eagerly await the mail day when we received letters from friends and family—and newspapers too, no matter that the events were weeks old. Catalogues from far-off city stores were received and every page was carefully perused.

About two weeks after Jack's departure, in the quiet of early evening, Dinah's piercing, high-pitched yackering heralded his return. It was an age-old bush wailing cry—that declaration of some happening or other—to everyone within hearing and to no one in particular, over and over. 'Packhorse com-m-m-ming! Packhorse im ere nah!' Dinah called as Jack rode up.

With the horses milling about, Ken went out to help him unpack.

# CHAPTER 47

# My Unique Household

The country was drying out: time to start mustering! The stockmen and other Aboriginals returned from Borroloola.

Ambrose and Marjorie came that year. Ambrose had leprosy so he hid out bush, well away from Dr John Hargrave's medical team, who came periodically to check for the disease. Marjorie was young and unreliable: as she pushed Dominique about in her stroller, she bounced over the roughest ground at a fast pace; both were downcast when made to stop. That stroller had a short life—it fell to bits soon after Marjorie's arrival.

Spider and Minnie also came that year, and were with us for years. Spider was very much a man of old bush ways. He had quite a reputation among local tribespeople as a skilled and fearless spear fighter, and was accorded a certain deference by younger men in camp.

In keeping with tribal custom of earlier times, Spider had hammered out his two front teeth, which he believed was a sure prevention against death by thirst—and so there wasn't the slightest possibility that such a terrible death could befall him, however dry the country he hunted. A good hunter and a good-natured man, he smiled his gap-toothed smile and went about life in an amiable way, although he wasn't so bright with matters that required serious thought and planning.

With an attentive audience, Spider would tell of old spear fights, becoming so engrossed that his eyes glittered with the excitement and danger of it all. His fingers gripped an imaginary spear, the tempo of his story would build and his listeners, feeling the rising tension, instinctively moved back. Then came that final mighty death-dealing cast of his spear and his audience could breathe out.

Well before Spider had come to live at Grasshopper, Ken had once witnessed him in a serious, tribe-arranged fight. He had stolen a young lubra who was already promised, but in that vague way in which the prize was enticingly withheld, while various suitors were assessed as to their worth and just how willing they were to part with any of it. Spider, not even a contender in this 'bride business', soon put an end to indecision and ran off with her himself.

Retribution was called for and a meeting place—or battle-ground—arranged. Spider arrived fully armed, with the stolen girl standing behind him, quite enjoying her moment in the limelight. At some distance stood the opposing spearmen. Tribal custom decreed the pattern of battle: the aggrieved men were to throw the first spear, against which only defensive action was permitted.

With a woomera, Spider skilfully fended off one spear after another, including a final attack with a big waddy directed at his head.

After the aggrieved completed their side of the battle, custom decreed it was Spider's turn. Out on a bare patch of ground, with no wind that might deflect the flight of a spear, Spider stood ready for battle—fearless, omnipotent.

'Who want him?' he demanded.

Silence. Was a woman worth risking a spear in the gut from a sure-thrower?

There were no takers, so Spider gathered up his weapons and made off with his prize, without payment to Elders either.

This was the ordained procedure to deal with this crime. If a spear had found its mark, that would have been tribal justice.

~

Minnie was Spider's wife, the prize from that battle long gone. She also lived close to old bush ways, and had a hole through the septum of her nose in the style of her tribespeople.

Over the years, the hole had enlarged from the weight of an ornament threaded there, although no bone or wooden peg adorned her nose by the time she came to us. In profile the light shone brightly and disconcertingly right through. This fascinated Dominique when she was very young, so Minnie would often unfold a tale of the hole's origins; depending on her mood, it was sometimes colourfully romantic, other times painfully frightening.

Dominique was always eager to present Minnie with chicken bones, wooden spoons, toothbrushes, odd pieces of jewellery— anything she felt could replace the original bone—but it remained unadorned, for Min felt her tribal days in the bush were past and she was now of the white man's world.

Minnie was good with the children, and all the dogs liked her, even the unsociable ones. When our basset hound joined the family pack, Minnie was dumbfounded: never had she seen such a canine.

'What you reckon, Min?' we asked.

She tentatively lifted a long drooping ear and carefully flapped it like a wing. 'He can have good listen, this un, proper long one earole.'

Minnie had once lived with a white man who'd named her Buttercup. She was happy to tell of him, and still seemed to harbour some good feeling for him, in spite of a terrible fight they'd had in which he'd swung the hobble chain that took out her eye.

Now she suffered often and painfully from Spider's first-aid treatments. Her judgement of distance was poor around horses, due to the loss of her eye.

On a trip with cattle, Minnie, Spider and Ken were the sole drovers when she was kicked right in the centre of her forehead by a shod horse. When Ken reached her, Spider was already astride her chest, two thumbs pressing her swollen head. 'Push im back brains,' he declared with conviction.

How Minnie survived Spider's violent nurturing belies belief, but she was a hardy bush-woman and always in good spirits. She especially enjoyed watering the garden, settling by each plant with a fire of a few twigs to keep her pipe alight, a ritual that could fill her entire day. Or Minnie would bustle off importantly to the vegetable garden, telling us, 'Me gotta go marry im up pumpkin now.'

Me and my pet brolga in 1932.

This is the old 'Leaping Lena' leaving the Pine Creek railway station in the 1930s.
I could quite possibly be on it.

Eileen G and me at the Darwin
Convent School, 1930s.

Darwin jetty in the late 1930s.

Here I am soon after arrival in Brisbane, following the outbreak of war, complete with sandshoes and koala.

Following the end of the war, my family headed to north Queensland.

Newcastle Waters pub in its heyday in the 1950s.

Me outside the pub in Newcastle Waters.

Ken riding at the Warwick
Rodeo in Queensland
in 1947.

Ken and me in Newcastle
Waters, 1951.

Jack Bailey's grave on the road from McArthur River. The road had to detour around the grave as he was buried in the centre of the road.

Our first bush house at Bauhinia Downs with Ken reclining out front, early 1960s.

Fanny with Kurt and Dominque all dressed up at the Borroloola races in 1967.

Ken escorting his daughter down the aisle for her marriage to Milton Jones of Coolabah Station, NT.

My family in 2012: from left, Kurt, Ken, Dominque and me.

She plucked off male flowers for this purpose and wandered through the dense vines, 'marrying' the male and female flowers.

I can certainly say that my household was unique, with a stockman who had pummelled out his two front teeth to ward off thirst and a housemaid with a hole through her nose.

─

With roads barely dry, Ken left in the Blitz to make what he hoped would be a quick trip to Cresswell Downs Station.

On his return journey, he purchased three goats and some hens from Mallapunyah Station, which would provide fresh milk and eggs. A real egg would be a welcome change from the army-style powdered stuff that tasted and smelled awful, and did nothing to inspire a cook to produce anything of merit.

During Ken's absence, several horses broke through the paddock fence and went bush, Dominique became quite sick with a fever, and my top lip tripled in size to resemble that of an African Ubangi woman. And, to top it all, the hand pump our house girls used with much effort to fill the water tank from the creek had fallen to bits.

Time came for Ken's return, but a few days later there was still no truck, so I sent Spider off, mounted on a mule. He found Ken some miles out, bogged deep in black soil, the goats tethered in shade nearby.

'How's everything at the station?' Ken asked.

'Good, all good,' Spider replied. Then, as an afterthought, he added, 'Dominique him got temperature 250 degrees.'

'That's high,' said Ken. 'Everything else all right?'

'*Uwai*, ebinthyn good!' Spider answered, before adding another snippet: 'Mob horse bin go bush.'

'Yes?' said Ken, with some uneasiness.

'Missus bin swell up big face.'

'What else?' asked Ken, with mounting alarm.

Spider thought awhile, desperate to find something equally catastrophic to report. Then, with his big gap-toothed smile, he remembered the broken water pump.

CHAPTER 48

# The Good Old
# Bush Life

My mother was somewhere in other parts of the world—we
rarely saw her now. People who knew her and were aware
of our financial straits sometimes enquired if she assisted in that
regard. No, there was nothing forthcoming from her direction,
other than nice gifts from foreign parts.

Mother believed she had done her duty toward her child and
it was better for a person's character to make one's own way,
with one's own successes and failures. I must say I agree with
that philosophy. How else, later in life, could I have taken the
pride I did in my achievements and actually proven to myself of
what I was capable?

There was a time in the dim past I would never have believed I
could take on anything more arduous than lifting a cocktail glass

or spreading my beach towel on the sand. The very suggestion I would participate in some of the bush undertakings I did would have left me a chittering idiot. I can say, not without a certain cynicism, 'Ah, for the good old bush life, to make a real woman of you.'

I hadn't been back to Borroloola since the flying doctor, on his monthly visit, had given me news of my second pregnancy seven months earlier. During that time I hadn't seen a white person other than Ken. There had been longer stretches without company, but this one seemed longest.

The isolation on Grasshopper presented a much more hazardous situation if medical problems arose during labour than it had at Top Springs, and Ken was made nervous by the thought the road might be unpassable when I was due. As a result, he loaded the old Blitz with several big fuel drums filled with water to ease travel over the rough road, and we began a slow, careful trip into Borroloola.

The Festing family were no longer administering the Aboriginal Welfare settlement. We were invited to rig our tarpaulin and make camp at the little bush general store down by Rocky Creek, where Keith Braybrook had become storekeeper—the same one that Jack Bailey had set up a few years earlier.

Ken and I were giving some thought to what inroads into our practically non-existent bank account a trip south to hospital would make, without even contemplating the accompanying medical bills. Worse still, we had recently received a bill from the Income Tax Department for our work on McArthur River. The bill was for £700—a sizeable sum in those days. I did give a fleeting thought to the tribal midwives doing their stuff, but a sense of self-preservation prevailed.

Around this time, Jack Camp, who owned Robinson River Station, happened by town and asked Ken if he had any cattle for sale.

'Sure have! Two hundred head, immediate delivery,' said Ken, although actually he had no cattle at all in hand at that time of year.

When Jack said he'd buy the cattle, there was a big rush back to muster whatever cattle Ken could find.

Meanwhile, Dominique and I settled into camp beneath our tent, with folding stretcher, swags and mosquito nets. The heat was horrific under canvas, the storms created a humidity that left one perpetually dripping with sweat, and the Borroloola mosquitoes, renowned for their ferociousness, were in clouds from late afternoon.

Pregnant white women and little white girls were alien beings in the lives of the few white men there, but they rallied around, full of kindness and interest, visiting daily and bringing small bush gifts to amuse Dominique.

We took our meals in the store with Keith, where a perpetual stew simmered steadily throughout the day. Occasionally it was given a rolling boil and odd bits of things that came to hand were gaily cast into its bubbling interior. When the stew became too aged and the enclosing heat of the iron shed caused its fermenting barley to give forth ominous spitting sounds, a can of something was opened and we all fared very well.

It would have been ungrateful of me not to sit down to the house menu. I had no complaint with it, having been endowed with a cast-iron digestion by my early nursemaids.

⁓

Another white man came to join us in Borroloola. A full-bearded Lithuanian, his surname was Blumental, though to everyone he was 'Crocodile Harry'.

Crocodile Harry had fought in the German army during the Second World War and been badly wounded in action. Deep scars criss-crossed his chest and back, which he jokingly passed off as the results of crocodile maulings.

After emigrating to Australia, he'd settled in a country town, where on Anzac Days he enthusiastically marched in the parade, with good-natured tolerance from local returned servicemen who presumably thought that a soldier was a soldier, and had endured equal horrors whatever army he fought for.

Harry took up crocodile hunting, a profitable business then. He sailed his small boat up the McArthur River and into Borroloola with his Alsatian dog, Splititz, dropping anchor in the wide, deep waters.

Jack Mulholland, Roger Jose, Keith Braybrook and Harry would come to chat with me in the evenings and we formed a little clique. Harry brought Splititz to play with Dominique, and it was amusing to see these hard old bushmen settled quietly in a circle watching a little blonde child and a dog playing together with such attention.

We celebrated Christmas together. The stew was tossed out to be renewed after the festivities, some cans from the store shelves were opened and we enjoyed a good dinner. Late at night, Harry and Splititz swam home to their boat, in waters teeming with crocodile.

⁓

Meanwhile, Ken was on his way with the cattle for Jack Camp, and was camped out not far from Borroloola. Roy and Larry Boy had crept off in the night, with the temptation of corroborees, lubras and company too much to resist, giving little thought to Ken and Jackinabox being left to battle on alone.

Jackinabox was always a staunch old friend to Ken—he would never leave anyone stranded—and, of course, where Jack was, there was always Dinah. Those three had kept going without much sleep, without much tucker and, as Ken said, with 'bugger all much of anything at all'.

Over a waterhole nearby their camp, in daylight flying foxes hung in clustered thousands on trailing branches, their over-powering stench hanging in the air. Crocodiles cruised hopefully beneath them; woe betide the bat who fell, or swooped for water and wasn't quick enough about it. It wasn't an enviable roost to be bottom fox.

On Christmas Day, without awareness it was a festive occasion, Dinah's hunting had produced a nice bag of five flying foxes, which she'd killed with a long firestick. Placed intact on hot coals, fur and wings peeled back, they were good tucker that Ken gratefully accepted as Dinah's contribution to their Christmas dinner—although the little fox heads were still attached, their sharp teeth showing under curled-back lips, catching the eye with every bite and quite dampening Ken's enjoyment.

Soon after Christmas, Mull drove me out to Ken's camp in his open Jeep and I bounced around like a very round ball as we swept up at high speed. It was very different to the care Ken had taken with water-filled drums and slow, steady driving in the old truck!

Cattle were delivered to Jack Camp and paid for. Then, with Dominique, I flew out to Brisbane. Ken joined us later in Brisbane for our son's birth.

CHAPTER 49

# A Bush Child
# Comes Home

Our son began his journey into this world on my birthday, 5 March 1963, and made his grand entrance at 1 a.m. on 7 March—another monsoon-time baby. We gave much thought to his name. It had to be short and easy for Aboriginals to pronounce and we decided on Kurt.

Soon after his birth, our family returned to Borroloola by plane. The Aboriginal Welfare officer braved our terrible track and drove us out to Grasshopper in his four-wheel drive.

It was scorching hot and very dry for March that year, and there was no air-conditioning in bush motors then. We stopped at every receding gilgai and waterhole along the road, where Ken would lie his tiny three-week-old infant son along his forearm, little arms and legs dangling, before pouring water from his head on down to keep Kurt cool throughout the long, hot journey.

That was Kurt's christening in the billabongs of old Territory bush where the course of his destiny was firmly established.

~

After we arrived home with Kurt, I dusted off Dr Spock, smoothing out dog-eared pages that had dealt with past emergencies, all ready for new developments—none too disquieting, I fervently hoped.

The lubras settled on Ket-Boy as a nickname for Kurt and later prefixed everything of his with this name. He was given a pony named Stan, which immediately became Ket-Stan, and so on.

Ken had intended to head back to Borroloola in the Blitz to get a load of fuel and stores, but heavy rains arrived after just one day back. The country was awash and it was too late for a road trip by motor vehicle.

Despite the dryness of March, a bumper wet was recorded that year, and I settled into our bush home with a new baby and a three-year-old to see it through; one hoped all would be without problems.

Ken and an old bush blackfella mate, Don, had to ride and swim their horses through miles of floodwater to Tanumbirini Station, hoping Hurtle Lewis might have a better-stocked storeroom. But Hurtle's cupboards were bare, so they turned back. The return trip took them five days in pouring rain, their swags soaking wet.

To cross the flooded creeks they had to tie everything into a bundle: a tarpaulin laid flat, their pack saddles placed upon it upside down, pack-bags and swags too, the sides drawn up and tied at the top with rope or swag straps—exactly like a huge plum pudding. They swam beside it, guided it across creeks, then returned to swim the horses across.

When Ken reached home, Dinah was contentedly fishing on the homestead side of the creek, in spite of everything being rain-soaked. Ken dived in, swam under water and sprung out with a shout in front of her fishing line. Into the air went the line, with a terrifying scream from Dinah, who believed that every debil-debil of Aboriginal lore had come to carry her off.

Ken was not to be easily forgiven—for days after, whenever they passed each other she mumbled sulkily to herself.

⁓

Devilish deeds were very much part of old Territory life. Sometimes funny, sometimes cruel, oft times very cunning in their execution.

Johnson was an Aboriginal stockman in Ken's bush camp and one of his best men, but quite the Lothario, a devil with the lubras, especially those belonging to someone else.

One dark night in the mustering camp out on the Limmen, all hands and their wives were settled around the camp fire. In the still quiet night a horse was heard making its way down to water, its shape just visible in the shadowy starlight, hobbles clinked rhythmically with each step, then clearly came the sound of splashing as it pawed at the water's edge, and then there was another jingle of hobble chain.

Lydja, the young wife of an old man there, suddenly rose from her seat by the fire, picked up the billy-can and announced she was off to the river for water. Ai-yaai! This was another of Johnson's devilishly arranged trysts. Bent over with a blanket covering his head and along his back, hobbles in hand clinking convincingly with each horsey step.

Johnson's unique disguise brought reward of an amorous nature. A romantic interlude that was a little hurried perhaps, but with a momentary pause now and then to tinkle his hobble chain, brought quiet positive result, and proved well worth the effort for this old philanderer. A disguise never unmasked.

The myall little piccaninnies could be little devils too, often up to some mischief. Those who had spent time at the mission station with their parents were well versed in the hymns of the Anglican faith and would gather down by the rubbish bins to lustily sing their own versions of popular songs of praise, with little understanding of their content.

We grew tired of 'Onward Chris Us Sojers', so Ken taught them something new, and they took this up with renewed enthusiasm, the quiet bush echoing to:

*I don't care if it rains or freezes*
*I am safe in the arms of Jesus*
*I am Jesus little lamb,*
*Yes! By Jesus Christ I am.*

# CHAPTER 50

# Alone Under the Milky Way

Were you ever out in the great alone under the Milky Way? Alone is different to loneliness. Loneliness can pervade a life filled with people. Not until you have lived far out in the bush, expecting the return of horsemen in days' time—in fantasy you imagine no return, and you will be there alone on the earth forever—can you know real solitude.

For too long I didn't seen a white-skinned adult other than Ken, and he was away bush a good deal. I had no radio and no contact with anyone beyond our bush world.

Wander down to the creek in the bush stillness of midday, where drooping branches of paperbark trees hang motionless in the heat. Then a short, swift breeze will excite the leaves to a frantic whispering that wearily sighs away. It's so quiet here you can hear the silence, and would whisper if you spoke.

At night, darkness descends, slowly covering everything familiar. Surroundings change and imaginings become decidedly unreal.

High above, too high to be heard, flies an aeroplane bound for foreign places over the sea, its wing lights flashing on and off. Imagine real people within those flickering lights, seated in warm comfort and companionship—before the plane disappears into the night.

Alone is not good for too long. I could handle solitude better than most, I think, but I have seen women crushed and defeated by the isolation of bush life, and it can create strange behaviour in men. Tommy Ryan comes to mind. His was a busy teamster's life, out of Borroloola. Then, one day, he turned his team loose and settled in a small hut at a place called Tawallah, way off the beaten track.

With a small herd of goats to give meat and milk, he settled into a solitary bush life. He rode occasionally into Borroloola until the last of his horses died of walkabout disease, his goats eaten by dingoes. He was always alone, never ventured to where a traveller might pass. One becomes more introverted as periods of isolation lengthen. Thus are true hermits born.

Far out on Grasshopper Plain one day, deep within a smoky curtain of shimmering heat haze that rose upwards in waves, two smudges wavered into form, dissolved and floated together again, like figures deep under water. Two people on foot were advancing slowly from the direction of the river.

Our boys and lubras watched and speculated with the trepidation they always had for the unknown, human or otherwise. Ready to run, prepared to hide, they whispered, watched and wondered, 'Who that un, who im?'

The figures were a married Aboriginal couple, Fanny and Brown, who'd come from Rose River Mission Station on the coast—quite a journey on foot. Fanny was Roy's aunt, and one of the relatives who had left the boy with Ken all those years before. The mood became jubilant with much excitement at new people, news to hear and questions to be asked about relatives at the mission.

Next morning Fanny came to the kitchen door, her great mop of wiry hair and smoky dark skin glistening with the liberal application of dugong oil. 'Me Fanny, Missus Ken.' We were friends from that moment, and she stayed on—as the fairytale ending goes—for ever after.

Fanny was a truly remarkable person. Aged around thirtysomething, she was thin, wiry, strong as a man, and could ride and work cattle. She was quite fearless—brave as a lion, really. Her mane of hair grew straight outwards like a halo of teased wool.

Fanny's husband, Brown, was very much older than her, and she fetched and carried for him, saw to his comfort and food. Brown wasn't too fond of work and was not a brave man. He had no need to be brave, for Fanny was there to face all dangers for him.

With Fanny's arrival, much of my concern regarding the children eased. She had no children of her own and took delight in fishing with Dominique and Kurt, and taking them to collect lily roots, crocodile eggs, konkerberries and bush plums. She told them stories of animals, real and magical; of debil-debils and bush blackfellas—all much more comforting, instructive and exciting to a child of the bush than stories of unfamiliar fairies, elves and such.

Fanny walked beside Dominique's pony and ran fast as a wallaby to head it off whenever it bolted. She carried Kurt everywhere on her hip. If a snake or danger presented, her voice calling 'Dominie, Ket-Boy!' to draw them close could pierce eardrums of leather.

She spoiled Kurt. When he gave vent to a tantrum, she would stride fully clothed into the nearby waterhole with him perched on her hip—as effective a way as any to restore good spirits in a fractious child.

CHAPTER 51

# Twenty-Chebbin Dog Johnny

An Aboriginal family of four emerged out of haze on the plain one day, obviously having lived off the land and walked on foot for some time. The leader of this little group was a tall, thin man walking ahead of the rest and carrying only his spears. He came forward very purposefully and with a somewhat imperious manner for a bushman who'd been living lean for some time.

His name, he said, was Johnny. 'You know that un gotta dog.' And gotta dog he certainly did: around him milled a veritable flock of dogs, in all colours, sizes and sexes, all skinny and in varying states of health.

We knew who Johnny was because Ken had actually brought him into the country years before from Mainoru Station, but had lost track of him. He was known as Twenty-Chebbin Dog

Johnny—although whether this was a true summation of his dog numbers, I never did discover; it was close enough. Johnny was well known among coastal tribes: he was unpopular and somewhat feared.

In his wake trailed his small family. At a respectful distance came his brother Sam, a spectacularly unfortunate person who flapped along on feet encumbered with fully webbed toes. Far from bright, Sam's main function in life was to follow his leader in a subservient manner, carrying Johnny's didgeridoo on his shoulder.

Bringing up the rear were Johnny's two wives, saddled with all their belongings. His older wife, Ebly, carried her baby. Mary, who was little more than a child, had a sullen expression, to which she was quite entitled and some sympathy as well, given the treatment she received from the others.

They asked for work—though probably the tobacco and abundant supply of beef on a station after a long period of bush goannas was more of an attraction.

Johnny's orders to poor old Ebly and to Mary came with a sharp word, a gesture toward the billy-can when required, or an impatient wave of dismissal. He was domineering and demanding, rather like that outsize cockatoo of old bush lore. This mythical parrot was a mighty creature: 7 feet tall, no less. He would fix his beady eye on his keeper, lean way down from his perch, and demand in a menacing parrot voice: 'Polly wants a biscuit, right fucking now!'

Johnny too was to be obeyed without question—and right now. And he was not a man to transgress for any reason. Poor Mary once undertook the risky business of making off with a little of Johnny's tobacco. When this daring theft was discovered, she took refuge high in a tree where Johnny, expert spearman that he was, impaled her leg to a branch.

We gave Mary work in the Aboriginal kitchen, while Ebly remained in camp with her baby, Johnny did general station work and Sam was assigned the simplest tasks possible, such as delivering wood—already cut by others—in the wheelbarrow to the kitchen. Invariably he wouldn't show up, and if one had the audacity to suggest he do his work, he sulked and was to be found in his swag, blankets over his head, out in the hottest midday sun.

Johnny was the didgeridoo puller—he who makes the didgeridoo sing is a puller, not a blower—and Sam was the carrier. It was Sam's duty to prepare the instrument for concert, so to speak, and he'd liberally pour water through it to improve its tone before each performance.

When Johnny made corroboree, Sam had to sit forward of him and take the weight of the didgeridoo's great length on his shoulder. It was an unusually long instrument, wider at the end than most, rather like a long trumpet; the usual method with a shorter instrument is for the puller to spread his big toe and balance the weight of the didgeridoo between this toe and the others.

When Sam was asked why he hadn't shown up for work, his excuses were vague and unimaginative: 'Too much corroboree,' or, 'Didgeridoo too heavy, shoulder bin bugger up. No bin schleep (sleep) long time.'

Perhaps a sleepless night might be true. Sitting all night by the fire to avoid falling afoul of the terrifying Aboriginal goombidigdig women may well have tired him. Though desirable, these women were unkempt and horrifying, with long, sharp fingernails and hair falling to the ground. Compelled by insatiable sexual appetites, they roamed the night to capture a sleeping man, for what purpose Sam was only too aware.

They were to be avoided at all costs, for they were death to the unwary. This was possibly not such a bad way to go, in the opinion of some men, but such an end was far too frightening for poor Sam to imagine.

⌒

During Johnny's absence from the station while out working with the men, his dogs grew out of control, devouring everything in sight, stealing food, fighting, fornicating and multiplying. They were a threat to stock and to those in camp—Fanny had been bitten quite badly by one of them—and it became clear that this mangy, diseased flock needed at least to be culled.

Around that time we heard about lubras on a station near Borroloola who'd gone fishing, leaving a baby boy alone in camp. On their return, they found a hungry camp dog had chewed away the boy's scrotum. With this story still fresh in my mind and with the men away, I decided to shoot the lot.

I began determinedly, but some way through I gave the rifle to Brown to continue the cull. The very thought of shooting even one of Johnny's dogs generated a palpable terror in Brown. Only after I'd assured him several times that he was to tell Johnny the Missus had shot them, would he carry on.

They were all shot, every last one, which improved the hygiene of the camp. And without the dog fights and their loud howling throughout the night, peace came too.

Some days later, when the stock camp returned, Brown lost no time informing on me to Johnny. Late that night, when all was quiet and the house in darkness, I heard a sound outside by the kitchen door. In the pale shadows of moonlight, I saw a figure, just a shadowy outline, and heard the special clack of spears, old language of menace from a spearman and meant to threaten.

A pistol was always by the door, which I picked up on my way out. 'Who there?' I asked.

'Johnny.'

'What you want, Johnny?' I asked, although I had a pretty fair idea.

'You bin kill my dog.' This a statement.

'*Uwai*, too much dog, they must go,' I replied.

He clacked his spears again and shuffled his feet nervously in the dust. He was alone without his family, so he had serious intent. He came closer, raised his arm, moved his spear closer to my chest. He was taller than me, naked, and very black beside me in my white nightgown. Suddenly he gave forth a furious tirade in his language.

I knew Johnny was a volatile, impulsive person, and raised my shiny silver Colt .45 with its 15-centimetre barrel, six bullets nestled within. As I put firm pressure on the trigger, my uppermost thought was that if he thrust his spear, I would involuntarily pull the trigger—so if I went down, he would too.

In the shadowy light we stood close together, his pungent bush smell hanging heavy between us as we stared at each other.

'You're not the first man I've shot,' I lied, holding my heavy pistol with both hands, finding it hard to keep it steady. I was doing my best to give weight to my threats, in spite of the tight ache of fear in my throat, and my less-than-fearsome appearance in fluffy slippers and frilly nightgown.

Then, abruptly, he dropped his arm and strode off into the night.

After he'd disappeared I sat in the dark, desperately quiet, with my pistol. The house had no lock, no lights that didn't take a while to put on; the night was still, with only an occasional heart-stopping rustle when the breeze fluttered the canvas curtains on the gauze windows. And so the night passed.

In the morning Johnny and his family were gone. Ken was fencing some kilometres out and saw Johnny circling in the distance. He had an idea the man was up to no good, and sent word that if Johnny wasn't gone by evening, he would come out after him. But we never saw him again.

Many months later, just before sundown, the lubras came to tell me there was a stranger to see me.

'Who stranger? Blackfella?' I asked.

'*Uwai*, blackfella.'

He came forward and said, 'I go long mitchen [mission] see my lation [relations]. One rain time [one year] then nudja rain come, I never see my mother longest time now.' He was on walkabout to the coast.

'What you want?' I asked.

'I bring you present, Mighus Ken,' he replied and unfolded a dirty cloth to reveal two beautifully carved pipes, the bowls perfect buffalo heads with carefully crafted horns and a hole in top for tobacco.

'Who bin give me this present?' I asked.

'I bin carry im ghish un longest way for you. Twenty-Chebbin Dog Johnny, he bin talk, gibit ghish un long Mighus Ken, gibet long him pinger [into her hand] Johnny bin make him himself.'

I still have them.

# CHAPTER 52

# Along the
# Old Coast Track

The Northern Territory government, in collaboration with the Lands Department, had decided to open the vacant miles of northern country to pastoral lease, incorporating the existing grazing licences with new boundaries and conditions.

Early in 1960, Brian Egan of the Northern Lands Branch had come down from Darwin to work on this project, mapping and drawing up the new blocks. Brian and Ken were old friends from way back to their Gatton College days.

As Ken had worked the Limmen grazing licence for some years, the court granted our lease and we returned to a station with entirely different borders. Where we had roamed virtually free of boundary restrictions, we now had neighbours and mustering was restricted—even though we were many kilometres apart—to within our own borders. As they say, good fences make good neighbours.

Our station at Bauhinia Downs was about 4000 square kilo-metres in area. It was 50 kilometres wide from east to west, and 80 kilometres north to south, with the Limmen River flowing diagonally across it.

Over the northern boundary lay the newly formed Nathan River Station, within the Valley of Springs. On our western boundary was Tanumbirini Station, where Hurtle Lewis lived his solitary life in a little iron house perched on a stony hill. Tawallah and Balanbirini (later renamed Balbirini) stations bordered Bauhinia to the east and south. Both were created from country resumed from the wandering miles of the huge McArthur River run, where Ken and I had made our home a few years earlier.

Our station at Bauhinia Downs shares its name with the bauhinia tree, whose tiny butterfly-shaped leaves flutter frantically with every gust of breeze, as if to launch themselves clean off their branches into flight. As to the 'Downs', there was no real downs country, as on the Barkly, only wide plains stretching out from the riverbanks.

At the beginning of the twentieth century, Alf Scrutton, already an old man, had settled a camp there, after years riding the wilds of Cape York with the Jardine expedition.

Ken knew this country well; he'd ridden over every one of Bauhinia's wide miles, knew every spring, every ancient art gallery, every bone-littered cave hidden for aeons past. Ken was an excellent bushman who could, as they say in the bush, 'track a duck through water'. Dan Sprig, the police officer at Roper

Bar, pronounced Ken the best bushman he ever knew. Old Don, a bush Aboriginal, said of him, 'Can't lose im that young pulla, im proper longa bush oright.'

~

Ken and I decided to move our household from Grasshopper Plain, although it was still within our boundary, and settle on the better homestead site of the old Bauhinia Downs. Of the little that had been built there, nothing remained except a few scattered, overgrown graves of men of the old bush that lay forgotten under the spinifex grass—no one to visit them with a prayer or a flower, no one to mourn them. Bauhinia was vacant land with a name and wild cattle, nothing more.

Ken and the boys set off with the first load to build a small temporary house. The old Blitz girded its ageing loins and made several trips through bush from Grasshopper to Bauhinia. One entire load consisted of huge drums planted with trees I had grown in anticipation of our final settlement, including my much-travelled tamarind tree. Some trees were well advanced by then, but overhanging limbs snapped the tops off the taller plants, so they arrived all pretty much the same height. They were to be the foundation of my new garden.

Time came to make our final trip from Grasshopper Plain. We had the usual big load with the addition of several lubras, four-year-old Dominique, nine-month-old Kurt, dogs and a brolga, who squawked piteously when he thought he was to be left behind, but refused to fly along and had to be lifted onto the truck, where he fluffed his feathers and settled quietly for the journey.

As we moved off, our little house on the plain looked small and forlorn with its vegetable garden of beans and sweet potatoes, and a wild growth of pumpkin vines. No water would come its way without rain, so the green lawn would shrivel and die. That little house could tell some stories of one woman's lonely life in the Territory's far Outback.

Our friend in his grave under the laundry floor could lie quiet again with no children's laughter nearby, no lubras shouting to horsemen, no more 'trousa' to be washed above him. We had come there clattering noisily out of silent bush and after a couple of years we just as noisily departed. Now he could settle down to another hundred years of peace and silence.

～

It was almost Christmas when we left Grasshopper Plain. Storm clouds were gathering out beyond the hills, and heat pressed down around us like a warm, damp sponge. With our high load crashing through low branches, we travelled on slowly.

When there were some miles still to go, the thrust bearing on the Blitz overheated and seized up. We knew we had to get through the bush road before it rained or we could expect to stay out there—with a long walk and possibly a swim ahead if the creek came up—so Ken kept the old Blitz ploughing on.

We and the rain arrived at Bauhinia together. The debil-debils of bog and disaster had been foiled once again. In places far distant, people were preparing to celebrate Christmas.

Our new house stood on a hard stony ridge that looked impervious to holding moisture, but the continuous rain seeped silent and unseen down through the depths of the high escarpment. When walking upon its deceptively firm surface, one could sink to the knees with every step.

We woke one morning to find our beds had sunk into the earthen floor. Kurt's cot was a slippery slide and he lay curled asleep in a ball at the lower end. While busily preparing tea on a stove angled drunkenly in its alcove, Fanny was ankle-deep in the ground.

We weathered that first wet on Bauhinia as we had others.

With two good men—Jackinabox and Jimmy Gibb Johnson— Ken went out on horseback. In good time he threw 40 big, solid scrub bulls, tipped their horns and walked them 225 kilometres to Cresswell Downs Station, where he sold them for £8 per head, less than the price of a kilo of steak today. That grand sum kept us going for twelve months.

# CHAPTER 53

# Bauhinia Downs Station

'Along the Old Coast Track to Bauhinia Downs, where
vigilance was the price of continued existence.'

OBSERVATION OF W. MILLAR, WHO TRAVELLED THE OLD
COAST TRACK EARLY LAST CENTURY TO TAKE PART IN A
MUSTER AT BAUHINIA DOWNS

Thirteen kilometres along the valley from the Bauhinia homestead, the Limmen River tumbles over the high western range into one of the largest rock holes in the north, surrounded by towering sandstone cliffs that glow a searing red in the late afternoon light. Over all is a bush silence that can stir a sense of uneasiness in the lonely and superstitious.

Out beyond the tumult of the waterfall, the surface is as smooth as glass. Freshwater crocodiles mass there, their hooded eyes and the tips of their snouts visible over the wide dark water. When endeavouring to measure its depth, a line was run out at about 80 metres, but the bottom was never reached—just as the Aboriginals were certain it never would be; for them it had no bottom, no end. They called this place Manaparoo.

Billy Miller, an old bushman friend of my father's, knew this country, had mustered cattle there, and wrote of Manaparoo as the most sinister and lonely place he had ever been.

Travelling through with a young Aboriginal boy in 1890, he suffered a bout of malarial fever and was forced to camp, too ill to mount his horse. On the high escarpment above the water, armed tribesmen stood silhouetted against the evening sky, and the boy shook with fear and pleaded with Billy to ride on, although this was impossible. He then begged Billy to do without a fire, for it would alert the hovering tribesmen to their whereabouts, but the shivering and cold of Billy's fever put fear from his thoughts and a fire was lit beside his swag. Early next morning, they were mounted and away before daylight.

Billy wrote of Manaparoo:

It is a place that fills you with instinctive dread. Even now, if the name Manaparoo comes to mind, I shut my eyes and see it, and feel again the weird sensation down my spine, and the irresistible urge to look back as though something unseen and malign was following.

In the enclosure of high cliffs was deep shade, moist and chill even on hot days, and there was always an air of unnatural stillness. With the roar of the waterfall beyond, it could heighten imaginings as to what might linger there unseen, as indeed it did for the Aboriginals.

But for our family, Manaparoo was a favourite place to fish for barramundi; a place to take visitors to the station; a place our children knew and loved all their young lives. With the house lubras we came for picnics, lit a fire, cooked big catfish on the hot coals, collected sugarbag from hives among the rocks.

We swam in the deep water among the huge number of quiet fresh-water crocodiles, whose call could be imitated with a deep drumming sound in the throat; often an answering call would float back over the water. But never would the Aboriginals venture into those dark waters, nor peer down and see a face mirrored back, for that would tempt the evil within.

When our children were learning to swim, Ken would row them out into the central depths in a dinghy and off they would tumble to splash happily about. He might row off some distance, then call out loudly, 'What's that behind you?' Small arms and legs would thrash the water with lightning speed to reach the boat.

Fanny objected strongly to her charges being left to battle the dreadful magic of those spooky waters, and raged about at the water's edge. Dominique and Kurt both became excellent swimmers!

~

This is a country of thermal springs that stretch in a long line between Borroloola and the Roper River. Geologically speaking, they're pretty old and haven't always surfaced from the same orifices. Water travelling its underground passage breaks through in places where the crust is thin and a thermal pool is born.

Some springs cascade down through high rocks in waterfalls to create pools below. One of these pools—its Aboriginal name Erekini—was about 300 metres behind our homestead, and no resort swimming pool could compete with it.

Deep within a stony escarpment, water gushes up from a depth of about 1000 metres, so hot that a lubra's dog was scalded when it splashed in, and afterwards its hide peeled and fell in shreds. Crystal clear, pure as water can be, it rushes down a rocky gorge and falls tumultuously into a perfect circular rock pool, gnawed out of stone by thousands of years of pounding water. Fifty metres wide, 9 metres deep, the pool is encircled and shaded most of the day by high cliffs, pitted with bat caves and dripping ferns.

How many can boast of a thermal swimming pool with waterfall in their backyard? The very soft water was tested and found to contain some soda, no other minerals at all. The great depth from whence it came accounted for its heat. It flowed hundreds of thousands of litres an hour, all year round.

With such an abundance of water situated so high, no pump was necessary for our water supply. Instead we had a siphon hose that continuously carried water to our garden and tanks.

To the local Aboriginal people, Erekini was a waterhole of special significance, as Uluru and other ancient places are special, and they would not enter the water.

In 1912, when Dr J.A. Gilruth, administrator of the Northern Territory, made his epic overland trip in a chauffeur-driven motor car, he came down through Bauhinia. In his written report, he predicted Erekini would become a major health spa and tourist attraction in years to come. All those years later, it hadn't progressed further than our family swimming pool.

We kept Erekini as pristine as it had been for centuries, so I was distressed to learn that, presumably for the benefit of tourists, a plaque with the name 'Poppy's Pool' had been cemented into rock. I trust someone will care enough to remove it. When Gosse climbed Uluru, he did not cement his footprint and chisel his name there. Who is Poppy, anyway?

~

High above the valley on a quartzite plateau, almost directly above where our house and spring were, hot water oozes out onto an immensely wide, flat area of black peaty soil, fed from several orifices.

This soil is densely covered in rich, succulent green grass—and is most treacherous. One step onto this deceptively inviting lawn is a step into a hot morass; steaming water wells up in the indent of a footprint. I know of no one who has taken more than a step or two onto this emerald stretch.

The atmosphere is humid and oppressive on a still day, and there's no obvious rock on this oozing sponge of earth; no bubbling or flowing water visible. Huge paperbark trees grow on the periphery, in spite of water so hot a hand cannot be held there for more than a moment.

But the most peculiar feature of this strange sheet of water is that although situated close to the highest escarpment, it lies like a huge, steaming green blanket and doesn't overflow in any sort of waterfall to the valley below.

The old bush Aboriginal called this place Umbaloorama. After moving to Bauhinia, we cleared what was termed a 'jump up' road—a steep ascent from the valley through to the plateau above—to Umbaloorama. Past here a further 2600 kilometres of our country fanned out, which was called Broadmere.

In the late 1870s when Nat Buchanan brought cattle through the Old Coast Road to Glencoe, the Territory's first cattle station, his party made camp by a spring in the Limmen Valley. One afternoon all the men went out to collect stock, save for a young stockman, Travers, who remained to settle camp and prepare a damper for dinner.

Returning in the evening, the stockmen found him beheaded with his own axe, his sightless eyes staring up at them from the dish of damper dough. The Aboriginal raiders were gone with a good deal of their supplies. They buried Travers at the foot of a stony hill, although no sign of his grave remains today. The local Aboriginals called the spring where Travers was murdered Gorrialladotgowaloo—place of the flying-fox dreaming.

The stony hill where Travers was buried has another tale to tell. It looks like any other along the valley, not unduly high, but it rises immensely steep with a narrow horse pad ribboning up to its summit.

I once rode up this track with Ken, our horses slipping and scrabbling for a footing through a loose gravelly surface. Up, up we rode to reach the top where, unexpectedly, an amphitheatre opened before us. Well grassed, with a spring running water through its interior, it was a splendid place to hide a small mob of cattle—and a chap by the name of Skuthorpe once did just that, with a mob dodged from under the nose of Tanumbirini Station. He also erected a camp at the foot of this hill, where a patch of flat stone is all that remains today.

Few of life's ventures run true to plan. Skuthorpe and his ill-gotten cattle were found by a Borroloola policeman; a wandering tribesman may have told of it, or played out the story from start to finish in corroboree. Or perhaps George Conway, Skuthorpe's partner in this duffing crime before they fell out, talked too much. It was George who told Ken of it and directed him to the exact location of the hidden pasture. However it came about, this truly secret sylvan pocket was discovered. It still bears the name Skuthorpes Pound, but I doubt there is anyone who knows its whereabouts today.

Tom Hume, the half-caste son of a teamster, knew this country and the few who travelled it better than anyone. He told quite opposing accounts of local happenings than those recorded in official reports; his first-hand accounts sure beat dusty written reports any day. Tom told us that Skuthorpe lay buried near my garden fence—just another of those forgotten men who lie wrapped in blanket or swag-cover out under the dry grasses of the Territory.

~

George Conway was an old cattleman who, like Bullwaddy, Bathern and others of early Territory days, contributed enormously to opening up northern cattle country. He came over the Territory border in around 1902. He married a European woman and lived in wild country with his wife, who sickened and died suddenly. He told us bush lubras had poisoned her. He never remarried and ever after had a lubra as a companion.

Years on, his home was a bush camp where he lived with two lubras called Rooney and Florida. Such liaisons were illegal, co-habiting with Aboriginals was a definite no-no as far as the law was concerned, but there were few single men in the bush who did not turn to native women for companionship.

Rooney and Florida ruled the old man's life, dealt him terrible punishments when they saw fit, but generally took good care of him. His life had always been harsh and not short on danger, and George bore a galaxy of scars from old wounds. On his head were healed craters and white tracks, evidence of past encounters with humans, animals and nature.

George would take you on a tour of his anatomy, explaining in detail the origins of his battle scars, and the exciting dramas that accompanied each one. 'See this one,' he would say, 'nearly finished me that time, a gin [native woman] waddied me from behind, but Rooney stitched me up orright.'

Most years he mustered Elsey Station, and later had his camp rigged in bushland on Moroak Station. With his own Aboriginal stock camp he mustered cattle for Les MacFarlane.

George owned an old blue cattle bitch, of which he was very proud. Her pups were much sought after, and one day George wanted to show off her latest litter of new pups to interested visitors. The old bitch had settled her pups under George's camp bed, and had wandered off for a brief respite from the demands of her family, so the pups were quite alone.

With his audience standing by, George proudly threw back the blanket covering his bed, to reveal his prized pooches. But instead of six new pups under the bed was a mammoth boar pig which belonged to the station and was allowed to roam free. Huge and ugly, he lay there smiling and replete, having eaten all the pups.

George's fury was something to behold and the big pig, getting a clear message of his displeasure, jumped up and took off. George snatched up his pistol, his bandy legs in full flight, his shots flying wildly after the huge porker, which was running for its very life with George's bed balanced precariously on its back, mosquito net somehow still attached soaring out behind, like a sail in high wind.

George had another occasion on which to unsheathe his pistol in a hurry. Mustering in the bush, his horse bolted, took the bit in its teeth and was away. With no chance of halting its wild flight, and with his horse flying straight towards Lancewood scrub (terrible stuff Lancewood, treacherous to ride through its dense splintering growth), which loomed ever closer, he knew he wouldn't stand a chance in there. Out came his pistol and he shot his horse right between the ears. As it crashed to the ground George, only a little fella, flew through the air and skidded to a halt, wrapped around a slender Lancewood tree – another case of quick thinking, another scar to display.

George was once accused (whether true or not) of shooting an Aboriginal man and was taken into police custody. Ever loyal, Rooney's steadfast defence of his innocence prevailed and he was released.

Rooney was not to be dominated though and once, while hugely angry with George, she devised a unique punishment for the old man that ensured she was safely away from any immediate reprisal. After climbing the tree above his camp-bed, she balanced on a limb, and interrupted a nice nap George was enjoying below by copiously urinating upon him. He waved his arms about in terrible rage and made awful threats but she knew there was no way George could climb the tree in his feeble state. Rooney sat it out for a time until all was calm, then descended, and life continued in its usual benign way.

George greatly admired Ken, and told me once he thought him the finest young horseman he knew who put up the best rough ride out in bush he ever saw. High praise from an old bushman who had seen it all.

George lies today in the Elsey cemetery near the town of Mataranka in the Territory.

# CHAPTER 54

# Money is Like a Sixth Sense

'Money is like a sixth sense without which you cannot make a complete use of the other five.'

W. SOMERSET MAUGHAM

We had borrowed very little money, having lived thus far with a certain frugality and believing that doing so a bit longer would do us no harm. However, we did need breeders to build up our herd, and for this a bank loan was necessary. Our application meant that the pastoral inspector from the Development Bank was due for a visit, and of course we took steps to impress him as to our worthiness.

Visitors were rare beings at that time, given we were so far out at the end of a dead-end bush road, so the inspector's arrival caused quite a stir, with children and dogs all coming out to stare, and lubras hiding shyly and peering around corners with curiosity. He came to the door and was about to enter when he stopped, startled at the sight of our borzoi hound. The Russian was an unusual sight to be sure—lean as a greyhound, taller than a calf, and coolly aloof and unwelcoming.

'Your dog looks like a garfish on legs,' he said, then almost collapsed with amusement at his own wit.

Ken, never greatly enamoured of the Russian, who was under suspicion as a sneaky calf-killer, was nevertheless offended on her behalf. 'You're not so hot yourself,' he observed. This wasn't a good start to a meeting where the granting of a loan was as yet undecided, and it brought Ken my sternest frowning look.

Curiously, not only was the loan granted, but the pastoral inspector was also insistent that we take a loan of additional funds to build a larger homestead. We decided against this because it wasn't a pressing priority and could wait.

Soon after, the Russian was caught red-handed and had to go.

It was unfortunate that the old law exempting Territory cattle stations from paying income tax had been withdrawn just before we settled Bauhinia. It was also unfortunate that the 1000 breeders we'd signed, sealed and contracted to buy were sold to a higher bidder.

So instead we purchased a bulldozer and fencing materials. We also bought a 12-volt lighting plant and everyone gathered around to hear its first rackety sound. 'Might be good un ghish un,' said the lubras, and there were smiles all around. The lighting plant provided power for a few lights only and was the first engine, apart from the Blitz truck, ever to be heard on Bauhinia.

～

In the 1960s the market for bull meat was thriving, with ground beef for hamburgers much in demand in the United States. Early on at Bauhinia, our bush bulls were still thrown from horseback, then walked 30 kilometres to where they were loaded on trucks and sent off to the Katherine abattoirs.

On these trips to the loading yards, two old bulls took the lead. Alexander knew exactly where to guide his mob and strode out with real purpose, quite like that other Alexander (the Great) leading his army forth.

But on reaching the yards, there was no way Alexander was about to be loaded onto a truck; he turned around, put his head with its great sweeping horns down, and set off right back home. This went on for several years, until one day Ken announced, 'Well, old Alexander made it to Katherine. I saw his carcass hanging in the meat works.' Such heartlessness!

Alexander's mate was a great ragged old bull whom the stock boys called 'Tongue-go-round' for his incessant bellowing as he took the lead to the yards. He was somewhat more crafty than Alexander, for it took quite a time longer to cajole him into a truck and off to the same sad fate.

～

'Nine. S. M. W. Nine, Sierra, Mike, Whisky, calling Victor, India, Delta. Do you read me? Over.'

In my father's day, a message from the doctor, if considered urgent enough, could be tapped by Morse code over the telegraph line. 'Enough quinine and citrate of iron to cover a sixpenny piece' was prescribed for general bush illness. As few carried money in the bush, the amount was a guess.

With the arrival of outpost radio and antibiotics in 1963, the days of bush medicine and long treks over unpaved roads to see a doctor ended. Instead, stations were issued with large metal medicine chests, the contents of which were numbered and named, as in a pharmacy. The doctor had only to advise the patient, 'Take two Number 4s every two hours.'

A medical session took place each day on outpost radio between us and the doctor. As anyone could tune in, this could be a very public airing of your ailments for all to hear. So it was a busy and friendly medical session in those early days; after the doctor had departed the air, a voice might pop in to commiserate with the patient, or even suggest a bush remedy for what ailed him—for it had done the caller a world of good and was worth a try.

A man we all knew who lived on St Vidgeon Station, which was quite isolated then, was describing a serious problem he had with his feet to the radio doctor. Reception was poor, and he repeated loudly, 'Me feet Doc, it's me feet, they're real bad, might be infected.'

'Well old man,' the doctor replied, 'if your *teeth* are as bad as you say, I can't see any way but for you to come into town and have them removed.'

'Removed? Removed you say? I'll wait until I go south at Christmas time and see a doctor down there. Over and out!'

Generally, though, we were well pleased with our medical advice. It was a good service for bush folk, especially as an aircraft could be sent in an emergency. We'd come a long way from the days when a sick man had to be taken miles on horseback or by wagon and be lucky to survive the trip.

Our newly installed outpost radio also enabled us to send telegrams, so there was no more need for driving—or riding—240 kilometres into Borroloola and back to send one, with a day or two waiting for a reply.

Hot on the heels of our outpost radio came another outback service—with our souls coming in for attention this time.

While living in our first house on the property, we bathed in the creek not 100 metres from our door. Its water came down still warm from Erekini Spring, and with flat stones handily placed by nature on which to deposit our toiletries and towels, the tumbling creek made a fine bathroom.

Late one night with everyone away and Dominique asleep, I was returning to the house after my bath, quite naked, when the headlights of a car swept high as it turned the curve in the road to our house. Some way off, to the rear of the house, we had a small yard to house two milking goats, and the best way for me to avoid detection was to make a quick dash and crouch behind the goat yard, then wait for the lights to switch off and discover who the visitor was. It couldn't be Ken—this was no truck. I crouched, uncomfortably cold among the prickly spinifex, and alarming the goats, which took me for a dingo.

The car's lights were switched off and darkness descended, so I decided a quick return to the creek for a towel was my best option and made a run for it. The headlights suddenly blazed on, shining like giant searchlights with my naked self at centre stage. I had a moment's fluttery panic about what to do. A dash to the house—no, back to the creek—no, no, the house!

The visitor was Brother Paul of the Anglican Bush Brotherhood: a young unmarried Englishman who'd been educated at the prestigious Winchester School and was an ordained minister. This was Brother Paul's first visit to Bauhinia on his ministerial rounds of a large bush parish. Having heard of a family living way out, he was quite fearless to take on rarely travelled roads in order to bring the benefits of a church service.

He had not been long in Australia, so the poor young man must have had his ministerial sensibilities shocked to bedrock by a naked woman way out bush at night, cavorting wantonly in his path like a rabbit caught in headlights—a saucy rabbit, he must have thought.

Dressed, I regained some dignity and we proceeded as if nothing amiss had ever occurred—not a word from either of us. Next day, as he'd travelled so far, I felt the least I could do was to attend his service, which turned out to be a long Anglican mass for a congregation of two people—a totally bewildered four-year-old girl and one long detached from the divine influence of the church.

The good brother had a fine folding altar that his father had made for his son's bush work before he left England. He set it up with a certain determination, perhaps thinking prayer might help to stabilise this immodest bush person who wandered the night unclothed.

Throughout the service I intoned my responses with some smugness, for they'd been indelibly imprinted during years in our school chapel. I hoped to impress the good brother and perhaps repair my image a little.

I must say the Bush Brothers did fine work. They travelled endless miles over poor roads in the Outback, marrying, baptising, burying and just bringing comfort to people. We enjoyed their visits; they were mostly good company.

This was a long time ago, so surely Brother Paul has been rewarded with a bishopric for his good work; quite likely he is even an archbishop in a gentle church in England, for he must surely have earned his purple robes working to bring grace to the more unworthy of his bush flock.

It is an unfortunate thing God did not come to me. I invited him in on several occasions, but he thought better of it and travelled on by. However, I do ask my church-going friends to pray for me, for I know it pleases them and gives them a pious purpose. If one day I am taken with a divine awakening, it would be a great victory for them through their prayers.

⌒

In such isolated country the arrival of a traveller was always an event. Hospitality was a necessary part of bush life, to the traveller as well, and everyone gathered around to see and to hear. We would sit together late into the night, eager for news and company.

Like most cattle stations north of the Barkly Stock Route, Tanumbirini, on our western boundary, wasn't easy to reach by motor vehicle back then. The bitumen beef road that now runs from the Barkly Highway through to the Stuart Highway at Daly Waters was just a hopeful dream for northern cattlemen, so to reach Tanumbirini by road was a long haul.

You turned off the highway at Newcastle Waters, 65 kilometres on to Beetaloo Station, a further 180 kilometres to OT Station, and finally 68 bone-jolting kilometres following the old wagon road, cleared a long time back with an old horse-drawn fire plough (a triangular wooden or metal frame weighted with a 200-litre drum of water and camp gear). This was a painfully slow trip, as I know first-hand, and not one to take for a light-hearted Sunday drive.

There were still overgrown horse pads from the plateau above Bauhinia and each year Hurtle Lewis rode on down from his lonely little homestead on Tanumbirini to spend a night with us on his way through to Borroloola for his annual spree—or 'dronk up', as he called it.

As he unsaddled his horse and unpacked his old packhorse, Hurtle would greet the kids: 'Well! Here's old Hurtle the Turtle come to see you.'

Then he'd settle down for a long night catching up on the news of the past year while we had a good dinner. He always anticipated a delectable dessert, which for him was a special treat, and made any effort on my part worthwhile. I always prepared something he would find unusual. Once, a colourful parfait I placed before him was greeted with amazed delight, and to all he met along the track, he told of the 'puddin' in glasses' the Missus had made for him.

Hurtle, like all bushmen, loved to talk. In the isolation of his life there was little opportunity for conversation. Although he could neither read nor write, he was curious, and he had definite ideas of what was acceptable behaviour.

Reflecting on fatherhood, Hurtle looked with suspicion on hyphenated surnames. To him, there was an indecisiveness and an uncertainty there. 'What for, eh? They call themselves Campbell-Jones, Armstrong-Smith—y'know, they've got to decide just who is the father, which one it is, no good tossin' up between two, lettin' people think you're not sure. If they're not sure,' he advised, with confidential sympathy, 'they should settle on one. Who's to know, eh?'

His opinion: one father, one name; two names, anyone's guess. I once told him I knew an Englishman with three names linked in his surname.

'Well now! Someone's been busy there, eh?' he replied with a disapproving shake of his head and a quaint disregard for his own lifestyle of casual assignations along the bush bridle tracks.

CHAPTER 55

# A Veritable
# Noah's Ark

'In order to keep a true perspective of one's importance,
everyone should have a dog that will worship him, a cat
that will ignore him, and a horse that will tolerate him.'

DEREK BRUCE

O ver the years, pets have paw-tracked through our household in
a veritable Noah's Ark procession of poddy-calves, orphaned
foals, wallabies, glider possums, dingoes, horses and brolgas—and
dogs too, of incredible variety, some useful, others merely decorative.
All have their special niche in our family's memories. Without
animals you are out of touch with nature and the creatures of your
bush environment, and this can be a truly sad and lonely thing.

Brolgas came, some went. One old man brolga at mating time
looked upon the musterer's helicopter as competition. He hid in

the saddle shed, his big body unseen. His long neck swivelled out around the door to gaze skyward, as if to say, 'Now that's a bird to leave well alone.'

When we drove home after time away, Brolga flew along just above us, swooping and dipping in high excitement—an airborne welcoming committee. I can tell you, that was a bird with real attitude: strutting about, shooting his cuffs and behaving in the most arrogant way.

Unfortunately, for some reason he took a dislike to our stock inspector, Peter Flanagan. When Peter rode his horse through our gate, Brolga would glide straight as an arrow toward him with obvious intent. With the horse panicking, colourful language flowing, arms flailing and the odd grey feather floating gently to earth, Brolga would swoop off, quite sure he was the victor in *that* skirmish, and stride about with a 'to hell with you' attitude, stropping his long beak warningly on stones.

~

Apart from brolgas, ducks, chickens, an emu named Paddington, and the odd turkey, we had no birds as pets.

I don't like parrots—beautiful as they are. Never did. They are destructive, raucous, bossy creatures, and I was never moved to encourage one to settle in and be a pet. However, a station we often visited had a pet galah that roamed at will, even striding up and down the long dining table during meals. He was a dreadful, scantily feathered bird who, for reasons unknown, developed an unreciprocated affection for me. At lunch he would perch on my shoulder, nibble lovingly on my ear and cosily mumble parrot endearments to his stiffly unresponsive chosen love.

When a large pot of warm custard was brought to the table—the standard dessert there—the galah would perch on the pot's edge and thrust his head completely beneath the yellow liquid. Then, with a squawk of delight, he would give a vigorous shake, splattering custard all about. A firm slap with the custardy serving spoon from our host would send him huffily back onto my shoulder to further custard-besmeared endearments. I was vaguely afraid of him, yet our hosts were ridiculously pleased by his infatuation with me, so I made no move to dispatch him. 'Oh, he does love you,' they would say in flattering tones.

The galah objected to my departure. With the car windows firmly closed against him, he perched on the rear-vision mirror and urgently pecked for entry.

'Faster, faster!' I urged Ken, who thought it all a great joke.

There the galah clung desperately, as if at the wheel of a racing motorcycle, head down in his feathery shoulders, eyes closed, feathers straining back fit to ping clean out of his body. Then, dislodged by wind, he flashed backward past my window, for all the world like a stuffed bird.

He went home—presumably to await my return.

～

Juno was a brindle Great Dane–staghound cross, named for the Ancient Roman queen of the gods. She roamed the hills and kept snakes at bay for twelve years.

On the days the stock camp was in, the Aboriginal boys

stripped down to a naga, took up their spears and went bush for a day of hunting. 'Can we take Juno?' they'd ask, and off the old girl would go with the near-naked hunters.

If a portion of goanna or kangaroo wasn't handed over for Juno to bring home to chew on, she would remember this and refuse to join in the next bush hunt, and would have to be led off with a rope through her collar.

Juno was a great hoarder. Despite living in a land of plenty, she buried caches of odd bits of things for later attention—relics of the Sunday hunt; children's small toys; even soap, for which she had a special fondness and stole from where the girls left their towels and bathing things. On occasion she would silently carry off an egg from the fowl pen, with bulging cheeks, before carefully burying it.

On the floor of our house we had two large leopard skins which had been brought out of China by a Methodist missionary years before. Luxuriously furred, with long tails, clawed feet and huge toothed heads, and set with a taxidermist's glass eyes. Juno would recline on these exotic pelts with the long striped tail behind her and the ferocious head between her paws, surveying her realm with the exquisite disdain of a majestic great sphinx surveying the plebeian and unworthy.

Juno regularly gave birth to large litters. When Dominique was very little, she sat through the night in her dressing-gown to aid her in delivering yet another family of pups. So the mysteries of propagation and the intricacies of birth were revealed to Dominique early in life, as they are to most children of the bush.

The dear old thing's reflexes slowed with age, but her instinct to protect us remained alive. A king brown snake got the better of her one evening. She had a lingering death, but without obvious distress. We sat with her as she lay quietly for a long time. She gave my hand a long, slow, dry farewell caress, which said she knew nothing could be done and we were not to blame. Then she lay her head on Ken's lap and died. And though she left us, her loving spirit lives on.

We wrapped her in a blanket and buried her in a deep grave down by the cashew trees. Ken fashioned a marker with her name embossed with welding lead.

Some years after we left Bauhinia, I was asked by someone about the lubra who was buried down by a cashew grove, close to the homestead. 'Oh, she must have been a big woman, or maybe just very tall,' the person said.

'Why so?' I asked.

'Well, her name was Juno—it's on her grave marker.'

So Juno lies serenely among the cashew trees, with all the respect and gravity due to human remains, and with no one to know her secret.

Should we not all strive to be the person our dogs think we are?

A beloved member of our household was a large, not overly active white bulldog. His name was Ugly Bugly and strangers were made wary by his appearance, especially the big, prominent lower teeth that protruded over his upper lip, but he had a gentle nature.

His only real activity was to awaken, as if by an inbuilt alarm, at four o'clock each afternoon. If he could have told you, he would have explained it was his bounden duty to escort, from the kitchen to the verandah, the lubra carrying the afternoon tea-tray. He stood, then—eyes lowered, stomach sucked in—portraying with an actor's skill a starveling stray, with just an occasional deep-chested snort to remind you of his great need.

Regular visitors became concerned for Bugly if he didn't present himself with the tea-tray. He ate and grew fatter, slept and grew lazier, and dreamed a bulldog's twitching dreams of his ancestors' past battles with fighting bulls and great black bears.

~

When we'd moved to Bauhinia from Grasshopper, we'd brought along our few hens and housed them in a very small pen close by the homestead.

A fearful cackling and fluttering woke me one night while Ken was away. In the pen I found an especially large snake, which I guessed was a python, intent on a chicken dinner. So, clad in a nightgown, with my .410 shotgun in hand and a torch gripped under chin, I entered the tiny enclosure and shut the door. If the snake escaped, his chicken dinners would continue, which was usual when a snake was onto a good thing.

With an insecure grip on the torch, and the snake much alarmed and somewhat belligerent—it darted about, paused and reared up with its neck flattened like a cobra's—I had to duck under roosting rails and fend off frightened hens to try for a shot. I hit it!

I took the dead snake out for Ken to see on his return. It was so unusually large, a hen would have been a mere snack for it.

Next day we made the chilling discovery that my 'python' was a giant king brown, the biggest I ever saw!

Later we built a huge fowl pen that opened onto the running creek where the chooks could water. Each year we had 100-day-old chickens flown in. We lost some to the turtle hawks and giant snowy-white sea eagles, but were resigned to share in small numbers.

Then the chickens began disappearing noticeably faster. My father was making a rare visit at the time and found some crocodile tracks in the pen. Soon after, he caught a 3-metre-long freshwater croc who'd been enjoying a steady diet.

In spite of the eagles, hawks, snakes, blue-tongue lizards and crocodiles, we had plenty of chooks, ducks, even turkeys, and no shortage of eggs for everyone.

CHAPTER 56

# Bush Race Meeting

Around 1967, Ken, Bernie Jansen, Tas Festing and John Francis, the local police officer, set about forming a picnic race meeting in Borroloola. Roads had improved, and a bitumen beef road enabled cattle trucks to transport stock to Katherine and Darwin. Bush race meetings were popular and well attended: from the tablelands and stations around came keen racing men and their entourages.

We chose emerald and white as our colours, and the jockey silks we'd ordered duly arrived in the post. The jockey Ginger McLean came down from Darwin to ride our horse, Dandy Jack, in the Borroloola Cup. Ginger's flaming red hair made a happy contrast with the green of his silks.

I purchased a smart hat from a Sydney store. Unlike the hat my mother had hoped to wear at the Rankine races 35 years earlier, this one didn't need to come by camel train, but more prosaically on the regular mail plane.

The big day dawned with a good crowd for our first meeting.

Our stock boys were not as sophisticated as their tribespeople from the big stations on the tablelands. They'd never been out of Borroloola, so they'd never been to a race meeting and were naive in its specifics. They did not take losing a race lightly and felt it a personal slight if the Bauhinia colours weren't first past the post. In the festive atmosphere of race day they wore their new green shirts and white moleskin trousers with a sense of importance and belonging—they were the Bauhinia Boys and all should know it.

Dandy Jack won the cup that day and Ken won the Stockman's Race, which in tonier climes was known as the Gentlemen Riders' Race—not a title appropriate for a race in Borroloola in the 1960s. We were not without gentlemen, of course; it was just that the title had too pompous an air to it.

Every bush race meeting in those days ran a Blackfellas' Race for Aboriginal stockmen. They were welcome to ride in other races, and did, but they would tell you this race was for blackfella only, did not permit whitefella. Roy won on a brown gelding, Christopher, and was lavished with praise and a prize.

Dominique and Kurt were wildly excited when Fanny rode in the Ladies' Race. She competed against the white Missuses, who were all good riders, and beat the lot. She'd insisted on wearing her dress over the top of her riding trousers—she may have been a modest dresser, but she could ride, could our Fan.

Trophies were presented on the track. I hung my new hat carefully in camp. In the morning it bore evidence that birds—big birds—had roosted above, so it was tossed in the fire with other party debris.

Amusing stories emerge out of the hectic days of bush races, which are retold for months. Our stock boys in their Bauhinia colours had, with some cockiness, caused a fist fight with visiting lads. During the battle their green shirts suffered terrible damage. Ruska appeared with one remaining sleeve attached to a primly buttoned collar and was thoroughly pleased with his first race meeting.

The Borroloola races soon became a popular annual event. The Territory administrator attended one year, spending the night with us at Bauhinia. He arrived, driven by his chauffeur, about 60 years after Administrator Gilruth and his chauffeur had made the trip to Erekini Springs.

~

We had delayed sending Dominique to boarding school for too long, and at the beginning of her eighth year she went off to Queensland—with no great enthusiasm, I might say. The vision of her standing in the rain in her yellow raincoat and sou'wester hat, waving a tearful goodbye, is one of those painful moments that remain with me, as I'm sure it did for all bush mothers.

We all missed her, and Fanny's reproachful, 'When Dominie coming home?' at least once a week did nothing to help.

Pat Festing's six children and others from the surrounding district also went to boarding schools. At the end of their school holidays, a despondent group of children would gather on the Borroloola airstrip.

Dominique and Kerry, the youngest Festing daughter, once made a valiant effort to return home. When the plane landed at Wollogorang Station—the first touchdown out of Borroloola—they spotted the familiar face of a huge Aboriginal man, somewhat facetiously named Big Splinter, on the airstrip. Recognising him from Borroloola, they regaled him with an improbable story about their baggage having been left behind and it being imperative they return home.

Splinter was all for driving his compatriots to their home country and was fussily preparing to take them in his vehicle when the pilot nipped escape firmly in the bud with a 'Nice try, girls.' Splinter was much disturbed to see their tearful little faces at the window of the departing plane and was never quite sure he'd done the right thing in not making off with them in a rescue bid.

Whenever I drove into Borroloola I would hope Splinter wasn't around the store, because if he saw me he would hover outside, awaiting my appearance, then rush off to my car, open the door wide, and stand there stiff and attentive with his big bare feet and dusty old singlet, like a doorman at a posh hotel. It might be that I wasn't yet ready to leave, but such attention couldn't be ignored and I had to enter the car like royalty. I would drive up the road a way, or to the Festings' house, only to return later when Splinter was not to be seen.

The last time I saw Big Splinter was in the company of the Borroloola policeman, who was making a social call into Bauhinia on his way through to Darwin. Splinter was under arrest for biting a man's nose off in a fight. We had a chat, I gave him some food, and he waved cheerily as they drove off.

# CHAPTER 57

# A Bush Christmas

B ush Christmases had always come soaked in monsoonal rain, searingly hot in the midst of parched aridity, or just poised between storms with nothing to whinge about other than how hot it was, because it always was.

Chinese station cooks had been the order of the early days, presiding with keen authority in many kitchens. Station cooks were well aware of their value—a good cook was hard to replace and you didn't wander carelessly into his domain. Food was prepared in steamy kitchens on huge woodstoves, with no refrigeration.

At Christmas, quantities of liquor were set out under wet bags to cool in the breeze. Way out bush in camp, a bottle of Christmas beer could be suspended on a string in a waterhole to cool, and no one complained. A plum pudding turned out of a camp oven was jolly good tucker.

With the advent of cold-rooms and freezers, ceiling fans and gas ovens, everything changed—for the better, of course.

⌒

One early Christmas on Bauhinia, in our first little house, Santa Claus was expected in spite of torrential rain. Amid high excitement, pillowcases were hung at the foot of each child's bed in readiness.

A small glass of sherry was placed within easy reach to lift the big man's spirits after a boggy journey, and soggy grass was cut and left as a sustaining snack for his hard-travelling reindeers. With the bush child's knowledge of such things, it was decided there was no need for a water dish this year; the gilgais and billabongs were full, so a reindeer could find a drink easily enough.

Everything was ready; expectations were high.

Early in the evening, in pouring rain, Ken drove out in the Blitz to Billingarra Creek, now running a banker with floodwater, to await the arrival across the creek of two crocodile shooters, John Jamieson and Ted Dixon, who were to spend Christmas with us. Santa's delivery depended on them returning in time to retrieve his gifts, hidden high in the rafters of our house—I had no way of climbing up there. Ken settled down in the truck to wait.

The next morning it was almost daylight and not a reindeer in sight. Santa's non-arrival would be a tragic disappointment for two small children. Although usually they were no more than a few days' horseback ride from Borroloola and the companionship of other kids, they were a world away in our small bush house in the isolation of the wet season.

I paced about in a fever of nervous impatience, tossing down Santa's sherry to ease my edginess—although an empty sherry glass would present a poor image of a Santa who bore no gifts, just scoffed the booze and rode on.

Meanwhile, back at flooded Billingarra Creek, Ken swam across to help Ted, who couldn't swim. Halfway over, amid swirling debris, Ted became agitated and was disinclined to continue. It wasn't fear of drowning that caused his panic, but with a wet and slippery grasp on his rum bottle it was going, going, gone. The bottle was swept way downstream, perhaps even to the Limmen River.

The men returned just on daylight and the last pillowcase was settled in place—Santa reigned.

We always made a great occasion of Christmas. Like most parents, we devoted our efforts toward a festive family occasion. Newcomers to the district or those with nowhere to spend Christmas Day were gathered into our fold; we welcomed all those who fell under the label 'strays' to Christmas dinner.

⁓

Ken was keen to introduce Brahma blood into our shorthorn cattle. Though not generally popular at that time, Brahma were resistant to tick and a hardy breed for the tropics. At the first ever bull sale held in Mount Isa, Ken bought nine stud Brahma bulls—huge, sleek beasts with great humps on their shoulders.

Within a few years Brahma were much in demand; they were fast overtaking the old shorthorn breed in the Territory. With good seasons, calves proliferated with distinctive Brahma characteristics.

However, good seasons came and went even in this country of monsoonal rain.

One year, Christmas had passed but the rains held off and the country was as parched as we had ever seen it. Clouds built; the air was hot and still with the expectancy of a storm. Away to the north, sheet lightning flashed like the distant flare of a searchlight; thunder thumped fists on clouds, beseeching them to open. We waited, hands outstretched, gazing mindlessly skyward, anticipating the first fat raindrop that precedes a downpour.

Then the clouds blew away to the horizon, with any hope of rain—gone!

In cities of the south, a newspaper might carry a single line: 'Drought threatens northern cattle country.' Who reads this and cares in a city where a clear day with no rain is a joy and lifts the spirits? For us paddocks got so bare it was hard to remember them green with feed. The cattle grew weak and listless, many dying in bare paddocks or bogged deep in mud of receding waterholes, too weak to free themselves and sucked deeper with every movement.

Dingoes thrived on the surrounding misery, growing fatter and more lustrous than you could ever expect to see a wild bush dog. This was their brief time to prosper, while all else suffered; the bush wasn't always so generous to the hungry dingo. Why else would bushmen refer to a meagre meal as a 'dingo's breakfast', which they would tell you was a 'piddle and a look around'?

Still the sun scorched brazenly down. In the dry, hot air, small birds dropped exhausted from above; lizards panted, heads held high, throats pulsating furiously; dogs made a beeline for the creek, skittishly lifting their feet high over the hot stony earth—then with blissful relief, like a woman taking her corset off, they eased themselves into the cool water.

Out on the run, the sun glared from a sky as hard and blue as the steel of a gun barrel: poised, hopeful, yet unable to find a beast fat enough to kill for beef. Instead the shots from the rifle mercifully disposed of the weak and dying.

On the plain, mirage clothed the seared country with a glittering expanse—heaven's daydream, they called it. Dust-devils ran in spirals across the baked earth. Hard-working cattlemen would say to you, 'No cattle for sale this year. Too dry, can't say what we'll do if it don't rain,' and from under their wide-brimmed hats sweat ran in thin rivulets down dusty faces. When grass shrivelled and he saw his stock dying, a cattleman's spirit would shrivel up with it.

Drought didn't affect the flow of Erekini—the water gushed up as freely as ever. But without rain there was no grass and no feed for starving stock. With nothing to tell of rain, one way or another, we just looked at the sky and hung on the promise of every small cloud.

~

This was walkabout time for our Aboriginal staff, and they'd all gone to Borroloola. The children were still home on school holidays.

We first smelled the smoke, then saw billowing black clouds rise high in the sky, thick with debris, dust and burned leaves. Dozens of hawks circled above, on the watch for small game in the bushfire's wake. The sky darkened out beyond the paddock.

Ken left in the truck to take a look and soon returned, calling, 'Everyone needed, be quick about it.' We rushed around gathering bags and water, then headed off at top speed.

Through most of the night we worked against the fire in tinder-dry country. The children were very young but they were able to beat along the brown grassy edges of the road with green bushes. Using back burning, we prevented the fire leaping the road, which was about all we could do by then.

On the blackened earth there was powdery smoking ash and scattered burning logs. The greatest risk were the smouldering holes where trees had burned deep down into their roots, the surface deceptively sound, flat grey ash; one step onto this powder and down you could go, waist deep into a pit of red-hot coals. I kept calling to the children to keep back along the road's edge.

It was a long night, with most of the hard work done by Ken, who rushed from one flaming patch to another and was well singed for it. He and I returned to the road to find our two exhausted children sound asleep on the bare ground beside the truck. My shoes had burned through the soles, we were soot-blackened and smelled of singed hair, and we coughed for hours. There was ugly scorched country all around, but we hadn't done a bad job together.

After a long dry season with bushfires and dwindling stock feed came the first heavy shower—drops we'd longed for, which pelted down with gathering force. We stood outside and let the rain soak into our very bones, while the children ran about slithering in the mud, screaming with delight.

It then rained for 29 days straight.

Our bulldozer, left out on the run, went completely under water; stock drowned; heavy with debris, fences collapsed; stores could not get through; and anything damp in the warm humid air became fly-blown—even dry salted beef was fly-blown. Drenched, unhappy fowls clustered on high perches.

Aboriginals sat under the iron verandah roofs and stared contentedly out at the rain, chewing wannoo or smoking their pipes. They boasted of the rainmaker's success with his rain stones—usually brought out to work their magic when scurrying ants had been observed and heavy clouds looked ready to discharge their load.

We sailed in our tin dinghy across paddocks usually dry and grassy, crossing roads where dusty wheel tracks were drowned deep.

Our truck, returning from town loaded with stores, had to be abandoned out on the main road—too boggy. The country became so saturated that a heavy footstep here would cause the ground to quiver way over there, like a huge jelly. The truck remained out on the main road for three months.

Around the station, the pervading smell was of musty damp, wet saddle cloths, blankets, swags, sour drying mud, wet dogs— everywhere wet dogs.

I woke early one morning to a strange silence. The rain had stopped. I watched as a pale pink and grey line of daybreak under cloud eased apart to reveal a lone star shimmering, shaking the water from itself.

The wet, the real wet, was over. But the roads took ages to dry out and the children missed the entire first term of school.

# CHAPTER 58

# Working on
# Bauhinia Downs

I once had a gardener whose name was Syd. He was a rather special little fella—a tireless worker who would take up any work, no matter how difficult. I never, ever heard him complain about anything.

Syd was a skilled survivor or, in bush parlance, a tough little bastard. He'd fought in the Australian army in the Second World War, and when Crete fell was taken prisoner and spent four grindingly awful years of privation and freezing winters behind barbed wire in a German prison camp.

After Syd was released from the army, he lived for a time in a city boarding house opposite the botanical gardens. A pool with lilies and waterfowl lay close to the entrance, and the ducks there lived a precarious existence with Syd nearby. His hunting inclinations were always close to the surface, so with fine fat ducks of all description waddling about among the water hyacinths, Syd was wont to wander over there, a bag over his shoulder, to admire the botanical wonders.

In his small room in the boarding house, this ex-soldier fresh from the prison camps in Germany dined quite spectacularly, with a gourmet's appreciation, on exotic poultry.

Years later, even in a tropical climate he seemed never to have recovered from those four bleak years of extreme cold, with frost coating the inner walls of the prison huts and only one blanket issued to last through all that time. Like a man who has suffered starvation and takes a cache of food with him everywhere, Syd was rarely without a warm coat, and each year purchased a new one.

One year when the stock camp returned after walkabout, Willie and Kathleen joined our staff.

Willie was very tall, had a bushy white moustache, and bore the stern air of an authoritarian schoolmaster. He wasn't a stockman; he'd worked in the garage of Anthony Lagoon Station, and knew the workings of motors and machinery.

Kathleen was a plump, pretty middle-aged woman with a shy, sweet smile, and she worked in the house with Alice, Minnie and Fanny. I became very fond of Kathleenea, as I called her, and it amused Ken no end that when Kathleen shyly presented me with a flower from the garden, she usually departed the house with a generous supply of small treats.

My mother sent parcels to the station containing all sorts of things for the girls—jewellery and watches, handbags, clothes—from both her travels and her fashion-conscious city friends. The girls just loved it when the station mailbag was opened to reveal their parcels. Dresses were the most popular, and it was a sight to see the lubras setting off for a day's hunt with billy-cans, dilly bags, yam sticks on shoulder, splendidly decked out in designer cocktail dresses awash with beading and aglitter with sequins.

Years earlier, in Borroloola, Kathleen had a romantic liaison with an Irishman who worked in the old pub before it fell into ruin. He had long since died, but had fathered a son with Kathleen who, because of his European heritage, was taken from the camp and into care, as was usual then.

Kathleen's son became a successful businessman and married a white woman, which would have been quite improbable in the past. He once contacted Ken to ask if he could bring Kathleen into Borroloola to see him, as he was passing through the town, and of course Ken did.

Kathleen hadn't seen her son in years and barely knew him, so the visit was quite exciting for her and they spent the day together. Returning to the station, Ken asked her, 'How was this meeting with your son?' Kathleen assured him they had talked and he had given her 10 shillings.

He never came again in the years Kathleen was with us. Doubtless the gap in their lives had become too wide for her to deal with the reality of a white daughter-in-law; to her, a white woman had always been a 'Missus'. And for the young man, a black, barefoot, shy and uneducated mother, with little English, unable to adjust to separation from the tribe, would surely prove untenable, so there was never a suggestion of a change in their association.

~

Whenever the stock camp left the station Willie remained and informed all who cared to ask that he must stay to take care of the Missus.

In fact, it's possible Willie *did* save my life once when he, Syd and I were returning from the stock camp. It was raining buckets that day and our vehicle became hopelessly bogged, so we set off to walk home in the rain.

At the creek crossing we paused and, with some trepidation, took in the branches and debris wildly churning in the rising floodwater.

'I'm not going in there,' I said in tones that brooked no argument.

The alternative? Three people tightly packed in the cab of a truck, all through a rainy night. So I did go in!

The creek was rising fast and there was no way I could actually swim through the racing current. We clasped hands, with me between the two men. The water was way up to tall Willie's chest. Syd, a little fella, couldn't swim a stroke. We eased in and carefully began to wade behind Willie's long strides.

Then, just as we were almost across, where the water was deepest, my legs were swept from under me and I shot off. I would surely have been taken along by that swirling floodwater and drowned or been injured by the debris, but despite his slippery hands, Willie—stalwart as a bloodwood tree—held on, clutching a handful of my shirt. But Syd lost his hold and careened into Willie, clinging to him like a desperate waterlogged possum.

There could be a dramatic, detailed description here of our emergence from a watery maelstrom. But although we were truly endangered, it is enough to say that Willie brought us both out. So Willie was the hero of that day.

⁓

After Willie and Kathleen had been with us a few years, one day Willie came and quietly told me he had 'that bush sickness'.

'Do you feel sick, does your head hurt?' I asked.

'No,' he said and lifted his shirt to show the white patches on his back that told of leprosy. I had never known an Aboriginal person to come forward and admit this disease, but then Willie had spent most of his life at the stations.

He was taken to Darwin, where treatment was much advanced from the old days when years could be spent in isolation. In a few months he returned from the leprosarium. Although he'd been a teetotaller all his life, he came back a drinking man. The two cans of beer given each evening to the patients was his downfall, and alcohol of any kind became his weakness.

Soon Kathleen was drinking too.

At the Borroloola picnic race meeting, our house girls came hurrying to me. 'Quick, Missus, Kathleen dancing!'

Shy, gentle Kathleen—dancing? Never!

But sure enough, when I went with the house girls there was Kathleen, loud and drunk, within a dense circle of male onlookers.

I elbowed my way through and led Kathleen away just before the last 'veil' was cast.

Kathleen became blind in her last years, and she and Willie have both since died. Did that son from another world care? Did he even know? If not, he is not to be thought of too harshly, for life had set them on very different paths.

# CHAPTER 59

# 'Just Shoot the Bloody Thing'

Race meetings, rodeos and social gatherings were all timed to take place when the children came home on school holidays.

Fanny would get out her fishing lines and keep up a steady chatter about the children's imminent arrival. Almost as the plane landed, shoes were discarded, then home to an extravagantly enthusiastic welcome from Fanny and everyone on the station, as well as dogs and other pets.

Usually on return to school, there was some drama to relate in gripping detail to city friends—a buffalo attack, the race ball, a major fall from horseback—all crammed into two weeks of holidays.

For Dominique, the race ball involved a new dress and everything special. Once she was dancing very decorously with Peter, our stock inspector. The dance floor was crowded, music slow, when Peter excused himself in a most courtly way, stepped aside and had a fight.

Fisticuffs over, he stepped back on the floor and calmly continued to dance. All over in a few minutes, an opportunity presented to repay an old grievance—nothing like a bush dance to keep the party lively.

A rodeo and gymkhana made our race a two-day meet, and Dominique won the open bullock ride there in 1977—much to the ire of the men in competition.

Dominique got an even better story to take back to her school-friends on one holiday. 'There's an old bull buffalo in the paddock,' said Ken. 'We'll go take a look. He's a quiet old fella, so we won't shoot him.'

We drove off in the old, unreliable cabinless utility. Dominique was standing with Juno on the flat tray back. We drove up close to where the lumbering old buffalo with enormous horns was placidly feeding.

Without warning he charged at high speed, his great horns giving a tip to the truck tray with every step. The dog flew off to attack and Dominique very nearly went with her, as she lost her grip on the collar and was on her back on the wheeling vehicle.

The dog was jousting with the vicious old beast when Ken shot it. Not such a 'quiet old fella'! We used its hide and beef; kept the horns as a reminder of Juno's brave attack in our defence.

Ken, like most countrymen, had high hopes his children would ride well. He declared to an unconvinced Dominique that his big stockhorse, Nipper, was an 'old gentleman' who would never throw a woman. Dominique mounted carefully, Nipper gave a great buck and my daughter made a spectacularly high, rather graceful exit from the saddle. 'Old gentleman' indeed.

Sympathy on such occasions was always in short supply and likely to be along the lines of 'What did you do to the poor old fella? Maybe you had perfume on, or something else that upset him.'

Nipper was a champion camp-drafting horse, but there was that certain sly glint in his eye and he was always on the lookout for an easy win.

Whenever I heard Ken say, 'We'll get a killer here at the station. I'll bring the cattle up to the bauhinia tree at the gate,' before riding off on horseback, my spirits would sink. This was my least favourite thing to assist with.

Most of our killers were shot and butchered out on the run, then brought in to the beef-house or cold-room. But occasionally, usually during the wet season, we killed at the station. Someone on horseback would herd the cattle to a tree or some other place where a shooter could wait out of sight. If there was no one else available, I was the one up in the branches, rifle in hand.

I was a good shot, but this was something I really disliked doing because orders, not always given in a good humour, could be tersely snapped out—something like, 'Get the roan cow!' Then, with cattle jostling about, the horse stepping nervously and no shot fired, there'd come an exasperated: 'What in *hell* are you doing up there? Just shoot the bloody thing!'

There was definitely an expectation that you would take one shot and you would not miss, and this could test the soundest of female nerves. For me, there was the anxious possibility that, with the milling about of cattle, I might not only miss the beast, but make the disastrous mistake of shooting the man on the horse.

I cannot resist the boast that I never missed my kill, first shot, but praise for so ordinary a thing was never forthcoming. It was expected that 'you just shot the bloody thing'.

CHAPTER 60

# Our New Homestead

Around this time we started to build a new homestead, as life in our little bush house remained sadly lacking in home comforts. Ken and the boys carted endless loads of rock to the building site, and Ken began the task of smashing it with a sledge hammer to create a base above the underlying seepage from the stony hill behind.

John Sanders settled in for two years as resident carpenter to build the house and separate guest quarters. The kerosene refrigerators were retired and a new cold-room installed that could hold several sides of beef. An electricity generator arrived that, as far as I was concerned, was magically started with the touch of a light switch in the house; no more swinging that crank handle in the distant engine room. And our new bedroom was larger than our old bush house.

From Thailand we imported impressively carved teak furniture. In keeping with the somewhat carefree services of the day, a large buffet marked 'N.T. Australia' sailed off to northern Tasmania. Some months later it arrived without drawers; later still, these made their appearance wrapped in newspaper on a cattle truck.

Quite some years since we'd ridden into Borroloola from the Limmen with Hurtle, the old horse pads through bush were barely visible, rarely travelled, so a motor car was the way to go. We bought the first Toyota LandCruiser wagon sold in the Territory, leaving the old Blitz truck abandoned and rusting.

~

A radio telephone was to be installed to replace outback radios on remote cattle stations. This was a long time before mobile phones and there was great excitement on the station.

Workmen arrived from Darwin and put up a high aerial mast with ungainly wide stays to support it. Though it was anchored in the middle of my rose garden, we dared not voice a single complaint. Now we could inform friends and family that our telephone number was 'Radio Telephone 1325'.

There were some drawbacks, though. You couldn't just pick up the radio telephone, ring a number and chatter away. Calls had to be booked and a long wait was usual. But we had a telephone link—wasn't that something.

~

The Civil Aviation Department cleared an airstrip for us, which served us very well except in extreme wet weather.

Our homestead, directly under the highest escarpment, was difficult to spot from the air. There are a dozen tales to tell of lost aircraft in this part of the country before modern navigational aids came into general use.

Late one day, alone on the station, I heard an aircraft circling. Presuming it was signalling to land, I drove over to the airstrip to find an American pilot in his small plane. He had flown across the Timor Sea to Darwin, refuelled there, and set off for the newly formed mining settlement of McArthur River.

Flying from Darwin across Arnhem Land to Borroloola covers empty country that seems to go on forever. As you look down from an aircraft window, the continuing sameness of the landscape below can make you feel as though you are stationary in the air. The pilot felt completely lost and was desperate for somewhere to land when there, below him, was an airstrip with windsock flying gaily in the breeze. He couldn't believe his eyes.

I found him almost in tears with relief, and took him home, revived him with tea and gave him fuel for his plane. With maps spread out on my dining table he recovered his bearing and the confidence to fly on. 'This day,' he said, 'will forever remain in my memory.'

He had flown across the sea to land in a foreign city, passing over vast emptiness he could not have imagined, without the navigational aids he was accustomed to in his own country—then to take civilised afternoon tea under a flowering Poinciana in a beautiful garden, while looking out over a couple of thousand kilometres of empty Territory bush.

He also spent an hour repairing a damaged refrigerator for a woman he had just met and would never see again.

He took off then and, with a farewell dip over the house, faded into the darkening sky and into what is now just a tale to regale.

⌒

I extended the garden ever larger as time went by, so it spread out over two and a half hectares.

Each year the Katherine Show Society ran a competition for best Territory station garden, which many stations entered. The judges boarded a plane in Darwin, flew out and landed on the airstrips of the competing stations, and closely considered each garden before flying on to the next. Many, many kilometres were covered in this competition, as it had a widespread number of competitors.

I won the competition for two consecutive years—I still display my trophies with pride—and Bauhinia became known for its splendid garden. Johnny Festing, the small son of Tas and Pat, referred to Bauhinia as 'the bot-a-nickle gardens'.

⌒

In the changing times of our later years on Bauhinia, visitors came from all over the world. They included Japanese businessmen whose names grace modern motor cars, and miners from mining groups in France, Italy and India, who prospected in the modern way with helicopters while living in elaborate camps.

Biologists came too, seeking rare bush animals and birds. John Calaby, an expert in wildlife, was delighted to trap an especially interesting native mouse *in* my house.

A large green frog who spent his days quietly settled in a moist place—a bathroom toilet bowl—provoked visitors' interest too, especially as he was given to leaping at anything that dangled from above, which he would then cling to with little suction feet. Green frogs were a common sight in the toilets of bush households, but city visitors could be unnerved by an encounter.

One young man visiting from the south couldn't pronounce his R's. He came urgently to tell me there was 'a big gween fwog' in his toilet. Henceforth, it was referred to in our family as 'the fwog'. Even when removed and taken a long way off, the very next day Fwog would have settled right back in.

Bauhinia was no longer an isolated outpost. We mustered all our cattle using helicopters—no one threw wild bulls from horseback now. With good roads, social life in the bush had improved, with camp drafts, rodeos, race meetings and rural shows.

We sold Broadmere, a 2600-square-kilometre section of our station, which left Bauhinia a mere 1300 square kilometres.

~

Kurt and Dominique have a closer relationship as adults than they did as children. They had quite different interests on the station, and although they both went mustering with the stock camp, they had their own ponies and dogs.

Kurt was a true child of the bush. A very adventurous little boy, as bush children often were, he had endless country to explore, swimming holes, horses and other animals, and the companionable Aboriginals he had grown up with.

Kurt fished with Fanny and hunted with Juno, who went every-where with him. He would wield first spear, Juno would perform the coup de grace, then they'd bring home whatever the kill—goanna, snake—to give as a treat to the lubras to cook on their campfire.

But sometimes he returned with live things to care for, including blue-tongue lizards, which settled down and raised successive families in the garden outside my bedroom door. They greeted the unwary with a wide blue mouth and angry hissing, and fared very well on eggs they stole from the fowl pen. I would rather they had remained in the bush.

On one of his occasional visits to Bauhinia, my father brought Kurt the kind of scooter you mobilise by pushing off with one foot. Kurt took off right away.

Not too long later, he returned on foot.

'Where's the scooter?'

Kurt gazed off at the horizon, dreamily waved his arm in a wide, slow arc—as the very old Aboriginals did to describe distance—and said, 'He bin loooongway.'

In spite of much searching, the scooter was never seen again. Perhaps a thousand years hence it will be dug out of the earth by an eager anthropologist, who will exclaim in excitement at the juxtaposition of Aboriginal relics and a metallic wheeled contraption.

As he grew older, Kurt developed persistent chest problems. The Flying Doctor treated him, as well as city paediatricians. When he had a particularly frightening attack, we bundled him into the car and drove the 1000 or so kilometres to Mount Isa Hospital nonstop.

When Kurt went off to boarding school, our only cheering thought was that he'd have access to immediate medical attention.

Within a few years he was free of his chest problems and maintained good health. He became a champion runner, excelling at the cross-country competitions, and continued to love hunting and fishing at home.

Then he became interested in motorbikes, which proved not to be such a good thing. Out bush one evening, he crashed while chasing after a dingo. His leg was broken completely through. He spent all night in the bush, but managed to crawl to the road. Ken found him and the medical plane took him to hospital.

Many of the young Territorian bush kids we knew have succeeded outstandingly in the cattle industry.

My friend Peter Sherwin, a young drover, took Victoria River Downs cattle through the Murranji Track and in 1984 became the station's owner. Victoria River Downs is the largest cattle station in the Territory and possibly the world.

Handsome and charming, Sterling Buntine now possesses one of the Territory's most prestigious cattle stations, as well as other properties. His name has been included in the list of Australia's richest men. Can't do better than that.

Danny Groves shines as a well-regarded cattleman, successful in every aspect of cattle- and horse-work—a success story of the Territory kind.

Johnno Keighran, in Ken's opinion, is one of the best all-round cattlemen in the Territory. His father, Jack, was an old Territorian of my father's time, and his mother was an Aboriginal woman of the Mara tribe. He mustered Bauhinia with Ken and is one of the few left to reminisce with about the 'good old days'.

Our Kurt Hammar is another example of a bush kid made good. And the list goes on.

~

My good friend Vi grew up on the Mornington Island settlement. Her mother was Aboriginal. Vi married a European cattleman and they worked very hard together, happily to eventual success.

Vi once said to me, 'Jack, why do we live up here? We could go south, live an easy life down there in a cool climate, never look at a cow again.'

'We couldn't bear it, life would be too dull,' I said. 'We've shared some experiences in the bush together, haven't we? One day I'll write a book and you can read about us.'

'God forbid,' said Vi.

# Epilogue

Recalling times past has been a sentimental, sometimes sad journey for me. The Territory, a stern country for those who long laboured there, a graveyard of broken dreams for many, has been generous to us. There was an enfolding warmth, a true sense of belonging, living in the old Territory.

For 30 years we lived in the beautiful Bauhinia Valley with its myriad geological wonders, until one day around Christmas time—the same time of year we had driven in with the wet season's storms close behind us to start a life there—we drove out through the garden lush with recent rain, past Juno's grave among the cashew trees, and on under the cassia trees, cascading yellow summer flowers, that I'd planted years before for Dominique's future wedding day. Out over Ballingarra Creek, where Willie had saved me from drowning.

Someone once said: if you must leave a place you have cared about, a place where all your yesterdays were played out, and buried deep, leave quickly, don't look back, never go slowly; and so we went quickly and were gone—forever.

All that remains of my wonderful garden at Bauhinia Downs Station is the tamarind tree I grew from a seed that I carried in my pocket throughout the months of muster on the Limmen, 60 years ago. It lives on through fire and flood as we did, and hopefully will live beyond our time, for the tamarind grows for hundreds of years.

The Aboriginal stockman is no longer the mainstay on the Territory cattle station. Our old blackfella of the far bush is gone now.

'Blackfella!' my city friends huff with disapproval and pursed lips. 'Say "Aboriginal person".' What do they know, who have only seen him pale-skinned in city clothes on their television screens?

'Can't call you blackfella now,' I say to Olman.

'Waffaw no more blackfella, you whitefella, ent it?' and he is much amused by these people of a city he has never seen, for we are old friends who have shared much in good times and not-so-good times.

~

Kurt remains a true son of the old Territory. He is 6 feet 5 inches of amiable, successful bushman, and is known, as was his father, by a variety of Aboriginal names and several others as well, none critical. Through a lifetime's understanding of Aboriginal people past and present, he almost exclusively employs Aboriginal stockmen in his cattle-mustering camps and works successfully beside them.

The name Kurt Hammar has an immediate familiarity from the tropical country of the Limmen River to the rugged Kimberley.

Along the Gibb River Road in Western Australia and in isolated areas of the Kimberley there are a number of undeveloped cattle stations, some owned by Aboriginals, some by Europeans. With his 'Hammarco' operation, Kurt musters cleanskin shorthorn cattle, and ships bulls to markets in Indonesia and Malaysia.

Hammarco, worth some hundreds of thousands of dollars, is an entirely mechanical operation. Helicopter pilots locate cattle, men in stripped-down Toyota LandCruisers—called bull buggies—race in full throttle, knock down, leg strap and tip the horns of bush bulls. They feed hay to these beasts and provide them with water in troughs, and they adjust to captivity before they are shipped out from Darwin, Broome or Wyndham.

Over the years Kurt has developed uniquely successful mustering techniques and become the country's leading exponent of this type of cattle trade. In the last fourteen years, Hammarco has exported upwards of 89,000 head of scrub bulls, and that's a lot of cattle by anyone's reasoning.

Although lately Kurt's work has him located in the west, he and the love of his life, Meghan, have made Katherine their home for the last 24 years. They have two fine sons who will undoubtedly follow in their father's Territory footsteps. They can tell, as the old bush nursemaids would tell, 'His father, belong father, belong nother long time father—this im country!'

~

The old roads that meandered through interminable Territory bush aren't there now. These roads—old cattle pads or forged by wagon wheels—would begin wide and encouraging to the outback traveller, but after a few miles they would grow indistinct and lose themselves in a tangle of spinifex and overgrowth. With what seemed too much effort to carry on, they gave up entirely and it was for you to make your own way on.

If for whimsical reasons you took out a map, 'UNSURVEYED' was emblazoned there, which you fancied had an apologetic or perhaps a defensive air to it, but it did not deter you and you pushed on in your given direction with all the optimism of a Leichhardt or a Stuart.

Dominique has travelled those roads.

When she was a small child, we took her in the old Blitz truck to places a white child had never ventured. Later in her life she travelled outback roads through bush that advanced further into more bush.

Dominique has had her own adventure with life. Her own Territory.

After years of city boarding school, she returned to a nursing career in Darwin. When she was 21, she met Milton Jones, a bush-hardened eighteen-year-old Territorian.

Together, with all the uncertainty of a new undertaking, the two of them went bull-catching to make their fortune. Back then bull-catching was done in an open, cut-down bull buggy and a truck. Dominique was Milton's strapper, so it was she who, when the bull had been run down and held by the vehicle, leaped out to strap its back legs together before it was pulled up a slide onto the truck and unstrapped.

Though bull-catching could be an adventure, it involved hard physical work and living in swags in all weather for long periods.

It's a nomadic life—dirty and dangerous, with discomfort in vast proportions. It was not the life we'd envisioned for our genteelly raised daughter, who had modelled high fashion in the insouciance of city life.

Dominique and Milton were married on our wedding anniversary, 14 August, in Katherine, with all the usual festivities of a country wedding, in a town where everyone knew most everyone else.

Milton acquired Coolabah Station—a small station by Territory standards—right on the main Western Highway, and this became their home. They farmed crocodiles, so collecting crocodile eggs from riverside nests became a necessity for this faint-hearted female. It entailed trudging through tall, steamy river grasses, confronting a crocodile in maternal protective mode, then departing on foot clutching a large box of eggs at a speed loosely compared to lightning. This was how it was done then, in the days before a helicopter was used to lower the egg-thief in relative safety.

Then Dominique and Milton purchased two cattle stations, Bedford Downs and Lansdowne, in Western Australia's Kimberley region, as well as a meatworks and a helicopter business, and managed several cattle stations for American businessmen. The two of them had a long hard road to success, and no story of Milton's life can be told without telling of Dominique's encouragement and steadfastness with every endeavour he undertook.

Altogether it was a joint effort, but someone once said that Milton would have succeeded without help from anyone, which is a placatory and easy thing to say when the happy state of success has long been reached.

Life with a young man unable to read or write, with few social graces and no money at all, could only be challenging. It can be said that Dominique shared Milton's life with grace and fortitude for 21 years. Business success does not necessarily ensure a harmonious life and so, after many adventures, much adversity and success, they went their separate ways.

Dominique and her two children, Beau and Alix, live in Katherine, although the children go to boarding schools as we all did. Dominique's house is surrounded by a beautiful tropical garden she created herself. Ken and I spend time there every year, for the Territory will always be home to us too.

Dominique has battled feral bulls, crocodiles, fire, and flood that inundated her station homestead; been discouraged by adversity, and blessed with success and good health; and remained as strong, durable and feminine a Territory woman as I have ever known. Perhaps she will one day tell her own story.

~

I have always felt a certain disquiet with the term 'passed away' or 'passed on'. It has a whispery indefiniteness to it; the connotation of a gentle, restrained exit.

This could never be applied to my mother's exiting anywhere, and she certainly called a thing as it was. I am sure she would prefer I said that she died—and she did, three years after my father. Their relationship had faded to a vague friendliness, and they lived their lives apart from each other.

I sometimes think of the women of early days in Territory bush, who receive little recognition today for their hospitality to all who travelled bush roads, and for their caring and comfort in sickness. They brought order and gentleness into the rough and lonely lives of bushmen.

With the white woman there came onto the isolated cattle station of those early times a linen tablecloth, china tea cups, a bedspread from a trousseau, and flowers and shrubs planted in painted flour drums. These small things—nothing in city life—were immeasurably uplifting in the far Outback and gave meaning to that quote from an old Territory newspaper: 'A far greater need than Railways, Naval bases, Gold and Garrisons is the Territory's need of white women.'

My mother was never your regular motherly housewife—a dimity-aproned mother producing cookies in the kitchen she definitely wasn't! This upset me not at all. She was a good friend, good company and had a great sense of humour, which was essential to survival in the old Territory.

Homely, nurturing—never. There wasn't a maternal bone in her body. But she was dutiful in every way. I was educated at good schools and never wanted for a thing. I prefer her as she was. She did a great deal for people, especially in the bush. She just had no aptitude for close relationships, no skill for family life. She lived life as she wanted it and deserved the good life she worked hard for.

After her death I opened her crocodile-skin suitcase with its great claws across the front—that croc had taken my father's best shooting horse out in the buffalo camp on the Alligator River. Inside the case were old photographs of daring young men on horseback, famous aviators of the 1930s, a chemist's blue bottle of quinine, Aboriginal artefacts that were gifts from patients past, old business letters that must once have held importance, and letters from bank managers signed, if you can believe it, 'Your humble and obedient servant'.

~

My father was a hard man of the old Outback: capable, inured to harsh living, carefree and popular—and brave, something I am old-fashioned enough to expect in a man. His life held many adventures. Who could tell first-hand today of a life as thrilling as he could? He made molehills out of the mountains he climbed, never regretted his losses, never boasted of success. It fell to others to tell of his exploits, and for men to write of them too.

He did not share my mother's ambition for wealth and success in business, although he worked along with her and helped her achieve her goals in life.

He and I were not to meet for some time after my birth, for he was away dealing with the murder charge. With his name cleared and pure as a snowflake, I'm told he gazed long and hard at this infant, and told her, 'I am your father,' and my father he remained. He looked upon fatherhood as companionable and enjoyable, and I never heard him say, 'Don't do that,' or 'You mustn't,' nor anything in a censuring way—it wasn't in his vocabulary with me.

He spoiled me outrageously. Without my mother's good sense, the aspirations of the Anglican nuns to make a 'lady' of me, and the even firmer hand of Sister Annunciata and the Catholic Sisters of the Darwin Convent School, I may have become a first-class brat.

My father rarely presumed to give advice, so when he did, you tended to remember what he said. The tenets of his council were simple: 'Never underestimate a small amount of money. Never judge anything—man, dog, horse or situation—by its appearance. And lastly, learn to keep your mouth shut. Better people should wonder why you don't talk, than why you do.' All good council I continue to benefit from.

We had a great rapport, my father and I; we talked together about many things. Once when someone we knew died, I asked him casually if he would like a big funeral, expecting him to say something like, 'Just wrap me in my swag and bury me out bush.' So I was surprised when he said, 'Oh, I wouldn't mind a big funeral, and everyone would say, "There goes old Jack. He wasn't a bad poor old bastard."'

As it was, his funeral took place in a chapel by the sea, in a southern place, where no sun-baked old Territory bushman should finish his days with his boots off. The last post was rendered by an army bugler, which is always painfully moving, and the thought came to me: 'There goes old Jack. He was a great old bastard!'

He was my father.

~

The first ten years of my life were lived in the final chapter of the frontier Territory. Tribespeople roamed the bush and cattlemen rode the lonely miles of vast cattle stations. Northern Mounted Police lived dangerous lives, and my father hunted buffalo on horseback in 'no man's land' of Arnhem Land where few white men had ventured.

Dear, blowzy, tarty young Darwin of the 1920s and 1930s, with a bottle in her hand, always had a ribald quip for the bawdy company she kept. Tolerant of society's rejects, she wore a tiara of gold, pearls and rubies tipped rakishly on her forehead. Triumphantly she had overthrown all who'd sought to improve and polish her.

Then came a devastating war; the world heaved, settled, and was changed.

Darwin has matured now, grown up, smoothed down her skirts, straightened her tiara, adding to it diamonds of rare colour and beauty, discarded her bottle—well, not entirely!—and taken her place with dignity and grace in the modern Australian family.

In most ways the Territory has changed for the better. Chinatown emerged from the years of war clean and renewed. New residents came to Darwin: respectable, unencumbered with eccentricities. No more dare southern journalists write, 'Darwin the damned. Last resort of the Australian derelict.'

It is indeed a changed world.

~

Who now truly knows the hard sun-browned men who subdued the wilderness with packhorse, swag, rum bottle and Old Gulf Cure. Yesterday's adventurers are today's curiosities. If remembered at all, they will become tomorrow's history, or perhaps just 'Post and Rail' graves out in the dry spinifex.

It pleases me that I knew the last of these conquistadors of a frontier land and, with a young man of equal pioneering spirit, I followed their path. We should all be so fortunate in our lives to have created things we are still talking about today, a hundred years later.

*There's a land where the mountains are nameless,*
*And the rivers all run God knows where;*
*There are lives that are erring and aimless,*
*And deaths that just hang by a hair;*
*There are hardships that nobody reckons;*
*There are valleys unpeopled and still;*
*There's a land—oh, it beckons and beckons,*
*And I want to go back—and I will.*

ROBERT W. SERVICE

# Acknowledgements

It can be a lonely project writing a long story when most everyone in the tale has long departed this life; so I give thanks to Ken, my husband, for keeping me 'at it' when I tended to flag.

My thanks go to Louise Thurtell, publisher *par excellence*, for her interest and firm hand.

A thank you to my friend Shona Kravenger who spent much time typing my reams of pencil-written pages on to her computer. And to my family, just for being there.